For the Sake of Heaven

FOR THE SAKE

OF HEAVEN

by MARTIN BUBER

Translated from the German

by LUDWIG LEWISOHN

Meridian Books
THE WORLD PUBLISHING COMPANY
Cleveland and New York

THE JEWISH PUBLICATION SOCIETY OF AMERICA
Philadelphia

Martin Buber

Martin Buber was born in Vienna in 1878. Co-founder of the Jüdischer Verlag in Germany, he also edited *Der Jude* from 1916 to 1924. For a time before leaving Germany in 1938 he taught at the University of Frankfurt. In 1938 he joined the faculty of the Hebrew University in Jerusalem, retiring from his post after fifteen years to continue his translation of the Bible which he had commenced earlier with Franz Rosenweig. His published works cover numerous aspects of contemporary philosophy and religious thought, and include studies in Hasidic literature, which have served to revive interest in this Jewish religious movement. In 1957 he visited the United States where he lectured extensively. His most recent English publication is *Pointing the Way*.

MERIDIAN BOOKS

The World Publishing Company, Cleveland and New York
The Jewish Publication Society of America, Philadelphia
First Meridian printing March 1958
Second printing August 1959
Third printing April 1961

Library of Congress Catalog Card Number: 58-8531
Printed in the United States of America

To My Wife

PAULA JUDITH

FOREWORD

Upon the appearance of the Hebrew * and English **
versions, the intention of this book was misunderstood
by sundry readers and critics. A clarification seems desir-
able which I, alone, may adequately provide.

I did not write this chronicle, as has been said, in order
to "sum up my teachings in a specific manner." The
decisive motivation of this work was furnished by
objective factors which are, to be sure, spiritual in
character.

It was in my early youth that I began to retell what
seemed important to me out of the incalculably rich
treasure of Hasidic legendary material. At first I used
the method of epic freedom; gradually I sought ever
more to limit myself to the necessary, that is to say, to
what seemed imperative according to my notion of narrative form, with the purpose of lending to the data,
generally crude and formless notations and relations, their
appropriate configuration. Finally I concentrated on a
formal type which is found in Hasidic literature in
incomparable fullness but commonly without attaining
its authentic narrative style, namely, the "sacred anecdote." What counts here is almost always the blending
of an event with a saying. It is precisely this blending
which expresses the Hasidic intention which aims at the
oneness of outer and inner experience, of life and teach-

---

* *Gog u-Magog,* Jerusalem, 1943.
** *For the Sake of Heaven,* Philadelphia, 1945.

ing. The event must be narrated with extreme concentration, in order that the saying or maxim may arise from it in pure spontaneity.***

I have been accustomed to renounce material which neither was told anecdotally nor could be reduced to this utmost terseness of form. I have not been concerned merely to narrate but to narrate something specific, something that seemed to me of the utmost import, so that it cried out for narration, something which had not yet been properly narrated and to which to give its right form seemed my duty.

In this process I came upon an enormous coil of stories of interrelated content. They unquestionably formed a great cycle, even though they had obviously been narrated according to two different and, indeed, contradictory traditions and tendencies. This group of stories could not be eliminated, especially because the happenings that stood at their center were of the highest significance. The material had generally been treated from a legendary perspective, but the kernel of reality was unmistakable. It is a fact that several *Zaddikim* actually attempted by means of theurgic or magic activities (the so-called Practical Cabala) to make of Napoleon that "Gog of the Land of Magog," mentioned by Ezekiel, whose wars, as is proclaimed by several eschatological texts, were to precede the coming of the Messiah. Other *Zaddikim* opposed these attempts with the monition that no outer gestures or events but only the inner return of the entire human being to God could prepare the approach of redemption. And what is so extraordinary and remarkable is the fact that all these men, both magicians and monitors, actually died within the space of a single year. Thus there can

*** For a complete collection of the material as far as retold by me, see *Tales of the Hasidim, The Early Masters,* New York, 1947, and *Tales of the Hasidim, The Later Masters,* New York, 1948.

be little doubt that the spiritual sphere in which they were involved, although from different sides, consumed their mortal being. Hence it is not a legendary symbol but a simple fact of experience that in this conflict both sides were annihilated. The point of the conflict was, first of all, whether it was permissible to exert pressure upon the powers above to realize our yearnings and, furthermore, whether an influence may be obtained through magic procedures or through a change of the moral man. And these questions were not mere objects of argument; they were matters of life and death. These events were so concrete and their significance so profoundly searching that it did not seem to me that I dared to avoid the task of their continuous narration. I pointed to this matter in a note in my book, *The Great Maggid* (1921), which runs as follows: "I have renounced including among the stories of this book a series of events, the last of their kind, since they form an entire and separate whole."

In this instance the method used with other legendary material, of placing anecdote beside anecdote, seemed inadmissible. For what precisely it was my business to delineate was the outer and inner connections among them. These connections, however, were very fragmentary in both the written and the oral tradition. So what had to be done was to fill in, as well as one could, the gaps in the material in the spirit of what had been handed down, in order to establish the continuity of the chronicle. The "epic mood" became a duty in this case. But I could no longer, as in my youth, use a free creative activity. I was forced to obey the law of these inner connections, to supply lacks according to the meaning of what preceded and what followed, of the events and characters themselves. For purposes of completion material usually existed, too, even though it consisted only of single strands, usable details, meaningful hints.

Another element entered the matter. As I have said, there were two accessible traditions, representing the two aspects, one having the magic, the other the antimagic tendency, that is to say, the tradition of Lublin and the tradition of Pshysha. Both were, as aforetime, the traditions of the party of Saul and the party of David, the precipitation of a long conflict. Both evidently were related to real events; each selected those that seemed important to it; each narrated these selected events according to its vision of them. What I had to try to do was to penetrate to the kernel from both sides. This attempt could succeed only if I placed myself in the service of neither of the two tendencies. My only admissible point of view was that of the tragic writer who must delineate conflicting forces, each in its own nature, and whose antithesis is not between a "good" and an "evil" will, but lies within the cruel antitheticalness of existence itself. Assuredly, I was "for" Pshysha and "against" Lublin, especially since from my youth on I had found the character and teaching of Rabbi Bunam particularly winning in kind. But in my narrative I had to determine to be just to the reality of both aspects. No positive element of the tradition of Lublin was to be neglected; nor could I utilize the critical elements within the tradition of Pshysha, if these were not confirmed by something essential in the opposing point of view. Now this was undoubtedly a difficult task. But it was eased by a very singular circumstance, namely, this, that whoever penetrates deeply into what is handed down from the side of Lublin will observe that Lublin at its very heart submits itself secretly to its adversary, the "Holy Yehudi."

The writing of this book was rendered possible by the

fact that, just at the period when its theme took strongest hold of me, during the last year of World War I, I took a trip to see my son who was stationed in Poland and could, on the way back, familiarize myself with the physical scenes in which the story of this controversy took place. Thus I acquired the visual imagery.

Yet two attempts at writing the book failed. I put my notes aside without much faith in its ultimate completion, yet not without a faint hope. For it is my experience that books which are given to one to write, ripen slowly and ripen most powerfully when one does not even think about them, so that finally they, as it were, announce their inner completion and need, in a sense, only to be copied.

What, finally, already during my residence in Jerusalem, brought this book to maturity was once again an objective factor, namely, the beginning of World War II, the atmosphere of telluric crisis, the dreadful weighing of opposing forces and the signs of a false Messianism on both sides. The final impulse was given me by a dream-vision of that false messenger spoken of in my first chapter, in the form of a demon with bat's wings and the features of a judaizing Goebbels. I wrote very rapidly—only now no longer in German but in Hebrew (the German version was done later)—so rapidly as if, indeed, I was only copying. All that was visual stood clearly before my eyes and the interconnections yielded themselves readily.

No, it was far from my purpose to lend expression to "my teaching." To be sure, I had to supplement and to extend the teachings of the personalities in this book, but I always did so according to the intention of the documents and in order to complete their indications. I found it possible to do so because I do stand at a point of very vital oneness with those men. When, in my youth, I came in contact with my earliest Hasidic document, I accepted it in the spirit of Hasidic enthusiasm. I am a Polish Jew. To be sure, my family belonged to the enlightened wing, but in the most impressionable period of my boyhood a Hasidic atmosphere made a deep impression on me. Doubtless, there are other, less tangible threads. At all events, I am morally certain that, had I lived in that period when one contended concerning the living Word of God and not concerning its caricatures, I, too, like so many others, would have escaped from my paternal home and become a Hasid. In the epoch into which I was born such things were forbidden according to both generation and situation. Not the premises were lacking in my case, but the inner possibility of preserving them untransformed. My heart is at one with those among Israel who today, equally distant from blind traditionalism and blind contradictoriness, strive with a striving meant to precede a renewal of the forms of both faith and life. This striving is the continuation of the Hasidic striving; it takes place in a historic hour in which a slowly receding light has yielded to darkness. Assuredly not my entire spiritual substance belongs to the world of the Hasidim. This has commonly been the situation of those who desired to resuscitate a past and transform it into a new reality. But my foundation is in that realm and my impulses are akin to it. "The Torah warns us," a disciple of the Holy Yehudi and Rabbi Bunam, namely, Rabbi Mendel of Kozk, said, "not to make an idol even of the command of God." What can I add to these words!

Another reproach that was addressed to me was that, whether consciously or not, I had changed the figure of the Holy Yehudi under the sway of a "Christianizing tendency." I may reply that I have described no single trait of this man which does not exist in the tradition, which also includes those sayings of his that remind one of some in the Gospels. Whatever in this book the Yehudi may have in common with Jesus of Nazareth derives, not from a tendency, but from a reality. It is the reality of the suffering "servants of the Lord." In my opinion the life of Jesus cannot be understood if one does not recognize the fact that he—as has been pointed out by Christian theologians too, especially by Albert Schweitzer —stood in the shadow of the concept of the "servant of the Lord" as we find it in the Deutero-Isaiah. But he emerged from the hiddenness of the "quiver" (Isaiah 49:2), the while the Holy Yehudi remained within it. It is necessary to visualize the hand which first sharpens the arrow and then slips it into the darkness of the quiver, and the arrow which huddles in the darkness.

I, myself, have no "doctrine." My function is to point out realities of this order. He who expects of me a teaching other than a pointing out of this character, will always be disillusioned. And it would seem to me, indeed, that in this hour of history the crucial thing is not to possess a fixed doctrine, but rather to recognize eternal reality and out of its depth to be able to face the reality of the present. No way can be pointed to in this desert night. One's purpose must be to help men of today to stand fast, with their soul in readiness, until the dawn breaks and a path becomes visible where none suspected it.

evidence." Thus apart that I feel sure that no single text, if the man spoke that he was a teacher, in which the reed appears so vivid and so personal that of all we have of ... whatever might be, to which any have an intimate intelligence of ... Indeed, there are ... nevertheless ... in ... If it are of the ... of the subject ... concerned the content in my opinion, the life of Jesus cannot be understood, and is ... but recognise the fact that he will not have profited and by Christ in the religious ... expected by ... their separateness stood in the ... shadow of the complex and the ... raising the form we we find it in the Harmony ... it is not convinced than ... still possesse the "places" ... Verily, ... the solid, the High ... but ... it remained no that in it is necessary to ... that the ... which the first displays the error and the ... middle and the ... and of the ... and ... and the intellectual middle, in the ... fashion.

It must have the conform ... My critical ... ... another ... the features of this group, He who ... that one great teach- ing historians a ... the ... of this ... movement will always be ... and have also, and if ... some to ... indeed that in this ... of ... the ... not to possess ... and ... that other ... remaine except it ... that ... of ... of ... to it in ... ... its ... ... so we can be ... to it in that of ... of the ... that ... time of our ... of ... in ... and ... mad in ... and in ... and ... the claim ... and ... would ... ... while ... maybe expected, it.

CONTENTS

THE FIRST PART

THE "SEER"

TIME was when swamps surrounded the hill on which
the castle stood in the northeasterly part of the Polish
city of Lublin. None dreamed of settling on those inhospi-
table lands. Then it came to pass that, nigh four hundred
years ago, Jews, who drove their trade in the city but were
forbidden to dwell within its limits, took it into their heads
to buy ground out there. Lot after lot around the hill was
drained. Beside a house of prayer and study rose first the
houses of great rich Jews, next of the poorer and very poor-
est, seeming to cling and nestle and cleave closely to the hill,
so that at last the immemorial castle with tower and church
rose from amidst its fast and castellated walls out of a very
coil of Jewish lanes and alleys and Jewish vaults.

Now if one were to traverse the main street of this Jews'
town, which bears the name of "Broad," he would come
upon a house which outwardly is indistinguishable from its
neighbors. If, however, emerging from the dark and narrow
entrance hall, he were to step into the courtyard about which,
like all the other houses, it is built, he would see before him
a low, extensive building with a wooden roof, and at once
the long series of tall, dim windows would show him that
this is no house in which men dwell, but one in which they
assemble. If he were to open the door he would behold a
hall with spotted walls and a ceiling of smoke-darkened
beams.

On the ground floor of the house that fronts the street,
with but an attic above it, there dwelt, in the days of the Napo-
leonic wars, the Rabbi Jaacob Yitzchak, called the "Seer."

The building in the courtyard was his *Klaus*, his withdrawing-place, as it were, in which he prayed and studied with his disciples. They took no part in the offices or studies of the Chief Synagogue; they were hasidim, the "pious" ones, one of the many hasidic congregations, of which each clung tightly about its rabbi, as about a very kernel. The established order wanted no dealings with them nor they with it, yet from a distance they fought both subtly and powerfully for the souls of the rising generations.

Jaacob Yitzchak was called the "Seer" because in truth he "saw." It was told that, when he was born, he had been able to see from world's end to world's end. Thus had man been destined to see when on that first day of Creation, ere yet a constellation was in the firmament, God's Word caused to arise the Original Light. When man encompassed his own ruin, God hid that Light in His treasury, whence it will shine, when the day comes, upon the redeemed. The child who "saw," however, was so dismayed by the flood of evil which he beheld engulfing the earth, that he besought the gift to be taken from him and his vision to be restricted to a narrower span. But as Jaacob Yitzchak grew up, actually from his twelfth year on, he had not been able to endure even this narrower seeing; for seven years he had hidden his eyes under a thick veil; he had unveiled them only for prayer and study, and in those seven years his eyes had grown dim and short of sight. With this stricken vision, behind which the seeing soul endured in undiminished strength, he looked upon the forehead of each of the numberless people who came wayfaring to him to beseech that a wonder come to pass — whether they were the poor who asked that this burden be taken from them, or the sick who needed healing, or the barren who prayed for increase, or sinners who strove after purification. Then he would take each slip of paper, on which each suppliant had written his name and that of his mother and had named his desire, and hold it close to his eyes, of which the right was somewhat larger than the left, and read the few words again and again and ponder them. Then he would give the slip back to the *gabbai*, the manager of his household, who arranged these meetings and was mediator and keeper of the slips. And at such moments the suddenly transformed eyes of the Rabbi, the strangely enlarged pupils, the tenseness of the cornea, bore witness to the fact that he "saw." What did he look upon and whither? For at this moment there was nothing left in the broad chamber that might receive his glance. He gazed (so it is related) with those eyes of his which "were within his power" into the depth of time and saw the origin and story of the soul of each suppliant, of which the mortal dwelling place, the body, stood before him there. He saw each soul's ultimate descent and root, whether it had once proceeded from the side of Cain or of Abel; he saw how often during its pilgrimage it had entered a human frame and how each time it had wrought ill or well at the great task which it was destined to accomplish.

But because we speak here of terror in the face of the world's excess of evil and of the distinguishing between the souls that were descended from Abel or from Cain, let it not be thought that the "Seer" turned his face from sinful men and would have no dealings with them. It was known to all men, on the contrary, that he was more passionately concerned with nothing on earth than with sinners. When complaints were addressed to him concerning such who made no secret of their wickedness, he was accustomed to say that dearer to him was the evil-doer, who knew that he was evil, than the just man, who knew that he was just. And the full meaning of this saying reveals itself when one considers that the "just one," namely, *Zaddik*, is the actual title of rabbis of the hasidic sect.

From time to time, therefore, Rabbi Jaacob Yitzchak would add: "There is many a one too" — he did not say *Zaddik*, but the overtone implied the word — "who is evil and knows not that he is so. He is among those of whom it is said that at the very gates of hell they will not experience the *teshuvah*, the inner return to good. Such an one has the conceit that he is taken to hell to save sundry souls from it. Once he is inside, however, they will not let him out again." He would laugh his brief, clipped laugh: "No, they will not let him out again." And he went even farther in his distinguishing love, making no secret of the fact that a passionate opponent of the hasidic Way was closer to his heart than a lukewarm adherent. The former, if once the spirit were to come over him, might become a glowing hasid, while of the latter nothing more was to be hoped. Thence it was clear how greatly the Rabbi was concerned with inner glow, with passion, even indeed with what is called the evil impulse or tendency, seeing that without it there is no manner of fruitfulness, whether of the body or of the spirit. Nevertheless he never neglected to point out that fruitfulness alone does not suffice; the test is the quality of the fruit brought forth. Nor did the Seer cease at the mere praise of passion. Among the stories which hasidim still relate to each other in our time, with the same mysterious wagging of the head they used in his, the strangest is perhaps that of a very great sinner, who always found the *Zaddik's* door open and with whom he loved to converse at length. When people came to him and ventured to remonstrate, saying: "Rabbi, how can you endure such an one in your presence?" — his answer was: "I know all that you know about him. But what can I do? I love joy and hate dismalness of soul. Now this man is a very great sinner. Even immediately after the accomplishment of sin when nearly all men are wont to repent, though it be but for a moment, though it be only to plunge back into folly soon enough, even in that hour this man resists heaviness of heart and does not repent. And it is joy that attracts me."

Rabbi Jaacob Yitzchak did in very truth hate heavy-heartedness. It is related that once upon a time during a journey, he had not been able to fall asleep in a new bed just built for him. The carpenter, a God-fearing man, had built the bed during the nine days on which men bewail the destruction of the Temple, and the man's woefulness had stung the Rabbi as with a thousand thorns. So it came about naturally that dolefulness troubled him more than sin itself. Thus another time a man came to him complaining of how deeply he suffered from the visitation of evil passions and how he had therefore been plunged into deep melancholy. The Rabbi lifted up the man's heart with counsel and gave him direction. But then he said: "Avoid melancholy with all your might. It hurts the service of God more than sin. Satan takes less pleasure in sin than in a man's melancholy over having sinned again and so feeling that he is a slave to sin. Thus the Evil One has caught the poor soul in the net of despair."

At this point, however, a saying is to be added which he confided but to a single disciple, who handed it down. "This is a strange matter," said he, "and one that I do not understand. People come to me with mournful hearts and when they leave me their hearts are brightened. Yet I myself am . . . " And here, according to a sound he uttered, it seemed as though he was about to say "heavy of heart." But he caught himself and said instead: "And I myself am dark and do not shine."

MIDNIGHT

It was in the autumn of the year 1793, a few days after the festival of the Rejoicing in the Torah. To the surprise and dismay of his familiar friends, Rabbi Jaacob Yitzchak had celebrated the feast, not as he was wont to do, with a very great and all but boundless gaiety, but with the air of a sufferer who affects a merry mien so that no one shall be aware of his suffering. It had been remarked that, even when he danced with the scroll of the Torah in his arms, his tread had been heavy.

As on every night, so on this had the Rabbi arisen before midnight. For the truly devout are commanded to mourn over the ruined sanctuary and to search in the Law at this hour. Do not the partakers of the hidden wisdom know that at this hour the demons begin to roam the earth in the bodies of dogs and asses? Soon now through the night that "other side"* of things comes to the surface and seeks a road to the King of the World. Men lie in their beds and in the midst of their sleep have a foretaste of death. But when at midnight the wind of the North awakens, that is to say, when evil arises in its power — as it is written: From the North is evil let loose — then there arises a holy tumult in the world. He who in this hour mourns the exile of the *Shechinah* (the Presence of God) and thereafter bends his mind to the Law, by *his* virtue are the evil beings cast back into the abyss and he himself may draw near to the Holy One, Blessed be He. Concerning this matter the *Zohar*, the Book of Brightness, relates the parable of a king who caused a poisonous serpent to coil about the chest which held his most precious treasures, to keep from it the eyes of the impertinent. But to his friend he confided the power to render the serpent harmless and to contemplate his treasures as much as his heart desired. These are the reasons why it is well to arise before midnight.

As he did every night, so, too, on this night the Seer sat him down with naked feet near the doorpost to which is fastened the capsule which is inscribed with the Name of God. He took ashes from the hearth and strewed them on his forehead. After he had recited hymns of lamentation and such as cry out for help, he arose from the floor and repeated the

* The wrong side: evil, temptation, disintegration.

[8]

words of the prophet: "Shake off the dust and arise, thou prisoner Jerusalem!" Thereupon he returned to the beseeching of the Psalms.

It is prescribed that the midnight lamentation be uttered with tears and cries of woe. And so did the Seer utter it night after night. But when he came to the words "with the voice of jubilation and thanksgiving, a festively striding throng," or else "they bowed them down and are fallen, but we arose, we drew ourselves up," his voice was wont to be so full of gladness that joy triumphed over mourning. This time it was not so. He murmured the proud words with a weary air and when he had finished he heaved a deep sigh. Before he proceeded to the study of the Law, he said softly, as he often did: "Lord of the World, perhaps I am among those of whom it is written: 'What right hast thou to proclaim my Laws?' " Weeping overcame him and it was long before he could open the Book of Brightness in order to seek the significance of the passages which treat of midnight. He sat down on a low stool, so that his knees were high and supported his elbows. His head rested on his hands and he closed his eyes so tight that his lower lids felt the pressure. As always, there appeared to him first a plane or surface of the color of blood; this surface was next rent asunder down its middle; light flooded through, at first with the dull whiteness of milk, then radiant and purer, and at last there was nothing but the whiteness of that light. "Why didst Thou do that unto me?" Jaacob Yitzchak asked.

It was exactly a year ago that at such a nocturnal hour he had prayed that it might be revealed to him as to who was worthy of leading the congregation after his own death. He listened for an answer.

"Jaacob Yitzchak," said the familiar voice.

He thought he had been called. "Here am I!" he replied. The voice was silent.

[9]

Again he petitioned: "Make me to know whom I am to appoint."

Again the voice said: "Jaacob Yitzchak."

Until dawn broke he sat on his low stool. He heard no more, neither did he ask any more. On the next morning, contrary to his custom, the Seer stepped forth into the large hall of his *Klaus*, from the small chamber in which, himself unseen, he shared the morning prayers. In an instant his disciples thronged about him. Slowly he raised his hand; he was about to speak, when a tumult arose at the entrance door. A stranger, known to none, pushed his way through the departing crowd of worshipers. The man was wrapped in a prayer-shawl, which he must have donned in the street; he ran up to the Rabbi. Everyone took him to be one of the petitioners who lay in ambush, as it were, in order to relate their troubles to the Rabbi "in a favorable hour." They were going to bid the man wait. But the Rabbi waved them aside. When the man stood face to face with him, he regarded searchingly the strangeness of the figure. All saw now that the man was quite young. His hands were the reddish uncertain hands of a boy, but his mouth was molded to completeness. He had been running with his head thrown back and kept it in this position still. His earlocks swayed softly; he panted in staccato fashion. But his thin and pallid lips were so tightly compressed, that it seemed as though one lip must inflict pain on the other. And now, before the Rabbi had addressed him, he opened his mouth very wide and cried out in a voice which was like the sound of a cracked mortar of iron when its side is struck by a pestle: "Rabbi, accept me as your pupil!" It sounded not like a request; it sounded like a demand, not otherwise than the demand a creditor might make upon a debtor, except that the voice was a cracked and broken voice.

"Who are you?" asked the Rabbi.

"Jaacob Yitzchak, the son of Matel," answered the stranger.

All were amazed, for Matel had been the name of the Rabbi's mother. The Rabbi himself had turned pale. For a little while his eyes underwent a change, as in those hours in which he peered into the depths of time. But thereupon his glance became painfully confused; his lids twitched; he drew his spectacles from his pocket, a thing he did most rarely. He put them on and said: "I accept you as a pupil."

The year which had passed since that day had been a year of ceaseless pain. The new pupil bore himself not otherwise than a creditor might do, who was obliged to take repayment in kind, in board and lodging. He treated his fellow pupils with condescension. Whenever he caught sight of one of them a jeering smile appeared on his thin lips, which, however, he dropped after a brief space. Leaning against the door he watched closely out of his peering dull-gray eyes the many, many people who came from all directions to the Rabbi and who waited in front of the house or in the antechamber, and it seemed as though he were making a list of them in his mind.

He never approached the Rabbi, who observed all this, except with a very zeal of serviceableness, nor did he ever fail to ask whether he might execute some command. During the hours of instruction, which proved him to be as learned as he was acute, he proposed problems of that kind which must lead even the sagest master on and on to a coil of illimitable speculation. Yet he never pursued this method beyond a certain point. Unexpectedly he would drop the discussion and with a sigh as of admiration would say in a loud whisper: "It is as the Rabbi declares." Worst of all were the hours of private converse with the Rabbi which he asked for at almost regular intervals on the ground that he needed help against the temptations that beset his soul. He used these hours to tell stories out of his own life. And it seemed to the Rabbi that these stories were the events of his own youth or, rather, the evil distortion and caricature of

[11]

these. What he remembered as the arch face of a child was transformed into a stealthy grimace; there was no path so smooth but that it was not now pock-marked with holes and crevices. So soon as the teller of the tales saw the change in his hearer's expression, he would make the confession: "Yes, Rabbi, I am indeed a great sinner." In such wise the year passed.

On its last day, however, on the day prior to this night in which the Rabbi brooded over all these matters, this disciple, unannounced by the *gabbai*, had made his way into the room of the Rabbi who was writing by the light of two tapers. It was before the time of the afternoon prayers, which the hasidim of Lublin recite later than is done elsewhere. The disciple had stood facing his master. The Rabbi paid no attention and went on writing.

"Rabbi!" said the pupil.

The Rabbi raised his thick dark eyebrows and continued silently to write.

"Rabbi," said the student, "when will you announce to them how it is to be with me?"

Carefully, so as not to blot his paper, the Rabbi laid his pen aside. He looked up and said: "Go!"

"How? What?" the other stuttered, and now it was a trembling falsetto voice that issued from his thin lips. "I? I am to go?"

"Go!" said the Rabbi and arose. His head with the deep straight furrow down the forehead loomed in all its power over that other who had fallen silent and now retreated with shaking knees. The Rabbi followed him to the door. "You are to pack your belongings at once and set forth," said he.

"I, I would but say farewell to the comrades," the other muttered.

"You have no comrades," said the Rabbi.

Of all this he was thinking now, of all that year including its last day, as he sat on the low stool with eyes tight shut and

[12]

stared into the white light. It seemed to him like one single happening seen in this single moment of time. "Why didst Thou do this thing to me?" he asked. No answer came. And suddenly Jaacob Yitzchak was impelled to laugh, because he had asked: "Why?" He laughed, and laughing rolled from the low stool and lay for long hours upon his countenance with outstretched limbs until the coming of the dawn.

THE WAGONER

Next day was Friday. Now Friday is, as everyone knows, no ordinary separate day, but rather the out-rider and herald of the day ahead. Right after morning prayer the disciples in Lublin set to work preparing the house of study for the Sabbath. The week's dust was wiped from the benches and the floor was scrubbed. While this was being done the Rabbi entered. Although he had performed his lustration at dawn, it was evident that he had immersed himself in the ritual bath a second time. His hair scarcely gleamed with moisture, but his feet still had the motion as though they were stepping out of water. He went up to the groups of youths and did a thing he had once done daily but had now long omitted to do. He asked each, one after the other, for his pipe which had just been cleaned and smoked a few vigorous puffs with each, returning it thereupon to its owner. The disciples had interrupted their work. They stood still and gazed at him in wonder.

Thereupon he went into his house and ordered the *gabbai* to begin to admit the hasidim who had come from near and far, many of whom had been waiting for a number of days; for of late the Rabbi had been unwilling to see strangers. Today, moreover, having pronounced each time the saying: "May the Holy One, blessed be He, and His *Shechinah* be One

[13]

again," he did not content himself with contemplating the faces and small written petitions of the people. He let them speak out; the advice and direction he finally uttered were clear and simple in each instance, even though they often took the listener by surprise. He counselled the lessee of a farm, who complained that he could not pay his rent, to buy the small estate on partial payments, assuring the man that the coming harvest would be so plentiful and prices so high that he had nothing to fear. Another declared that doubts tormented him and that they refused to be silenced. The Rabbi urged him to leave open the window of his chamber by night, for unrenewed air causes mildew to form upon the soul. Next they brought a boy to him, whose mind had fallen into disorder. Instead of seeking to subdue him, as is customary in such cases, by powerful adjurations, he went alone with the boy into the adjoining room. There he carried on a far-reaching conversation with him. At first the listeners heard the boy growl stubbornly. Next he cried out loud in amazement; finally he seemed to be telling a long story which was interrupted from time to time only by his own laughter or the Rabbi's. At the end of an hour the latter called in the boy's parents and directed them to let the child visit him daily at this hour. For the rest, they were to let him do unhindered whatever he would, seeing that he was sure to do nothing harmful. Hereupon the boy again broke out in gay, bright laughter and said with loud assurance: "I'll do no harm."

Already for some time there had been heard an increasing tumult in the street without. But the Rabbi had been so absorbed in the matter before him that he had paid no attention. Now the cries of "David! Rabbi David! Rabbi David Lelover!" reached his ears. He went out. In front of the house there was assembled a small group of hasidim who had evidently come recently from another town. In their midst stood a long rack-wagon, drawn by two powerful white horses. In front of it the drover could be seen. But an extraordinarily sturdy youth had taken the man's whip from him and held him by the collar in a grasp which, though it seemed casual, more than sufficed to prevent the drover from leaping into his seat and dashing off, a thing he evidently much desired to do. Opposite the drover, surrounded by students who continued to shout: "Rabbi David!" and clapped their hands and indulged in leaps, there stood a man, who was nearer fifty than forty. He wore a neat but badly patched *caftan*, secured by a girdle of straw, and on his thick locks of chestnut brown still bright with a youthful sheen he wore not the accustomed fur-rimmed hat but a rather shabby cap of cloth. His cheeks had not lost all the bloom of youth and neither his chin nor the hollows of his eyes nor his forehead displayed a single wrinkle. He had been speaking emphatically but quite without violence or passion to the drover. So soon as he caught sight of the *Zaddik* he turned to him and bowed in salutation. All those who had come with him followed his example, even that sturdy lad who held the drover by the collar and did not release him even now. The bystanders, who could not get their fill of gazing at the queer figure of the young man, perceived with astonishment that, though he himself was no mere youth and could not have been more than twenty years younger than Rabbi David, a blush suffused his face and throat at the sight of the Rabbi of Lublin. Having saluted him, David at once addressed the *Zaddik*.

"Rabbi," he cried, "what is one to do with a man like this? He beats his horses! How can one bear to do such a thing? On the way hither to you more and more hasidim with their bags and bundles kept getting into the wagon. Finally I could no longer bear to see the horses draw so patiently the ever heavier load; I beckoned to the people. 'Brothers,' I said, 'let us dismount and walk for a little.' They all heeded me, leaving only their luggage in the wagon, and we walked

[15]

behind. Now you might think that the horses would have begun to go faster. Far from it! They adapted their pace to ours. Horses are wise animals, aware animals, not without understanding. And now what do you think happened? This drover fell into a rage. Instead of being glad that we were careful of his precious property, he began to beat the horses in his anger. 'What are you doing?' I cried out to him. 'You must know that the Torah forbids us to torment any living being.' 'It is proper,' he replied 'that travelers sit inside of the wagon.' 'We shall not deduct anything from the fare agreed upon,' I said. 'It is not proper this way!' he cried. 'Nevertheless,' I said, 'why do you beat the horses?' 'They are my horses,' he made answer. 'That is no reason for beating them,' I said. He cried: 'They are mere senseless beasts!' You should have seen the horses. They wagged their ears and pricked them up and knew well enough that what was happening was their concern. 'Do you fancy,' I asked him, 'they draw the wagon because they are afraid of your blows? They draw it because they will to draw it.' And what answer did he give me? 'I cannot and will not argue with you,' he said and began beating the horses again. And at that moment —"

At this point the drover cut him short. "Holy Rabbi," he said, "have pity on me and let me get in a word too."

"What do you say to that, David?" the Rabbi asked.

"Let him say his say," David of Lelov answered.

"Speak, Chajkel," said the Rabbi who knew by name all the drovers of the entire region.

Therewith Chajkel began to speak, even though that grip on his collar was not loosened, while David of Lelov took off his cloth cap, remaining covered by his small skull-cap alone, and, fetching oats from some capacious pocket, filled the former with it and held the food out to the horses.

"Rabbi," said Chajkel, "do I not know right well who he is? I'm not from Lelov myself, but do I not have to go there

[16]

week after week? And every time I get there, do I not hear
him spoken of? Of whom should the people of Lelov be
speaking if not of him? I know well enough that he is himself
a *Zaddik*, even though he would be accounted merely a disciple of yours, and I say that he is crazy for all that! Do not
hasidim come running to him and write petitions on slips of
paper, and would they not be only too happy if he were to
accept their 'redemption moneys?' But he will take nothing
from any. Then what does he live on with his wife and all
the children, big and little? He tends his little shop and con-
sents to sell no more a day than will suffice to gain him that
day's need! 'Would you not rather buy at the widow's to
the right,' he says to customers, 'or yonder from that pious
man, who is far more upright than I?' And when he's rid
of the customer he sits down to study Torah. Look you, the
very whip, which he's let that fellow take — did I not buy it
of him? And do you know what he said to me when I bought
it? 'That whip,' said he, 'is made to crack over the horses
only, not to beat them with.' Are those not the words of a
crazy man? But now hear what took place on the journey
hither. Ought we not by rights to have got here yesterday?
For we set out from Lelov on Monday, the day after the feast
of the Rejoicing in the Law! But no sooner did we reach any
little town, but this mad *Zaddik* made me stop. Next he
gathered all the children of the place and gave them sweets
and gave each a little whistle. And that wasn't the worst.
He'd pack the whole crowd of them into my wagon and make
me drive them all over the town while they whistled. Was
that all? Oh, no! If we passed through a village in which
but a single Jew lives, he said each time that a brother of his
was living here whom he must visit, whether to ask after his
well-being, because the last time the man had been ill, or to
find out whether a daughter who, when he was here before,
was looking for a husband, had been married meanwhile;
and if it wasn't this thing it was another, and everywhere I had

[17]

to stand and wait. All right, all Israel is a band of brothers. All right! But a man's patience does give out! Was I to beat *him*? I beat the horses!"

"Is this thing which the man tells me true, David?" the Rabbi asked. "We may pass over the matter of the children. But is it true that he had to wait in the villages, because you had a brother dwelling in each of them?"

"It is assuredly true," replied David of Lelov, "and I will give you an accounting of how it came to be so. The first time that I repaired to your teacher and mine, the great Rabbi Elimelech in Lisensk, he refused, as you know, to receive me. He was revolted by the self-castigations which I had practiced in my youth. I went so far as to hide behind the great oven in the house of study. He caused me to be sent away. All the long Sabbath I waited in vain for a word from him. It was not until the next day, when I ventured to enter his house again, that he came forth to meet me and saluted me with pleasure. But before going on I must tell you what happened to me in the meantime. I did not sleep at all the night following the Sabbath, and Sunday morning I saw no hope of ever being received by Rabbi Elimelech unless I entered anew upon a period of preparation. Therefore I started without delay on the way home. In the first village through which I passed, a Jew, who was at the window of his house, caught sight of me and called out to me: 'Tarry a moment!' When I did so he said: 'Consider: here you have a brother dwelling among so many strangers. How can you fail to enter and ask concerning your brother's life and well-being?' I entered his house and we conversed concerning many things and had become good friends when it was time to say farewell. When I was back upon the high road a purpose arose in me with overwhelming force. And this was the purpose: never again on any journey to pass through a place where a Jew dwelt until he and I had recognized the brotherhood between us. And even as I vowed to fulfill this purpose there flooded my heart on a sudden that feeling which is called the love for Israel and to which I had hitherto been a stranger. With equal suddenness thereupon I was filled with a very great faith, which caused me to turn back to Lisensk and to enter the house of Rabbi Elimelech. It was now that, as I told you, he came forth to meet me and saluted me with joy. Since that moment I have kept my vow and kept it on this journey too."

"It is well," said the Rabbi and was silent for a space. But then he smiled and asked: "Is it true, too, that you took the man's whip away from him?"

"That is true too," David answered. "He had to be prevented from belaboring his beasts. To be sure, I did not take his whip from him myself. My feeble strength would not have sufficed. But I caused this friend of mine to do so. In addition, because the whole matter was to be put before you, I also said to my friend here: 'We must see to it that he does not escape us at the last moment. Therefore, so soon as the wagon stops, grab his collar and hold him fast, Jaacob Yitzchak ... !' "

"What — what is it you said to him?" the Rabbi asked.

"Why, I said that he was to hold the fellow fast."

"Yes, but what else did you say?"

David was taken aback. "What else? Only 'Jaacob Yitzchak,' that's all ..."

"What? You said: Jaacob Yitzchak?"

"Why not? That is his name. Here he is."

With these words he drew the man forward, so that the drover's collar and whip were released. Blushing hotly the man stood before the Rabbi. All eyes were upon him. He had the broad shoulders of a bearer of burdens, but a very straight back. His head was large but narrow, and brown hair shadowed his habitually pale face; boldly his nose projected directly from the forehead and his mouth was gentle. Everyone looked upon his large hands, which had delicate skin and slender fingers, and upon the strange power that dwelt visibly within them.

At this moment there emerged from a crowd of curious peasants who had assembled in the background a tall man in a white sheepskin coat and a white lambskin cap. With measured tread he passed through the crowd of hasidim who made way for him and faced the young Jaacob Yitzchak. He patted his shoulder and cried out in Polish: "Here for once we have a *Yehudi* — a Jew!" And on the instant he was no more to be seen.

From that day on young Jaacob Yitzchak was known in Lublin not otherwise than as "the Yehudi" and in the hasidic world not otherwise than as "the holy Yehudi." The youths, however, who soon gathered about him, were sure that that peasant had been the prophet Elijah who, as is well known, is fond of wandering about in the garments of the indigenous population and of speaking its speech.

At last the Rabbi spoke again. "Blessed be they who come," he said and gave his left hand to David of Lelov. "Blessed be he who comes," he said and gave his right hand to the young Jaacob Yitzchak. Chajkel, the drover, had meanwhile faded out of the picture with both his wagon and his whip.

DAVID OF LELOV TELLS A TALE

Soon thereafter David and the Rabbi sat facing each other in an upper room. Both smoked their short pipes and regarded each other in friendly silence. Finally the Rabbi broke the silence.

"You have never told me, David, why, since the death of our master six years ago, of the great Rabbi Elimelech, you came journeying to me and have done so ever since."

"There is not much to say on that subject," David observed, "and what there is to say is not greatly to my credit."

[20]

"Tell me just the same," said the Rabbi.

"Well," said David, "no one knows most of the story better than you yourself. When the long ascetic exercises, the repeated fastings from Sabbath to Sabbath, the tortures of the body too, had not only reduced me to a skeleton, but had made me arrogant and disconsolate at once, I heard that there were such people as hasidim in the world. I thought to myself: I must take a look at them. They must be strange beings who hold that the way can be trodden without ascetic practices. And once I came upon a hasid who was just returning from his Rabbi. 'What teaching did you hear from your Rabbi?' I asked him. He said: 'The interpretation of the scriptural words: And though thou wert to wash thee with lye . . .' 'Where dwells that Rabbi?' I asked. 'In Lisensk,' he replied. Thus I came to make my way to the Rabbi Elimelech. On the way I had to spend the night in the town of Lantsut, where you lived at that time. When the people told me about you, I went to you and begged you for a night's lodging. What happened thereupon I needn't tell you."

"Do repeat it," said the Rabbi.

"Well," said David. "You asked me why I desired lodging of you and not of another. I replied that, according to what I had heard, I could be sure that in your house all food would be prepared conscientiously and precisely according to the directions of the Torah. Thereupon you commanded your manservant to strike my face twice and to put me out."

"True, true," said the Rabbi.

"I did finally get to Lisensk. I have often told you that he would not receive me. But one matter I have not related even to you. As I was hiding behind the oven in the house of study that day, he came in and went straight up to the oven and beckoned me to come forth. So I stood before his countenance. 'Whence do you come?' he asked. 'From Lelov,' I answered. 'Who is it at Lelov who observes most faithfully and precisely all the prescriptions of the Torah?' he asked.

I could not but be silent, for I thought: how can I answer, seeing that in truth I am that one? He did not wait long. He bade his manservant to strike my face twice and to put me out. What followed I told you long ago."

"Things have been well with you," said the Rabbi.

"Have they in truth?" David asked.

"Yes," said the Rabbi. "But what I do not yet know is why after the death of our master you came to me."

"Well," David replied," because you too commanded my face to be stricken twice."

"It is clear to me now," said the Rabbi. "One more thing I would have you tell me. You sent me a message that you would come on Succot, the feast of Tabernacles. Why did you not come then?"

"It fell out thus," said David. "I was on the road hither, but I delayed even more than I did this time, and so I had reached a village not very far from here when Succot was upon us. A sense of dread came over me, because it was not being granted me to sit on this day at the pure table here in Lublin. But I considered and comforted my soul after this fashion: If the world knew what the Rabbi of Lublin really is, people would come from the four fringed corners of the world to be near him. In that case his table would be so very great that it would extend even unto this village and I, David, the least of them, would be sitting here, just where I do sit, at the farthest end of that board. Hence I am sitting at the Rabbi's table. So I passed the two festive days in great rejoicing. Then I went back home. For I said to myself: now the time for going to Lublin is past. Coming home, I found that my friend Jaacob Yitzchak had come meanwhile to visit me and was waiting for me in my room. So I said to him: 'After the day of the Rejoicing in the Law, Jaacob Yitzchak, we will both go to Lublin.' "

"Tell me something about this young man's character" said the Rabbi.

"What is there to tell?" asked David. "It is clear for all to see."

"Tell me nevertheless, David."

"I do not well know how to tell about another adult human being. I can tell about myself, but beyond that I can tell only about children. So, if you desire, I will tell you about his childhood, as much as I know."

"Tell me," said the Rabbi.

"It does not show, perhaps, that even in his boyhood he was a great student."

"It shows," said the Rabbi.

"Neither in his native town nor round about very far was there another boy who equalled him in power of research into the Law. But this was known to none. People said to each other that his father, an excellent scholar, must be wretched to have a son who does not understand what he learns. For in the house of study the boy listened with all his might, but reflected and was silent. A friend of his, a fellow student, the only one to whom he gave his confidence, told me of all this much later. Nor did any one know of the fervor of his devotion in prayer. In truth he was held to be careless, for he was often absent from morning prayers. In his native town it was customary to close the house of prayer after them. He would climb in through a window or a skylight and pray in front of the Holy Ark. Once his father, who hitherto had paid no great attention to him, surprised him thus. He opened the door of the synagogue and saw his son lying in prayer before the Ark. He did not enter but closed the door again softly. From that hour on he quietly observed his child's behavior. He noticed that the boy heaped his plate with food at each meal, but that he stealthily slipped most of the viands into his pockets or into a bag which he had prepared. He made inquiry and found that daily after the chief meal his son made his way to the quarter where the poor dwelt. There boys of his own age or older gathered

about him. He divided the food among them. After they
had assuaged their hunger he studied with them. This too
the father guarded in his heart. He did not speak of it to his
son. He let him have his way and ordered that he was to be
served copiously at every meal.

"A brother of his father lived in a far outlying town and was
a poor sexton there. But he was one of the thirty-six hidden
Zaddikim . . . Rabbi, why is it said that these hidden ones
sustain the world? Is the world not rather sustained by the
manifestly righteous who are our leaders?"

"The manifest just," said the Rabbi, "are themselves sustained by these hidden ones. Moreover, that within them
which serves to sustain men belongs to their hidden and not
to their manifest nature. All that sustains belongs to the
realm of the hidden. But go on with your story."

"This hidden *Zaddik*," said David, "would come to see his
brother from time to time. They would then take a walk in
the open country beyond the town and discuss the mysteries
of the Torah. Once they took the boy with them and he
walked along behind them. They came to a meadow on which
sheep were grazing. And they could not help seeing that a
great conflict had broken out among the beasts concerning
the sharing of the pasturage. The bell-wethers were ready to
ram each other with their horns. No shepherd and no dog
was to be seen. In an instant the boy had leaped forward;
in an instant he took over the governance of the meadow and
established order. He separated the fighters and composed
the quarrel. He assigned pasturage to each sheep and each
lamb according to its need. And there were some animals
who now made no haste to crop the grass but thronged
about the boy who scratched their coats and spoke to them.
'Brother,' said the sexton, 'the boy will be a shepherd of the
flock.' "

"And in all this time," the Rabbi asked, "did the world
get no news of him?"

"Well," said David, "these matters scarcely belong to his childhood any more. Moreover, where does the childhood of such an one cease? One thing is certain: he was still almost a child when they caused him to marry. His native town had by now ceased to satisfy his ardor for learning. He went wandering and came to the house of study in Apt, over which his former teacher presided. Here he soon became known. He knew more than any of the other students; his knowledge was a living thing, which he mastered independently. What, to be sure, was not known was that he pursued the secret ways of wisdom too, seeing that he did so by night either alone or with one companion. It was now that a prosperous baker and innkeeper took care to secure the famous boy as his son-in-law. This man, in point of fact, drove only the baker's trade. His wife, whose name was Goldele, managed the public house. She had a capacious memory in which she stored up accurately the life stories of all who frequented the inn. A newcomer was a suspicious character to her, until she had added his whole story to her stock. She was annoyed with this youth, to whom she had married the older of her two daughters, the very day after the wedding, because he was impenetrable by her. What good to her was a fellow about whom she could circle seven times without being able to figure him out? Nor was it as though he had acted reserved. He regarded her with a friendly glance; he answered all her questions readily. Yet was this the worst. For if a man keeps things from you deliberately, you can resort to tricks and stratagems. You cannot do that if he opens all the chambers of his soul and you find in none of them what you are seeking. And now a worse thing came out. In addition to the chief daily meal which the young spouses partook at the parental table, the woman would send them all kinds of delicacies, things beyond use and wont, such as rich pastries and rare wines. And she found out that the greater part of these things was given to poor sick people.

[25]

The notion of these rarities being consumed by those who had no appreciation of them — that was too much! She had been proud of her son-in-law, not only because people spoke of his great gifts, but because she hoped that an intercessor like him might be an investment in the world to come. Now it was clear to her that he could not be good for much. A man who wasted vintage wines on the vulgar could not be sound in his learning either. Nor was this all. He was often absent from congregational devotions. In his father-in-law's barn, which was full of straw and green fodder, he had prepared himself a little corner. It was there that he prayed with his mighty fervor when the time came that his whole soul was ready for prayer. And so it came to pass that Jaacob Yitzchak, whom no monition separated from his bad habits, was banished from the paternal board. His wife had to bring him food.

"One day, moreover, a matter came to light which caused all people, especially the hasidim, to fall into consternation. I must tell you that the ritual bath in Apt . . . But tell me, Rabbi, what is the mystery of the ritual bath?"

"The very fact that you ask as you do shows that you have thought out an answer. You would now know whether it harmonizes with mine. What is your opinion?"

"Since you desire me to tell my thought I will do so. But it is in nowise an answer. My thought is this: you descend in the bath, deeper and deeper you descend. And when you are at the very bottom, it is then that in very truth you bow down. That is all I know."

"And that is the right knowledge."

"But now I beg of you, Rabbi, give me the answer."

"You know, David, what our sages aver in the interpretation of a verse of scripture: 'God is the ritual bath of Israel.' "

"I do not perceive yet, Rabbi, what you have in mind."

"Immersion, David, the act of total immersion. Only it is not given us, as it is to the angels, to immerse ourselves totally. They, after they have performed their service, are totally immersed in the river of fire and do not re-arise until the time of their service recurs. Only during the space that he fulfills his service must each angel exist as he who he is, that is, as he who performs this service which none other can perform. Only as servitors are the angels persons and not at one with the fiery river of their immersion. But we do not descend into fire; we descend into water. We are not consumed nor do we know rebirth. Immersed we are still those who we are. But to immerse ourselves until not a hair of our head shows and to remain immersed as long as we can endure — such is our ultimate possibility. But go on with your story, David."

"The ritual bath in Apt," David went on, "is so deep that it takes ninety steps to descend to it. There is no way of ever warming the water. During a great part of the year a sheet of ice covers its surface, and they who would use the bath must break the sheet of ice. The hasidim never come singly, but in little groups of ten or more. And before they go down they build a little pyre of wood and set fire to it that they may warm themselves at it on emerging. Jaacob Yitzchak never joined these groups. He would always arise before midnight and go alone to the ritual bath. He would immerse himself without any fire and return home and pronounce the midnight songs and then for hours pursue the study of secret lore.

"Now it happened that near the bathhouse there dwelt a woman who cooked doughnuts all night in order to sell them early in the morning. She had been watching Jaacob Yitzchak. Hence every night she placed at the door of the bathhouse the kettle of boiling water into which she put the doughnuts before baking them in the oven, in order that the solitary bather might warm himself a little before he went home. Nor did he disdain to do so; for he had never, like myself, been prone to ascetic practices. For a long while the woman said nothing. But at last she confided the matter to a neighbor and soon the whole town knew. From this time on the hasidim treated Jaacob Yitzchak as familiarly as one of themselves. His father-in-law, however, a simple soul, fell at his feet and asked for his forgiveness.

"The next day he left the town and for many years he wandered from place to place as a *melamed*, a teacher of children. In one of these places the children told me about him. They said: 'This is a man you should know.' And so I did come to know him."

"Why did you not bring him to see me before this?" the Rabbi asked.

"I tried hard enough," said David. "For I saw clearly how, after all his years of study, he yearned to be set on the right path. But silence was all the answer he made me. For he is a stiffnecked fellow. He is not to be moved by someone else's will. But he is not to be moved by his own will either. The two acts of willing must coincide. He celebrated Succot in my house. I expected no answer from him when I said to him: 'Let us journey together to Lublin.' He looked into my eyes and said: 'Let us do so.' "

THE TABLE

In a side room of the inn at which the pupils of the Seer were wont to take their meals there stood a long, narrow, unpolished table, a very ancient table, covered by a thousand marks of age, but sturdy as the day it was made. There was nothing noteworthy about this table, yet it attracted the glances of all visitors of the inn who passed it. Perhaps this was so because the table stood there in such a fashion that one could not imagine its not having been there forever or ever ceasing to be there. It was related that the mysterious *Zaddik* who for unfathomable purposes followed the courses of rivers, visiting this inn whatime he followed the banks of the river Bystrzyca to Lublin, remained silent before this table. Thereupon he lifted his hands over it and said: "Remain standing till Messiah comes."

On this, as on every Friday afternoon, there sat about this table a small group of the pupils of the Seer. On all other days they ate in the Rabbi's house; on the Sabbath at his own table, on weekdays by themselves. Most of today's group were the younger disciples. David of Lelov was not among them. He was eating at the Rabbi's board. Present was the tall, thin Judah Loeb of Zakilkov, oldest of all those who were gathered in Lublin, himself once pupil of Rabbi Elimelech and one who, after the great man's death, had himself sought to "lead" but had soon abstained — he was sworn enemy of all festivity and so never partook of these meals at which the comrades pledged each other in mead or brandy. Among those former disciples of the Rabbi Elimelech, who had passed the Holy Days in Lublin and had not yet found it in their hearts to leave, there was the profound and subtle Kalman of Cracow, who was eager to get to know the younger men; there was the most faithful of all, the pious Mordecai of Stabnitz, who had brought the Rabbi to Lublin; there was the clever Naftali who, however, had not come to Lisensk until after the Seer had left his teacher and had established a congregation of his own. Moshe Teitelbaum was present too, he of whom it was related that he had long resisted the hasidic teachings and had even refused to permit the Rabbi Elimelech, whose attention was upon him, to instruct him in the mystic lore. It was of him that the Seer had said that he preferred his passionate opposition to a lukewarm discipleship. Now he was a light of lore and learning.

At the narrow end of the table, which usually stood against the wall but had now been drawn away from it in order to create space for the newcomers, chairs had been placed for Jaacob Yitzchak and for the friend of his youth, Yeshaya,

[29]

whose loyalty to him had originated in their native town and who had joined him on this journey to the Seer. Yeshaya was even more silent than his friend. He looked as though he had not dreamed to its conclusion a dream of the night and were now seeking to spin the vision to completeness.

Scarcely had these two taken their places than they heard the cries addressed to them: "Now each one of you place a jug of mead on the table." This being the duty of novices, the two complied.

Immediately a second cry arose: "Now each of you relate a thing you have experienced. But there are conditions we set: the story must be brief and concise; it must have to do with Lublin, yet Lublin must not be mentioned."

"I cannot tell tales," said Yeshaya softly.

"We can't permit that," they cried. "You must make an effort. If you do not succeed, you will have to practice during the following weeks until you have learned how to tell a tale."

"You will not be able to get anything out of him," Jaacob Yitzchak now declared. "But if you will permit me to substitute for him I will gladly tell you two stories in place of one."

"But in that case," they objected, "we would learn nothing concerning the story of his life."

"Whatever," said the Yehudi, "you will learn of my life will be equally true of his."

They discussed the matter for some time. At last it was agreed to accept the proposal on condition that as a penalty a third jug of mead be provided. Jaacob Yitzchak reflected as he contemplated symbols cut into the ancient table in front of his seat, symbols which apparently formed the initials of his names. Then he began.

"My first story will be called: 'How I Apprenticed Myself to a Smith.' When I was boarding in Apt in the house of my father-in-law, the baker, the window of my room looked out on a smithy. When I would take my seat at my window in the morning with my book, the fire of the smithy was already blazing and the bellows hissed and the smith, almost without taking breath, beat down on the anvil. The ringing of the hammer on the anvil was the accompaniment of my daily morning studies. But as time went on I could no longer bear to find the man already at work before I had begun. I arose somewhat earlier. It availed nothing. The hammering over there was in full blast and the sparks flew to the very street. I got up still earlier; it still availed nothing. 'I cannot let that mere mechanic put me to shame — me who am striving after the life eternal,' I said to myself and sought again to get the better of him. In vain. Thus things went on for awhile, until I arose so early that I had to light a candle to read my book. It was too strange to endure any longer. I went downstairs and entered the smithy. The man ceased working at once and asked after my desire. I told him of the experience I had had with him and begged him to tell me when he began to work. 'Until a short time ago,' he answered, 'I began at the usual hour. We smiths are all early risers. But then I saw that every day a little later than I you came to the window and began to read. Thereupon I said to myself that I could not very well permit someone who strains nothing but his head to offer me competition. So I went to my anvil earlier and earlier. Yet it availed me nothing, for always you were already there.' 'You cannot possibly understand,' I said to him, 'what I have at stake in my work.' 'Undoubtedly I cannot,' he replied, 'but can you understand what I have at stake in mine?' Thus I learned that it is necessary to seek to understand what our fellows have at stake."

"Oho," cried one of the students, who had been growling to himself for some time. "You are evidently one of those who would like to understand everybody and everything!"

"Not at all," Jaacob Yitzchak replied. "But since that experience it strikes me as unseemly to question another's understanding of me, while I have not yet come to understand him."

"You are right," Kalman said. "And you, Simon," he addressed the first speaker, "of you I have been told that, after copious potations, you once confided to our comrades that even the Rabbi does not understand you. That seems not a little curious."

"That was well said, Rabbi Kalman," one of the others agreed. "Now, however, Jaacob Yitzchak, tell us your second story."

"My second story," said Jaacob Yitzchak, "is even briefer and more concise than the first. Its title is: 'How I Apprenticed Myself to a Peasant.' You are to know that, after I left Apt and had set out on my journeying, I came upon a huge hay wagon which had been overturned and blocked the road diagonally. The peasant who stood beside it called out to me, begging me help him lift up the wagon. I looked at the wagon. Truly, my arms are not without strength and the peasant seemed quite a man, too. But how were two men to lift up that enormous weight? 'I cannot do it,' I said. The other snarled at me. 'You can,' he cried, 'but you're not willing.' That struck me to the heart. We had some boards; we inserted them under the wagon and used all our strength in this act of leverage. The wagon stirred and rose and stood. We piled the hay on it again. The peasant passed his hand over the sides of the oxen who still trembled and panted. They began to draw. 'Let me walk along with you awhile,' I said. 'Come right along, brother,' he answered. We trod along together. 'I would like to ask you something,' I said. 'Ask all you like, brother,' he answered. 'How did you happen to think,' I asked him, 'that I was unwilling to help?' 'I thought of that,' he replied, 'because you said you could not help. No one knows whether he can do a thing until he has tried it.' 'But how did you happen to think,' I questioned

[32]

him again, 'that I could do this thing?' 'Oh that,' he answered, 'that just popped into my mind.' 'What do you mean by that?' 'Ah, brother,' he said, 'what an insistent fellow you are. Very well, it popped into my mind, because you had been sent my way.' 'You will end by telling me that your wagon was upset in order that I might help you!' 'Well of course, brother, what else?' "

"Pretty stories enough," Simon Deutsch interposed. "But you have not fulfilled the necessary conditions. What have your stories to do with Lublin?"

The eyes of the Yehudi flamed. "What is it you have learned in Lublin," he cried, "if you have not learned this, that each has his own way of serving. Did not Rabbi David tell me how once upon a time disciples of a famous *Zaddik* came, after the *Zaddik's* death, to the Rabbi of Lublin. They arrived in the evening and found him standing on the road, where he was pronouncing the 'sanctification of the moon,' which was just emerging from among clouds. They observed at once that his custom in regard to the ceremony differed somewhat from that of their late teacher. They nudged each other. When, later, they entered the house of the Rabbi, he greeted them and said: 'What kind of a God would He be, who has but a single way of serving Him!' "

Another student had sprung to his feet and now lifted his hand.

"What have you in mind, Yissachar Baer?" he was asked.

Slowly and solemnly he answered: "It is true; it is true indeed. I myself besought the Rabbi to show me the way of service. The answer he gave was: 'There is none such. It will not do to tell one's comrade what way he is to pursue. There is a way of serving God by study, another of serving Him by prayer; one by deeds of loving-kindness toward one's fellows; there is a way to be pursued by fasting and there is one to be pursued by eating. And all these are right ways to the service of God. But each man is to observe well toward which one of these ways his heart inclines him. Thereupon he is to be active upon that way with all his might.' "

"It is so indeed, dear friend," said Jaacob Yitzchak. "Thus the smith served with his work in the smithy."

"Agreed," Simon assented. "But what has your second story to do with Lublin?"

As swiftly as on that other day he had flushed at the sight of the Rabbi, even so the Yehudi now became pale as death. "You are always talking," he said without lifting his eyes and very softly, yet in such a manner that his words were more audible than a mighty cry, "of the exile of the *Shechinah*. You lament that the *Shechinah* wanders about in exile, faints with exhaustion and lies on the very earth. And that is indeed no empty talk. It is really so. You may meet the *Shechinah* upon the very roads of the earth. And what do you do when this meeting takes place? Do you stretch out your hands? Do you help raise up the *Shechinah* from the very dust of the road? And yet who should do this thing if not the men of Lublin?"

Simon sank into a morose silence. But Moshe Teitelbaum bent forward.

"What do you mean by those things that you are saying?" he asked in a tone of irritable zeal. "We know that it is granted only to those very few, who are capable of the highest spiritual concentration, to cause the *Shechinah* to re-approach its source. And what do you mean when you say that we meet the *Shechinah*? We do know that from time to time it has visited certain individuals with its grace, as for instance, that Rabbi Levi Yitzchak of Berdichev, who found it in the Tanners' Lane. And what kind of a road is that, of which you say that upon it one may meet the *Shechinah*?"

Jaacob Yitzchak had fixed his eyes upon that point of the table, on which his initials stood. His pallor continued.

"The road of the world," he said, "is the road upon which we all fare onward to meet the death of the body. And the places in which we meet the *Shechinah* are those in which good and evil are blended, whether without us or within us. In the anguish of the exile which it suffers, the *Shechinah* looks at us and its glance beseeches us to set free good from evil. If it be but the tiniest fragment of pure good, which is brought to light, the *Shechinah* is helped thereby. But we avoid its glance, because we 'can not.' That is not strange when it comes to the rest of us. But Lublin may not avoid the glance; Lublin dare not doubt but what it 'can!' "

Among the others at the table there sat one who had come to Lublin from far away for the first time on the New Year. He did not partake of the drinks. He had been devoted to another master. But in the summer before the last, during the street fighting between Russians and Poles, this master had been hit by a Cossack's bullet. Since then the disciple had been the leader of his own congregation. In spite of that he had come to the Seer. This man's name was Uri, but his familiar friends called him the Seraph. He turned to the Yehudi.

"Concerning Lublin," said he, "one can say nothing until one knows it from within. No one knows a sanctuary until he has stood within it. He who knows Lublin, knows that it is the Land of Israel, that the court of this house is Jerusalem, that the House of Study is Mount Moriah and that the room of the Rabbi is the Holy of Holies, wherein the *Shechinah* speaks from his throat."

"It is indeed so," Kalman of Cracow agreed. "When it is given to a human being, as it has been given to our Rabbi, to purify himself utterly and to sanctify his two hundred and forty-eight organs and his three hundred and sixty-five sinews, then is he held worthy of being a vessel of the *Shechinah*, who speaks from his throat."

Jaacob Yitzchak was silent. His face was no longer pale;

[35]

his clenched fists lay on the table before him. Yeshaya sat beside him with closed eyes.

A disquietude ran through those who sat about the table. Several of the students had arisen; two or three from among them now approached one who had not hitherto opened his lips, although as a rule he was the most voluble among them and given to bubbling with jest and jeer. "Well, Naftali," they whispered to him. He waved them aside and continued, as he had done the whole time, to stare at the newcomer so intently, as though he desired to fix the image in his mind with such clarity that he might thereafter recall every detail of it at every instant. But after awhile he, too, began to speak. His face did not dislimn into flickering planes as was its wont, whenever he told his little stories. It remained calm and whole.

"We are full of gladness," he said, "and because we are glad we are kind to each other. And why are we glad? Because we are here. And what is this 'here'? Here is the place where the miracle takes place."

"The miracle," said Jaacob Yitzchak, "is not of such great importance."

"What would you call important," Naftali asked, "if not the miracle? I will relate to you a miracle performed by the Rabbi."

As was customary, when a miracle of the Rabbi was to be related, he sat on the table with legs crossed under him. He spoke:

"When the Rabbi was still living in Lantsut, a man lived there who had risen from poverty to great wealth. He owned many houses, but dearer to him than all these possessions was his seat in the synagogue which he had bought. It was close to the seat of the Rabbi. The wheel of fortune took a turn and he lost all his wealth. But he would not sell his place in the synagogue. He refused all offers with these words: 'That is my share of reward for all the weary travail of my life.'

Things went so far, however, that he was forced to beg from door to door. He also took to drink and the respectable citizens were ashamed to sit so near him. Consequently one of these bought up all the little promissory notes which the poor man had issued and summoned him before a Rabbinical Court and forced him to give up his seat in the synagogue. But when on Sabbath morning people would come into the synagogue, they always found the man already in occupancy of his old seat and they did not bid him leave it. On the Eve of the Day of Atonement, however, when, prior to the prayer which releases us from frivolous vows, the scroll of the Torah was brought out from the Holy Ark and all thronged forward in order to kiss it, the purchaser of the place used the poor man's momentary absence in order to occupy it. When the latter became aware of what had happened he raised a great cry. The crowd ran toward him in order to help him. Fist fights began and the tapers were extinguished. The tumult was hushed and the congregation was about to intone the evening prayer, when the Rabbi cried: 'In Heaven you are being judged!' The people broke out in tears, but all turned to their neighbors in entire loving-kindness and they prayed with souls bitter but renewed. After the prayer the Rabbi said to them: 'Great is the power of the *teshuvah* — the turning unto good. You will all be preserved unto life.' And so it proved to be. Of all those who were in the synagogue on that day none died in the ensuing year."

"The miracle," Jaacob Yitzchak repeated, "is not of such great importance."

"What then would you call important?" Naftali asked. "Did not the Rabbi himself say that the miracle bears witness to the indwelling of the *Shechinah*?"

"What is important," said the Yehudi, "is the weeping; the *teshuvah* is important, and love is important. It is important that the Rabbi set free good from evil and thus help to raise up the *Shechinah* from the dust of the road. The

[37]

miracle merely bears witness; hence it is not so important. How do you know whether the Rabbi does not hide himself behind all his miracles, in order that you may not see him, himself?"

This was too much for Meir, the younger brother of Mordecai of Stabnitz. "Enough and more than enough!" he cried. "We need not to be instructed by a fellow who has come hither from we know not where, and who can grasp neither what the Rabbi is nor what Lublin is."

The waves of tumult rose high. Nearly all sprang to their feet and talked to each other with violent gestures. Simon and Meir and several others had climbed on the table at both sides of Naftali and beat upon it with their pewter mead cups and cried out aloud.

Jaacob Yitzchak unclenched his hands and pressed his palms upon the table. The veins on the back of his hands stood out in high relief. A quiver ran over his right temple. Suddenly the opposite end of the table rose high in air. Those who sat at this side of the table tried to cling to it as they were swung upward, others at the other end jumped down or slid to the floor. The head of Simon Deutsch struck the ceiling.

"May your strength persist!" several of those who were standing close cried out to Jaacob Yitzchak. For an instant the table remained almost on end. Then it began to be lowered with a slow and even motion until the antique piece of furniture had resumed its accustomed place. They were all silent. Then Yissachar Baer raised his hand. "Long life to the Yehudi," he said solemnly, and although Meir, who was accustomed to initiate him in the mystic wisdom, looked at him angrily, he, too, repeated the words.

A sudden smile appeared upon the gentle lips of the strong Jaacob Yitzchak. "It is hard to be a Jew," he said. Then he looked back at the table and asked: "Who has cut my initials into the wood?" No one knew. "And why further-

[38]

more," he asked, "are the two letters *Yod* cut into the wood one above the other and not next to each other?"*

"Very naturally, because two *Yods* next to each other signify the name of God," someone said.

"In that case," Jaacob Yitzchak announced, "I will now tell you a final story."

"Tell us!" they cried out to him.

They had all peacefully re-assumed their seats about the long, narrow table. And Jaacob Yitzchak spoke:

"The way it is when two men drink each other's health and each feels equal to the other and neither of them considers himself superior, that is a matter which I experienced when I began to learn the alphabet. In the book before me I saw the letter *Yod*, which is so very like a mere point. I asked the teacher: 'What kind of a little point is that?' 'That is the letter *Yod*,' said he. 'And does that little point,' I asked, 'always stand alone or can two of them stand together?' 'Two of them may stand together,' said he. 'But how does one read them then?' I asked again. 'When two *Yods* stand together,' said he, 'that signifies the name of God, Blessed be He!' Soon thereupon I saw that at the end of each verse of Holy Scripture there stand two points, one above the other. I did not yet know that these are the points of separation; I considered each of these two points to be the letter *Yod*. 'Here,' I said to my teacher, 'there is printed constantly the name of God, Blessed be He.' 'Not at all,' the teacher replied. 'Mark my words: when two *Yods* (Jews) stand beside each other it signifies the name of God; but when one stands above the other it does not signify the name of God.' "

Kalman of Cracow and Mordecai of Stabnitz bade mead to be brought in and they all drank each other's health.

*

Yod is the name of the tenth letter of the Hebrew alphabet. In Yiddish it also means "a Jew," from the Hebrew *Yehudi* (German, *Jude*). Two *Yods* placed side by side frequently are used as a symbol for the name of God. The initials of Jaacob Yitzchak's name would have been two *Yods* placed side by side.

[39]

On the next day, which was the Sabbath, a crowd thronged the Rabbi's study, following afternoon prayers, about the table prepared for the holy "Third Meal." In Lublin it was customary to invite to one of the Sabbath meals even the opponents who, despite their opposition to Hasidism, had come to the *Zaddik* with some matter concerning which they were asking his advice and help. They took their places at the table as opponents, but it was said that none ever rose from that table as an opponent still. While the *Zaddik* was speaking they tried to hold on to their hostility with both hands, as it were. They did not succeed. His voice was like a mountain torrent, which swept away all in its path. But it was not his voice alone. All that took place in this room at this hour and all that did not take place cooperated with that voice.

The tables were so placed that in the hither part of the study two of them stood perpendicularly to the long wall. Two others joined these diagonally, so that a kind of gable was formed, but not wholly completed. Between these, at the farther end in front of the door leading to the Rabbi's private chamber, there stood a small table, at which he always sat alone. Thus no one ever sat opposite him.

As was the constant custom at this meal, one sole course was served, namely, fish. This custom was considered a mystery. In Lublin it was explained as follows: It is known that the souls of the righteous, who have not yet completed their pilgrimage, enter into fish. If one eats these fish in the right spirit of devoutness, the souls will be redeemed. But since, from the beginning of the Sabbath on, a "higher soul" takes up its abode in every Jew and dwells within him throughout the Sabbath, these redeemed souls may rest in a holy communion before, at the end of the Sabbath, they wing their way to Heaven.

[40]

Dusk had begun to fall. Behind those seated at the tables, the hasidim stood thickly crowded. There was whispering and silence and renewed whispering until the entrance of the Rabbi, who wore his Sabbath coat of white satin, brought a clarified silence into the room. The Rabbi pronounced the blessing over the bread, broke it, tasted of it, shared it with those who sat nearest. Then he stood with closed eyes and intoned the introductory saying: "Prepare the repast of perfect faith, the rapture of the Holy King." He lowered his voice as he named the names of the heavenly guests. Then he raised it again: "And the fields of the holy appletrees — they come to celebrate the meal with us." This was followed by the special hymn of the third meal which all the hasidim spoke with him: "Sons of the palace, ye who yearn...!" With extraordinary emphasis resounded the verses "Approach, behold my might; gone are the stringent judgments, exiled hence, no more shall those dogs, the impudent ones, make their way in!" And only now and without cantilation, simple as a prosaic communication, came the psalm: "The Lord is my shepherd, I shall not want." After this psalm he drank wine from the beaker and said: "I come now to fulfill the command of the third Sabbath meal which corresponds to Jacob, the father of the host of seventy souls." Hereupon he raised his voice and pronounced the next sentence with an emphasis so powerful that all his familiars knew that this would be the guiding text of the present Sabbath among all Sabbaths: "Through his merit shall we be saved from the wars of Gog and Magog."*

They ate and drank. Those whom the Rabbi desired either to delight or to honor he sent a piece of fish from his platter. This constituted, as it were, a special meal, which the recipient shared with the Rabbi. Thus within this great communal sacrifice, as which this meal was interpreted and within which the *Zaddik* functioned as high priest, there were

*See the Glossary.

included these special personal unions between himself and certain of his faithful. The head of a pike was sent in this manner to the young Jaacob Yitzchak and he blushed for the third time.

After the meal the Rabbi bade them sing the hymn: "God, who hides Himself under the secret canopy!" Soon thereafter he instructed Kalman of Cracow to pronounce the final blessing. Thereafter, as was his custom at the end of this meal, he drank a single glass of wine very slowly.

Now the twilight was deep. All were silent. Suddenly the the Rabbi drooped forward in his seat, so that his forehead touched the table. Without seeing, all were aware that his whole body trembled. They sat motionless and held their breath. No one dared to approach the Rabbi. In breathless silence a period passed. The darkness deepened. And very suddenly the Rabbi raised his forehead again. "The flaming of the circling sword!" he cried. Again he fell silent and again his limbs trembled, but now only those who sat near to him could observe it. Then he began to speak softly and with a hesitation so intense as though he were drawing one bucket after another out of a deep, deep well.

"It is written," he said, "that the serpent spoke to Eve: ' . . . and ye shall be as God, knowing good and evil.' Did not the first human beings know good and evil even before this? They knew concerning things that were bidden and things forbidden, those concerning which the Holy One, Blessed be He, desired that they come to pass, and those which He desired that they do not come to pass. Hence they did know good and evil, even as a human being in his merely human manifestation does know them. The serpent, however, said not until man becomes as God would he know good and evil. This, then, is clearly another kind of knowing from the merely human knowing. For it is written: 'He who makes peace and creates evil.' If He Himself creates it, it cannot be something concerning which he desires that it be not. It

[42]

must be another kind of 'evil' than that which Adam and Eve knew. One can only know this other evil, if one creates it. Consequently the serpent meant: You will know good and evil like one who creates both; you will know good and evil not merely as something that you are to do and something else which you are not to do, but as two forms of being, which are as contradictory to each other as light and darkness. Did the serpent speak truth or falsehood? God Himself later confirmed the fact that the serpent did not lie. Nevertheless its words were not true either. It uttered a lying truth. The Holy One, Blessed be He, knows the two things which He has created and goes on creating, namely, good and evil, even as He knows light and darkness, as two things, which at the very ends of the earth stand opposite each other and opposed to each other. But the first human beings, so soon as they had eaten of the fruit of the tree, knew good and evil as blended and confused. It is this blending and confusion which was brought into the world through their deed. This it is concerning which it is said that in the sphere of the planet Venus good and evil are intermingled.

"But what is this evil which God creates? It is the power to do that which He desires that it does not come to pass. Had He not created it, no one could commit a sin against Him. But He desires His creature to be able to oppose Him. He has given that creature freedom. He has given it the power to act, as though omnipotence did not exist. The creature is not deluded in thinking it can act contrary to God's will; it really can do so; it has the power. This is the innermost meaning which is pointed out to us by the saying that primeval being took on the limitation of cosmic form. We are taught that He apportioned space for the world within Himself. What is supremely important is this, that out of His omnipotence He saved a fragment of genuine power, which he apportioned to every human being. And that this portion of power is the genuine power of God is proven by the human being's ability to rebel against God. And without this genuine power, of which each human being has a share, the good would not exist. For the good exists only when it is done with this entire power. But what is this good which God creates? It is man's utter turning to Him. When man turns away from evil with that whole measure of power with which he is able to rebel against God, then he has truly turned to God. For this reason the world exists by virtue of the *teshuvah* — the 'turning.' It is the light, which breaks through the darkness. As it is written: 'He who forms the light and creates the darkness.' Creation is above forming. The darkness is created and the light is formed within it and drawn forth from it. As my first teacher, the *Maggid* of Mesritsh, may his memory be for a blessing, used to say: 'As the oil is in the olive, so is the *teshuvah*, repentance, hidden within sin.' But the darkness *is* in order that the light might be.

"The primeval serpent is a fragment of the darkness. We are told that it brought to naught God's purpose for the human race. How can that be, if He did not Himself give the serpent the power? It seduced those first human beings. But if they had resisted, it would merely have been a temptation, and the tempter is always empowered by God. In the Book of Samuel we are told that it was God who impelled David to count the people, but in Chronicles it is said that it was Satan who did so. And in the *Book of Brightness* we read that there is with God a principle, which is called 'Evil' and which confuses the world and lets it slide into sin and from whence arises all of man's evil impulse; and that this is God's left hand. But in the *Book of Radiance*, in connection with a saying of our sages that we are to serve the Holy One, Blessed be He, with both impulses, the good and the evil, the question is raised how anyone can serve Him with the evil impulse. Is it not the evil impulse which prevents man from approaching God and from serving Him? And the

[44]

answer is given that it is the highest service to submit the evil impulse to God through the power of love. Only he who does this becomes truly one who loves God. All tempting takes place by His will.

"But why was the serpent cursed?"

A quite special excitement overcame the disciples in the midst of the breathlessly listening crowd at this moment. For a guest, who had dwelt here for a whole year and in fact until the day before yesterday, a tricksy spirit, had propounded a similar question to the Rabbi during an hour of instruction on one of the interval days of Succot. "How are we to understand it," he had asked, "that in the Midrash we are told concerning the serpent that it was destined to punishment?" The Rabbi had brushed the question away like a troublesome insect. But now!

"Why was the serpent cursed?" said the Rabbi, and now he spoke even more slowly but with slightly raised voice. "Because it tainted the truth of temptation with a lie and thus distorted the word of God. It is God's will that in the process of temptation His word and whatever impels man to act in contradiction to it shall stand veraciously face to face. His seal is truth. He does not deceive Abraham when He tempts him. He really demands that which is dearer to Abraham than life itself — the sacrifice of the promised son, on whom depends the fulfillment of all promises. He really demands everything, in order to give everything anew to him who loves Him, after that loving one has truly given up all. It is his veracious messenger who wrestles with Jacob, on the journey commanded by God, unto the rising of the dawn and wounds him. Only out of the extremity of danger arises the grace which confirms the elected one after all his errant wayfarings. God practices grace and truth when in the camp of the night he attacks Moshe who, chosen by Him, is on his way to Egypt at His bidding, and seeks to slay him. Not until He has affianced Moshe to Himself in blood, as a

[45]

'Bridegroom by Blood,' does He set him free. The great grace of God is the grace of a pardoning. It is dreadful, dreadful, dreadful! Dread is the gateway to Him; there is no path to Him save through that somber gate. Only he who has gone through that gate can truly love Him, Him, and in the manner in which only He can be loved."

Once more the Rabbi lowered his voice. "It is written," said he, " 'strange is His work.' The primeval darkness, of which we speak, is a black fire. From it He hews flames, somber burning fragments of darkness, and sends them upon the ways of the world. Each fragment falls into the soul of a human being and consumes all that would resist Him. Such an one then sallies forth with all his might, and might streams toward him from round about until a great black river of fire floods the lands and sears the life of the peoples. But upon each of these fragments of darkness there is imposed a duty and a measure. For it is sent forth in order that, when it weighs heavily upon the earth, there should awaken in the depth of that spot on which it weighs most heavily the seed of light, so that this small white spark, at the point where the pure colorless fire is drawn from the blackness, may leap over into the innermost kernel of the dark and light may be formed therein and drawn forth. And thus there is imposed the duty and the measure upon each of these fragments that are hewn out not to exceed so greatly in weight that the awakening seed of light is extinguished. But because the darkness is fearful of the coming of the light, it will happen again and again that one of the hewn-out fragments will swell and, like its prototype the serpent, extend beyond the boundary assigned to it. And then it happens to them even as it did to the serpent. This it is what was written concerning Sennacherib, 'Assyria, rod of my wrath,' whatime it was said to him: 'I lay my hook in thy nose and my bridle on thy lips,' and concerning Nebuchadnezzar it is written: 'the king of Babylon, my servant,' and to him then are spoken the words: 'And

[46]

thou art driven forth from among men and with the beasts of the field is thy dwelling place.'

"And whatever the rage of the inundation of the darkness, it never succeeds in smothering the seed of the light. Evermore the light is born anew. But evermore it consumes itself again and is extinguished. It is extinguished, but its life enters into that power from which again and again the seed of light is awakened. And that power grows. It is full of soreness and sorrow from all the extinguishing of the lights; yet does it wax stronger and stronger. Even as it is told of the Messiah, that he sits at the gates of Rome in the guise of a leprous beggar and binds up his wounds. Yet does he grow stronger and stronger and were he to shake those gates they would burst asunder. For the Messiah is the image and the similitude of the power of which we speak. And the last increase of his strength is reserved for the great ultimate combat. For the strength of the darkness grows, too, and ever denser and greedier are the fragments hewn therefrom as they are scattered upon the ways of the world, and ever more mightily does their power summon forth the counter-power of the light. And it has been prophesied that an hour will come in which a gigantic flame of the black fire will roll over the seventy peoples; it will carry them along in its flood; it will challenge God Himself to combat. Thus will arise the man who is called the Gog of the land Magog. And to him, too, the Lord speaks that He will turn him aside and drive him forth and bring him from the sides of the north to the hills of the land of Israel, where he is destined to fall. But he will fall by the hand of him whose hand is armored as a symbol of the plentitude of power, as it is expressed in the last words of King David, 'with the iron and the wood of the spear.'

"We have been taught that God's action in respect of the combats of Gog and Magog corresponds to His action in our liberation from Egypt and to His revelation to the peoples after the victory of His revelation to Israel on Sinai. The

[47]

paths of that action go through the darkness, but the path of revelation goes through the light."

It was quite dark in the room now. Through the darkness gleamed the Rabbi's white coat and above his scarcely visible countenance his great luminous forehead. Again he lowered his voice. To all who were accustomed to listen to his words it seemed now as though he found it most difficult to say what still remained to be said, but as though he could not resist the urgency to say it.

"It is written," he began, " 'Truly, Thou art a God who hides Himself, God of Israel, Thou Redeemer!' He is the God of Israel in His character of Redeemer. But He is the Redeemer in the character of the God who hides Himself. His redemption waxes in secret; that, which occurs there, is a 'strange work.'

"In the *Book of Marvels* we are told that if in the name of God, *Shaddai*, one single point, the tiny letter *Yod* were lacking, there would remain the word *Shod*, that is to say, devastation. It is by virtue of this dot that the awful power of God, which at any moment could utterly devastate and annihilate the world, brings about the world's redemption instead. This dot is the primeval originating point of creation. Prior to any creative act it stood above the radiance of God which, unlike the primeval light of the world, was no created thing, but was from everlasting. The light of redemption will break forth from the darkness, but the light of God is anterior to the darkness and above it. Therefore it is written: 'He makes the darkness His hiding place,' for truly does He die and veil Himself in the darkness; and thus it is also written: 'He swathes Himself in the light as in a shawl,' for truly He has clad Himself in the light. But that dot is above the light. We come to learn about the darkness when we enter into the gate of fear, and we come to learn about the light, when we issue forth from that gate; but we come to learn about that dot only when we reach love."

[48]

The Rabbi fell silent. For a long while they sat in the darkness and uttered no sound. Then David of Lelov intoned the melody of our arch-father Jacob which, as is related, was handed down to us by the holy Ba'al-Shem-Tov. He had committed it to memory when, once upon a time, during one of the wanderings of his soul, he dwelt as a sheep in Jacob's herds and listened to the playing of Jacob's flute. All those present joined in the singing. The first stars were beginning to look in at the windows. After another period of silence the *Zaddik* arose. They stood up with him and pronounced the evening prayer with him. Thereupon, a lit candle before him, he performed the ceremony of the separation between the Sabbath and the profane days of the week. That single taper, which illuminated his figure alone among the deep shadows of the room, brought out in high relief his great stature and the power of his ruddy countenance. When in pronouncing the benediction of the separation the Rabbi came to the words: "He who separates between the holy and the profane, between the light and the darkness," those who stood near him saw great tears run down his cheeks. After that benediction they all joined in singing another melody, which also was preserved under the name of the Ba'al-Shem-Tov: "He who separates the holy from the profane, may He have mercy upon our sins."

THE QUESTING DISCIPLES

After the assembly had broken up, the younger students as well as a few of the older ones danced, as it were, arm in arm through the streets of the Jewish quarter and sang songs concerning the prophet Elijah, who is the master of all good tidings and concerning whom it is prophesied in Scripture that he will come before the great and dreadful day of the

Lord in order to turn the hearts of the fathers back to the sons and of the sons back to the fathers. But Mordecai of Stablitz whispered to his brother: *"He* is Elijah." When they came to the Jewish Gate they stopped and danced a circular dance.

Later, when night had come, all the disciples gathered in the Rabbi's dwelling and sat with him at one table for the "farewell meal of the Queen" which, similarly to the other three Sabbath meals — namely, that of the Sabbath Eve, that of the Morning, and that of the Afternoon — was named according to one of the arch-fathers. This meal is called The Meal of King David, the tradition being that, since God had announced to David that he would die on a Sabbath, the king established a meal of gratitude at the end of every Sabbath which still saw him in life. Closely pressed together they sat about a gigantic bowl of freshly prepared beet soup, called *borsht.* The plates were filled again and again, and with the soup they ate warm, freshly baked bread. Meanwhile they sang all the gay and sacred melodies which are suitable for this hour which bridges the gap between the sacred in time and the profane, partly in order to accompany home the Sabbath Queen who had visited them from above, but also in order to provide a last mortal delight to each of the single royal Sabbath souls. For in this hour those "higher souls" still dwell within those whom they are visiting and have not yet begun their heavenward flight. While they were eating they concentrated all the power of their thought on the task of drawing some of the radiant light of the Sabbath repasts to last them through the repasts of the coming week. During the singing, however, they were bidden to relax after all the concentration of the festive day and to give themselves over wholly to the songs. In this hour, too, anyone was free to ask the Rabbi any question that occurred to him, whether in earnest or in jest. It was customary, indeed, to prefer the

jocular ones. Furthermore it was permitted to ask the Rabbi
to tell a story; he had never been known to refuse.

"Rabbi," they cried, "do tell us the story of Rabbi Elimelech and King David!"

"But I have told you that story so often," he objected.

"But today," they urged, "there are newcomers among us,
who never heard the story."

"Very well," said he. "I will tell you the story once again.

"Rabbi Elimelech was not accustomed to hold this meal
which we are now eating in very high respect. He fulfilled
the command in the very simplest way, by sitting at his table
and dipping bread in hot, unsweetened tea. Once upon a
time there came to him on Friday afternoon a man in peasant
garb with a basket of fish and offered him fish for sale in the
Polish language and in the intonation of the peasantry of
the district. The Rabbi sent him to his wife. She bade the
stranger go his way, seeing that several hours before she had
bought all the food for the Sabbath and had no need of any
more fish. The man, however, was not so easily to be put off.
He returned to the Rabbi. There was something about him
which caused Rabbi Elimelech to send him back to his wife
with the message that she might as well buy some fish of him.
She persisted in her refusal. For the third time the fishmonger
entered the Rabbi's room; he took the fish out of the basket
and threw the squirming creatures on the floor and growled:
'You would do well to use some of these for the Queen's
farewell repast!' Thereupon the Rabbi Elimelech raised
his eyebrows, which were very bushy and which he was
accustomed to raise when he desired to get a close view of
anyone, and silently for a period looked straight at the man's
eyes and then said slowly: 'I no longer have the strength to
partake of your repast with all its proper ceremonies, but I
will bid my children to do so.' Thus it came about that the
sons of the Rabbi Elimelech eat fish also at the repast of
farewell to the Sabbath Queen."

"But why," asked one, "was he so intent, that his repast be eaten?"

"The reason is," the Rabbi replied, "that we, too, eat this meal as a sacrifice of gratitude, because we are still alive, and because our life is the bridge between David, who was called the anointed of the Lord, and the Messiah, that is, the 'Anointed,' the son of David."

"What I would like to know," Naftali said now, "is something concerning that nethermost bone of the vertebral column, called the bone of life, which, when Adam ate of the fruit of the tree, had no share in his enjoyment, because the act of eating took place on a Friday, whereas this bone enjoys only the repast that marks the close of the Sabbath. It has been said that one of the intentions of this fourth meal is to procure some enjoyment for the bone of life. Now this *borsht* is quite a good dish. But why is not something better done for so noble a member, which is said to be formed of the very substance of the heavens?"

"You will be able to figure that out for yourself," the Rabbi answered, "so soon as you recall vividly what else is told about this bone."

"We all know," said Naftali, "that when a man dies this bone takes no injury, that no hammer can break it, that no mill can grind it, that no fire can burn it, and that, for this reason, the new body of the resurrection will be built of it alone. But that by no means answers my question."

The Rabbi smiled. This smiling struck young Jaacob Yitzchak's heart more deeply than all else the Rabbi had yet said or done.

Still smiling the Rabbi asked: "How could a little bone be so heroic in its nature, if it needs a great deal to have any enjoyment?"

"There is something else that I would like to know," Naftali continued, "and it concerns that bird named Phoenix who, when Eve offered the fruits of the garden to all the

[52]

animals, was the only one to refuse, because he never ate between the end of one Sabbath and the end of the next. For this reason was he exempted from the doom of death, which was pronounced upon all living things. I would like to know what persuaded him to fast a whole week long."

The Rabbi's smile was so intense that it tugged at the very heartstrings of the young Jaacob Yitzchak. "Perhaps," the Rabbi said, "he never thought of fasting; he simply did not eat for that length of time."

"Fasting and not eating," Naftali observed, "that is the very same thing. I want to know why?"

"Once again you need but recall to yourself," the Rabbi replied, "what else you know about him."

"What I know," Naftali said, "is what every child knows, namely, that ever since then he lives continuously for a thousand years. Then his body shrivels and he sheds his feathers. But the roots of the quills remain in him; his limbs grow anew and his plumage is renewed and he lives on again. But what is to be inferred from that?"

"It is evident," answered the Rabbi, "that the Phoenix thinks of himself and of the necessity of nourishing himself only once a week, and that a thousand years pass until he is forced to think of himself thoroughly and this causes him to pine and shrink and then to be renewed."

Now Meir gave notice that he wanted to put a question. "Concerning the third Sabbath repast, the repast of Jacob," he observed, "we say, that it is on account of the merit of our father Jacob that we are saved from the wars of Gog and Magog. Why precisely through his merit?"

The Rabbi smiled no more. Gravely he answered: "That we invoke Jacob against Gog is grounded in his own history. That he endured in wrestling with the angel of God caused him to be armored against the weapons of Esau. He whose hip the Divine Hand has dislocated trembles no more before the power of the lords of the earth's peoples. And our Sab-

[53]

batical rejoicing in God, what does it mean but this: that we endure His dreadfulness by virtue of our love? Lame but inviolable do we issue forth from His hands."

The Yehudi could control himself no longer. "Rabbi," he said in an almost failing voice, "what is the nature of this Gog? He can exist in the outer world only because he exists within us." He pointed to his own breast. "The darkness out of which he was hewn needed to be taken from nowhere else than from our own slothful and malicious hearts. Our betrayal of God has made Gog to grow so great. Neither in the soul nor in the people does the power of the light prevail."

"Impertinence!" roared Simon Deutsch, who had begun to grumble at the very first words of the Yehudi. "He insults our Rabbi!"

With a wave of his hand the Seer restored tranquillity.

"You suffer too much, Jaacob Yitzchak," he said. "One should not permit oneself to suffer so much."

"What do I matter, Rabbi!" stammered the Yehudi.

Firmly the Rabbi took his right hand in his own. "We will talk to each other about you when it is day," he said.

PARALLELS

After morning prayers on Sunday morning, young Jaacob Yitzchak felt his heart beat and throb against his ribs. "Are you afraid?" he asked after the habit of his childhood. And a tiny voice, truly like the voice of a little child, made answer: "Yes, I am afraid." Later on he confided to his friend Yeshaya: "I would like to have cut and run just as Chajkel did when I let go of his collar. But the Rabbi said: 'Come with me,' and that was mightier than even my huge paw on Chajkel's coat."

Now the Yehudi sat facing his master. A gentle warmth

[54]

was in the room, intensified by the strong beams of the autumnal sun which poured through the window. The backs of the books crowded against one wall seemed to emit radiance.

"What was in your mind, Jaacob Yitzchak, "the Rabbi asked, "when you decided to come to me?"

"Rabbi," the other answered in some embarrassment, I cannot be said to have decided."

"Explain that," said the Rabbi.

"Decision," the Yehudi explained, "comes as when, at the end of a run, one leaps. But if a man says to you: 'Leap!' and you leap from your stance, that is not yet a deciding. To be sure, Rabbi David bade me come hither often enough. I could not. Then, suddenly, this time I could."

"And why could you not do so before this?"

"Because I was afraid."

"Of what?"

"Of you, Rabbi. Of your presence."

The Seer was silent for a while. Then he asked:

"And suddenly you lost that fear?"

"Yes."

"Why was that?"

The Yehudi hesitated. "Perhaps," he said slowly, "it was because this time Rabbi David did not say to me as he had done heretofore: 'Go to Lublin,' but 'Let us go to Lublin.' Oh, he had wanted to accompany me on other occasions. But this time he said it in such a way that I could not stop and reflect concerning myself."

"But formerly, even when you were still afraid, you desired to come here, did you not?"

"Assuredly."

"What was your problem then?"

"Rabbi," said the Yehudi, "that is easy to explain. When I left my native town and came to Apt, a holy man was living there, Rabbi Moshe Loeb who is now the Rabbi of Sassov."

[55]

"He is in truth a holy man," the Rabbi agreed.

"Rabbi Moshe Loeb," the Yehudi went on, "regarded me with kindness and gave me of his time and of himself. At that time I was in such a state that sometimes at prayer I was beside myself. Once the *Zaddik* came upon me in this state when I was alone and advised me energetically to desist from this way. For, said he, here in this lower world are we stationed and it does not behoove us to abandon our post. From that time on he let me accompany him upon his ways, when he went forth, for instance, to ransom those who were imprisoned for debt, or else when he began the day by visiting poor widows in order to wish them a good morning and to ask them what they stood in need of, and to obtain for them what they lacked. In these activities he paid no attention to whether those whom he aided were pious and righteous or were considered very examples of all wickedness. Indeed, he would not endure to have any human being called evil. 'A man will do evil,' he was wont to say, 'when the evil impulse overwhelms him. But that does not yet make the man evil. None intends evil. Either he slides into evil, he knows not how, or else he holds evil to be good. You are to love this human being who does evil; lovingly you are to help him escape this whirl into which the evil impulse has plunged him; lovingly you must help him recognize what is above and what is below. Otherwise than lovingly you will accomplish nothing. He will show you the door and he will be right to do so. If you call him evil and hate him and contemn him therefore, you will make him evil even when you desire to help him, indeed, especially in that case. You will make him evil, for you will cause him to cut himself off. The man who does evil does not become evil himself until he is imprisoned in the world of his actions, until he lets himself be imprisoned in it.' "

The Yehudi ceased speaking. When he observed that the Rabbi desired him to continue, he did so:

[56]

"And similarly Rabbi David spoke to me when in the course of my wanderings I came to Lelov. And I came to recognize the truth of this way. But it is not the entire truth. It is the truth concerning all that takes place between me and my fellow-man; for that is the place where Satan meets his limitation, seeing that love really exists and has no limitation. But it does not suffice me to know the truth concerning the evil that is in the world. The evil in the world is mighty; evil has power over the world. And I certainly gain no experience of evil when I meet my fellow-man. For in that case I can grasp it only from without, estrangedly or with hatred and contempt, in which case it really does not enter my vision; or else, I overcome it with my love and in that case I have no vision of it either. I experience it when I meet myself. Within me, where no element of strangeness has divisive force and no love has redeeming force, there do I directly experience that something which would force me to betray God and which seeks to use for that purpose the powers of my own soul. At that point I understand that the evil of the world is mighty and that I cannot master it by virtue of what I do to my fellow-man, because it, itself, uses the power of love in order to poison what we have healed. But it is impossible to leave things at this point."

The Yehudi was evidently embarrassed at having uttered what he never meant to utter. But now he could no longer hold it back.

"For this reason," he continued, "I once said to Rabbi David: 'What can man do to cause the world to be redeemed?' And his answer was: 'Look, as long as the brothers of Joseph said to him: We are true men, he thrust them from him in anger. But when they confessed: Yes, we are verily guilty concerning our brother, he had compassion upon them.' And true though this be, it did not at all content me. And I said: 'Yes, so it is. But that is not the whole. There still remains a mystery. And I must come upon that mystery,

[57]

to which you cannot lead me. I must reach the point of learning how to prevent the evil from using the good in order to crush it.' And he replied: 'Then you must go to my teacher in Lublin. He consorts with good and with evil.' When I heard that, fear overcame me. Until the moment came when the fear ceased."

"But do you not see, Jaacob Yitzchak," the *Zaddik* asked, "that God Himself uses evil?"

"God may, Rabbi. God can use all things, seeing that nothing can prevail against Him. But the good . . . I do not mean God's good . . . I mean the good that exists on earth, mortal good — if it seeks to make use of evil, it drowns in that evil; unnoticeably and without noticing it itself, it is dissolved in the evil and exists no longer."

"Yet ultimately it depends on God alone!"

"Assuredly it does. And I hear His words: 'My thoughts are not as your thoughts.' But I hear also, that He demands something of us, concerning which His desire is that it proceed from us. And if I cannot endure the evil, which He endures, then it becomes clear to me that here, in this impatience of mine, there is manifest that which He demands of me."

"You must now tell me, Jaacob Yitzchak, how you first found out that there is something which, as you say, would compel you."

"That was long ago, Rabbi."

"Go on and tell me."

Softly and hesitatingly the Yehudi related:

"When I left the city of Apt and my wife and children — she died soon thereafter — I lived first of all in the house of a man who had leased an estate and was the teacher of his children. In the house there lived, too — I don't know why — a married daughter. At table she often looked at me, not in a friendly way, but as though she were wondering about me. We never addressed a word to each other. One night, while I was studying by the light of a candle, she came into

[58]

my room. She stood still and looked at me silently, not at all boldly, but as though she wanted to throw herself down before me and did not dare. She was in her night garments and her feet were naked. I perceived that she was beautiful, a thing I had not known hitherto. A compulsion went out from her humility. I admired her beauty and felt a burning compassion for her humanity. Simultaneously that compulsion attacked me and now it used the forces of both my admiration and my pity. Suddenly I was aware that I was looking at her naked feet. 'Do not compel me!' I cried. The woman apparently did not understand me. She came nearer. And so I leaped out of the open window and ran a long distance through the March night. A long time thereafter, when I was a teacher of children in a place far from there, the woman came to see me and with tears begged me to forgive her. Something had come upon her on that occasion which she had never understood. 'I know,' I consoled her, 'the master of all compulsion incarnated himself in you. Thus he had first to compel you to become his vestiture.' "

"But why," the Rabbi asked, "did you say awhile ago, that that force would compel you to betray God?"

"God," said the Yehudi, "is the God of freedom. He, who has all power wherewith to compel me, does not compel me. He has permitted me to have a share in His freedom. I betray Him when I permit myself to be compelled."

"Once upon a time," said the Rabbi, "when in my youth, I had a similar experience, I found that one need not leap out of the window. On an icy winter evening, on my way to Lisensk to see Rabbi Elimelech, I lost my way. Suddenly I saw in the forest the illuminated windows of a house. In the house there was no one except a young woman. Until then I had looked upon no woman except the one to whom I had been wedded and from whom I separated myself because I saw upon her forehead not the symbol of the divine but a strange sign. After I separated myself from her, she did wander forth among the strangers. The woman in the house in the forest gave me food to eat and mulled wine to drink. Then she sat down beside me and asked me whither I had come and what my plans were and, finally, what I had dreamed about the night before. I was frightened by the magic which her eyes and her voice exerted upon me. The fright pierced to the very bottom of my soul, where hitherto there had been nothing but the dark fear of God and a shy attempt to love Him. When now this terror touched the bottom of my soul, love shot up like a flame and grasped the whole power of my being. Nothing remained without me; all the passionate power which rested within me was devoured by this flame. At that moment I looked up. There was no woman, no house, no forest. I stood on the road that leads straight to Lisensk."

"Grace played its game with you, Rabbi," said the Yehudi.

"And when did you reach the cognition," the *Zaddik* asked, "that God is the God of freedom."

"When I was eighteen," the young Jaacob Yitzchak answered, "They thought I was the best scholar in the house of study in Apt. They talked of making me head of the house if the Rabbi, as he planned to do, were to move to another city. But I myself knew that I had only studied and that I did not from deep within know that God whose lore was the lore I was learning. I had learned His words. It was well enough. I had prayed to Him. I had prayed fervently. But Him I did not know. This taught me that man cannot attain unto knowledge by study alone. Prayer brought me near Him, but it was not the nearness of knowing. This lack in me tormented me for a long time. Then it came to pass that I reflected on what is related of our father Abraham, may peace be upon him — how he investigated the sun and the moon and the stars, as to whether they were divine. Sphere upon sphere he found too light, and finally he saw that He rules above heaven and earth Who is the Leader of the Uni-

[60]

verse. I was absorbed by this thought for three months. Everywhere did I question and seek and I found that the compulsion tries to subject all to itself and that all strains its vision toward freedom. And suddenly, not gradually in spite of my questing and seeking, but unexpectedly and in the twinkling of an eye, it became clear to me that freedom dwells with God. It was revealed to me in an instant, and the instant was that in which, at the beginning of the morning prayer, I pronounced the words 'Hear, O Israel.' The thought of this complete divine freedom shook all my bodily being so that I thought my teeth would leap from my mouth and so that I could not complete the declaration to the last awe-inspiring word, 'One.' Not until I had made it thoroughly clear to myself, that we, though made of earth, have a share in this very freedom, could I go on praying."

"I had an experience similar to that, too," said the Rabbi. "When I had completed the study of the Talmud, I took a walk in a happy mood beyond the city and looked at the harvest fields. I met a student of profane knowledge, the son of neighbors, but some years older than I. 'What are you doing?' he asked. 'I finished studying the whole Talmud,' I answered. 'What does that amount to?' he observed comfortably. 'I did the same thing in my time. But then I changed my profession, and now I am a free man and a free-thinker.' This taught me that I had as yet accomplished nothing. I went into the synagogue and opened the Ark and threw myself down before it and prayed that the right way be shown me. As I was praying thus I had the vision of a figure which filled the whole house. But I was not afraid and offered him my salutation, for I had recognized our father Abraham. 'Seek thee a teacher,' said he to me, 'who will teach thee how to walk.' And so I went to the *Maggid* of Mesritsh, the man of God, who still dwelt in Rovno in those days, and learned of him how to walk on the way."

" 'The way,' you say, Rabbi. But can one go farther and farther along the way here?"

"What do you mean by your question?"

"I mean: how is it, if one is conscious of a plane which one cannot reach so long as one lives in this world and is imprisoned in this body? Ought one not to beseech God to take one hence? And yet it is assuredly true, as Rabbi Moshe Loeb told me: It is here below that we are stationed and it does not behoove us to desert our post. It is here that we are to combat evil — here!"

"Ah, Jaacob Yitzchak," said the Rabbi, "why do you bother with planes? When you begin to think in such terms, you reach no end. You must remember how Rabbi Michal appeared after his death to my disciple, Rabbi Hirsh of Zydatshov, and told him that in the beyond he was rising from world to world and each time the world in which he stands has all the appearance of an earth and each time there is vaulted above that world, in the guise of a heaven, a farther world which he does not yet know and that thus every heaven becomes an earth. Thus it is with planes. But the way, Jaacob Yitzchak, may be likened to the building of a road. You drag up your stones, you beat them into the earth, you roll the roller over them. Naturally you do not stick to the same place. You do get on. Such is the way."

He fell silent. So did the Yehudi. After a while a darkness came over the ruddy face of the Seer and the vertical furrow in his forehead grew deeper. He continued silent. At last he began to speak, and now it was he who hesitated before each word, as though he were testing the words, each for its usefulness before he permitted himself to utter them.

"But death, Jaacob Yitzchak, but death. . .

"Lisensk, Rabbi Elimelech's town, is situated near wooded mountains of moderate height. From time to time, early in the morning, Rabbi Elimelech would cross the bridge which spanned the river San in order to take a walk on one of the hills which slopes gently upward on the hither side, but on the farther side falls away sheer and steep. He would sit upon the wooded peak, which is shaped precisely like a cube. People came to call that place Rabbi Melech's grove and the cube-like peak Rabbi Melech's table, and will doubtless long continue to call them so. Annually on the 33d day between Pesach and Shavuoth, on the holy day of the scholars, schoolboys climb the hill and run and play there and shoot off their blunderbusses across Rabbi Melech's table. It goes without saying that, at the times when the *Zaddik* was there, no foot, whether of Jew or Pole, dared to approach the place. But at other times there were two students who, each solitarily, visited the spot and indulged in solitary meditation there. I was the one; the other was my older friend Salke, who watched over me with great solicitude; during a previous pilgrimage of our souls he had been my father. Once I was sitting there again and meditating, as I had often done, on true humility and self-annihilation. But on this occasion the ardent desire to give myself utterly so flooded my being that naught else but the sacrifice of life itself seemed adequate. I approached the edge of the declivity in order to plunge down. But Salke had stealthily followed me. He now raced up to me from behind and grasped my girdle and did not cease to persuade me until he had freed my soul from its purpose."

For a space, while the Rabbi was talking, the *gabbai* had been standing in the open door. "Rabbi," he now cried into the silence that had ensued, "the poor crazy boy is in a frenzy. He yells that he came to you and not to these people who stand and stare at him."

The *Zaddik* arose. He put his hand on the shoulder of young Jaacob Yitzchak and, as they stood thus side by side, it was to be seen that the Rabbi towered even above the mighty younger man. He left his hand there a few moments and then went out with head uplifted, as was his custom, while Jaacob Yitzchak followed him with lowered head. Thus was their interview interrupted.

THE SHIRT

During the days that followed, the older students who did not actually live in Lublin set out toward their various homes. Among these was David of Lelov, although he disliked leaving his friend uncompanioned in a company of whom not a few, 'as he had observed, did not look upon him with favor.

Before he bade him tenderly farewell he asked: "Is it well with you now, Jaacob Yitzchak?"

The Yehudi did not answer.

David repeated the question.

"The Rabbi is awe-inspiring," said the Yehudi.

David was startled. After a while he said: "He is the true human being." Then both were silent. Yeshaya joined them. During his stay here his pallor had become more intense. David started on the way home with a heavy heart.

After a period the Rabbi, too, set out on a journey. None knew whither. The disciples whispered to each other that this was probably one of those journeys on which no goal was given the coachman; he was told, as the holy Ba'al-Shem-Tov had done, to hold the reins loosely and give the horses their heads, so that they could go where they would. On such journeys all kinds of adventures were met, of which the coachman later would give only dark hints, touching upon the wonders which the *Zaddik* had brought to pass.

Before his departure the Rabbi did two things which no one comprehended. He directed that, during his absence,

youths who aspired to become his pupils or others who came
with affairs touching upon the Law, were to be received by
the young Jaacob Yitzchak. This was very strange, especially
in view of the fact that the Rabbi's oldest disciple, the very
learned Jehuda Loeb of Zakilkov, lived in Lublin. At the
same time the Rabbi sent one of his shirts to the Yehudi with
the command to don it. Jaacob Yitzchak was deeply dismayed by both commands. Even as the Rabbi was about
to enter the carriage he sought him out and thanked him for
the gift and begged him to appoint another to the office,
seeing that he was too inexperienced.

"You are the right one," said the Seer.

"But at least will you not wait a while?"

"It is well," the Rabbi answered, "to order what is needful
before the horses carry one away."

On the very next morning after prayers the Yehudi, having
donned the Rabbi's shirt, went dutifully to his house and took
his stand in the antechamber in order to fulfill, as need arose,
the functions of his office. At that very moment sundry
strangers entered. He looked at them to see whether there
were among them aspirants after the Rabbi's leadership.
And now something came to pass which frightened him as
nothing had done all his life long. He looked at one of those
who had entered, a very ordinary person, and looked involuntarily upon the man's forehead. In the next instant it
seemed to him as though a curtain were drawn apart. He
stood at the brink of a sea, whose dark waves assaulted the
very heavens. And now they, too, were split asunder as the
curtain had been and thus gave space for a figure, totally
unlike that visitor, but with the same seal upon its forehead
that was to be seen upon his. But already that figure was
devoured by the waves; behind it stood another, different
again but sealed with the same seal. It too vanished and
farther and farther the depths revealed figures after figures.
The Yehudi closed his eyes. When he opened them again

nothing was to be seen but that ordinary man and the people about him and the room with its habitual furnishings. For a long time he did not dare to look at the next visitor. So soon as he did so, the same thing took place. Again a curtain was torn asunder and again waves rolled in the abyss and again vision succeeded vision. At this point the Yehudi mastered the disturbance of his mind and decided to obey the plain and open bidding that had been given him. He observed and sought to grasp every figure. He let it sink into the depth of his memory; he forced his eyes to remain open as long as possible. And suddenly, when it came to the fourth and to the fifth visitor, he noticed that a change had been accomplished within him. His vision penetrated the depths independently; with inhuman swiftness it pierced those realms; it reached to the background of that row of figures and came upon the very being of the primordial.

When the time of the morning visits was over, the disquietude, which he had conquered, returned. He did not go home, but went into the Rabbi's house of study. He put on his praying shawl, fastened the phylacteries to his forehead and arm, sat down opposite the Ark and sank deep into speechless prayer. Now something very curious happened to him, which was in one way laughable and yet again also a new spur to him.

West of Lublin, and now a suburb of that city, there is situated by the side of a large pool the village Wieniawa, of which the real name is Tshechov, a huddle of low, windblown, irregularly placed wooden houses on both sides of the synagogue. When the Seer, who had first gone to Lantsut after he had left his teacher, Rabbi Elimelech, moved to the neighborhood of Lublin, he dwelt — at the command of an angel, as is reported — in this village. He was prevented from settling in the city by the resistance in those days of the bitter opponents of the hasidic ways. On the outer edge of this village there lived the man who leased the local inn.

This man's great trouble consisted of the fact that he had never amassed his rent in time. But ever since the Rabbi had settled in Wieniawa, the lot of this man underwent a change for the better. Ahead of pay day he always went to see the Rabbi, whose prayer had the effect each time of playing into the man's hands the money in some wholly unforeseen way. When the *Zaddik* left the city this thing did not change. Now it happened that in a nearby village there lived another lessor of an inn. In the days of which we are speaking here, it happened to him, too, that he did not have the rent ready. His wife persuaded him to follow the example of his colleague and to go to Lublin. Having arrived, he asked after the Rabbi. He was told that the latter had gone on a journey. He refused to believe this. For, said he, a Rabbi certainly does not go journeying. So he went to the *Zaddik's* house and was told the same thing. Again he refused to believe it and went to the house of study. There he saw a man sitting with his prayer shawl and his phylacteries on.

"Anyone who sits in this guise at the noon hour," said he to himself, "can be none other than the Rabbi." He approached the man and handed him a slip of paper with his name on it and the "redemption penny" and explained the nature of his errand.

"I am no Rabbi," said the Yehudi.

When the innkeeper heard that, it struck so sorely upon his careworn heart that he fainted. The Yehudi was amused and grieved at the same time by this queer happening. He revived the poor fallen man and helped him get up and said: "Very well then, if you insist that I am a Rabbi, a Rabbi I will be."

"Rabbi," the man asked with a sob, "what am I to do?"

"In such times of trouble," the Yehudi asked him, "did you ever recite psalms?"

"How should I not have done so, Rabbi?" the innkeeper replied.

[67]

"But did you ever recite psalms by night, when all is silent and no one interrupts you?"

"No, Rabbi, I have not done that. I am too tired from the labor of the day and I sleep very heavily."

"In that case," said Jaacob Yitzchak, "buy yourself a big rooster. When the rooster crows, get up and recite your psalms. Pronounce each word from the depth of your own heart and your prayer will not have been said in vain."

The man thanked him and went his way. For another hour the Yehudi sat in the house of study. From time to time he had to laugh. It was a sorrow-fraught laughter.

Next morning very, very early a man came running through the Jewish streets in Lublin. He was recognized as the innkeeper who had been there yesterday.

"Where is the Rabbi?" he cried.

"The Rabbi is gone on a journey."

"Where is the Rabbi with whom I talked yesterday?"

"What Rabbi are you talking about?" the people said in their astonishment.

But the man could no longer refrain from telling his story. "I have found a treasure!" he cried. By and by he was able to speak coherently. When the rooster had crowed, he had been drunk with sleep. In the darkness he groped about him and collided so violently with a certain spot in the wall, that a brick fell out and the man's hand being thrust into the hollow came in contact with a little metal box. He lit a light and lifted the box out. He broke it open and found a roll of silver guilders. These had apparently been hidden here by his grandfather during a period of war, in which the old man met his death before he could communicate the secret to his son.

The story of the treasure rustled through the streets. People asked who was this Rabbi. All kinds of speculation arose. At last the story reached the Yehudi. Now he could not even laugh any longer. It seemed to him as though the shirt burned his body.

When, a little while thereafter, he went into the bath-house, there followed him an exceedingly strange-looking man. Except for a goiter he was emaciated. He wore a tattered yellow caftan and a tiny cap upon his head which was almost bald except for the earlocks. The Yehudi scarcely observed him. He went into the bathhouse and was about to enter the water. At that moment the man entered and turned to him at once.

"Rabbi," said he in a hoarse, small voice, "give me an alms."

"Look into my pockets," said Jaacob Yitzchak, "you will find a penny in them."

"Rabbi," said the man and opened his caftan on his chest, "I have no shirt."

The Yehudi shuddered at the sight of that yellow body. "Take mine," said he.

The man took the shirt and vanished.

THE GAME BEGINS

Among the disciples of the Seer, Jehuda Loeb of Zakilkov was the oldest. He had gone to Rabbi Elimelech at about the same time with him. When the Seer left, he had remained in Lisensk. In those last years, during which the Rabbi Elimelech lived a life of complete separateness, the actual leadership of the students had been in Jehuda's hands. He called the most zealous among them, with whom he studied almost uninterruptedly, the bodyguard. No one knew whom they were to protect nor from what. After the death of his teacher they followed him to Zakilkov. A short time later, however, something quite incomprehensible took place.

The Seer asked a guest of his after Jehuda.

"His bodyguard is about him," was the answer he received.

"By Sabbath they will be with me," said the Seer.

In the following night one of the most loyal of that little circle slipped away and came to Lantsut. On the next day but one, three others followed his example. By the end of the week not a single one of the bodyguard was left.

"Are any of you still with him?" the Seer asked the last comer.

"None," was the answer.

"He himself will come, too," said Rabbi Jaacob Yitzchak.

It took another ten days until Jehuda appeared in Lantsut. It was evening.

"Admit no one," the Seer said to the *gabbai*, "I want to go to bed earlier than usual."

When Jehuda entered the house, he was not admitted to the Rabbi's presence. He did not raise his voice, for that was not his way. But he repeated his desire slowly and urgently. The door opened and there stood the familiar companion of so many years in his dressing gown, his pipe in his mouth and yet with an aspect of unknown majesty.

"What is it?" the Seer asked.

The *gabbai* withdrew.

"You rob me of my disciples," said Jehuda.

"I take nothing from anyone," the Seer replied. "I merely accept what is brought to me."

The other still stood in the doorway. "Think of Rabbi Elimelech!" he admonished him.

"If he came here today, he, too, would have to stand in the doorway," said the Seer. "As it is said in the Midrash: had Samuel lived in the generation whose leader was Jephthah, he, too, would have bowed down to Jephthah. One must know who is the leader of a given generation. Otherwise one remains a fool."

He pronounced the final word with broad emphasis. The visitor bowed his head and remained in Lublin. Yet he was not considered as one of the students. He was rather the Rabbi's student-colleague. Like him he wore a white coat on the Sabbath and sat beside him at the head of the table.

Jehuda was a gaunt man, prematurely gray. He spoke quite without gestures, almost without moving his mouth. When he walked, he trod with great regularity; when he stood, he never pressed down more heavily on one foot than on the other. His zeal for learning had remained unchanged from his youth on. It was evident that study was his only satisfaction. No one had ever thought of accusing him of the slightest, the most unintentional irregularity. When anyone addressed him, he always reflected for a space before he replied. He was not fond of looking at people, but he was fond of nothing else either.

On the day after the incident of the shirt in the bathhouse, Jehuda invited a few of the students to his house. Kalman, whom he had tried to dissuade from leaving, had had half an hour's conversation with him when he was already in the carriage. At last he had driven off, shaking his head. Among the older ones, in addition to Simon Deutsch, who growled to himself more violently than ever, Naftali had come. He seemed to consider the subject of the conference as a jest. For from the start on he laughed as he conversed with his neighbor and evidently on this subject. Yissachar Baer, whom Meir on the evening before had sought, with eloquent citations of hints from mystic lore, to persuade of the dangerousness of the Yehudi, had at first declined the invitation. Finally he came nevertheless. Meir, whose brother had left, sat motionless, but his eyes glittered. Among the youngest were two who were devoted to Jehuda with a special loyalty. One of them, Jekutiel, looked like the personification of stupidity which, however, had succeeded in becoming a virtue. The second one, called Eisik, made an open show of his cunning.

In fact, he seemed to desire not to let his patron forget for a moment how sly he was.

Briefly Jehuda referred to the occasion of the conference, namely, the intolerable behavior of the newcomer, who acted as though he were the Rabbi himself. "As long as the Rabbi was here, he stared at him uninterruptedly, clearly for the purpose of imitating him. And no sooner does the Rabbi leave, than he begins without delay to look at the foreheads of visitors, just as the Rabbi does — as though it helped *him* to see something. And next he immediately goes in for the performance of miracles . . . "

But now, as on that other day when they were sitting around the long table, Yissachar Baer jumped up and raised his hand. He was so excited that for a while he merely stammered. By and by he controlled himself and was able to speak coherently: "Nay, that is false! 'Tis Satan, lord of evil suggestions, who says that through your mouth. The miracle-making power chose the Yehudi against his will. Do not harry him!" Backwards and with uplifted hand he walked toward the door. Once more, before he disappeared he cried: "Do not harry him!" and waved his hand as though threatening the assembly.

With a clipped laugh Naftali said to his neighbor: "He's in love with miracles for their own sake, the hotheaded boy. He's worse than I. He is more concerned over the miracle than over him who performs it."

All this time Jehuda had not moved an eyelash. It was as though Baer's utterance had not reached his ears. Nor did he seem to have heard Naftali's observation, even though what he said now sounded like a reference to it. "Even the Egyptian magicians were capable of signs and wonders," said he. "Yet these had nothing but a superficial appearance in common with those of Moshe. There is no worse danger than the false miracle. We must be on our guard."

He stopped. Into the silence fell a cry of Naftali, which

astonished them all, as did every utterance of his that was not tinged with laughter. "The Rabbi is on his guard for us all. He knows what he is doing."

Jehuda hesitated before he replied. "Where there is a great light," he said at last, "the powers of darkness gather round about, seeking to devour it. But how can they approach it in their own dark guise? They must themselves put on a garment of light. And light is pleasing in the eyes of the light."

For a space Meir had sat as though poised. Now his moment had come. "Have we not been watching for a whole year," he asked angrily, "what the powers of evil have effected in the way of deceiving the *Zaddik*? Did not their emissary live and move among us, and did not the Rabbi endure him because, as he himself said to me, he was forced to assume that the horror had been sent from above? That onslaught of those powers having failed, they are now weaving a web of finer yarn."

"I have a thing to tell you," said Simon Deutsch. "I spent the evening yesterday with kinsmen in Wieniawa. On the way home a bold beggar approached me and demanded an alms. 'I don't give to fellows like you,' I said. He clung to my heels. 'The young Rabbi,' he lisped, 'gave me a shirt.' 'What young Rabbi?' 'The one with the broad shoulders.' A dreadful suspicion rose within me. 'Show me the shirt,' said I. He opened his coat. Into the collar of the shirt a blue strip had been embroidered. Later I questioned Eisik's sister Rochele, because all of the Rabbi's linen passes through her hands. It was really his gift. Do you recall how the fellow insulted the Rabbi at the farewell Sabbath meal and how, out of the goodness of his heart, the Rabbi would not take note of it? Now that man has shown his true contempt for everything connected with the Rabbi by the way he has flung the precious gift to a vulgar beggar!"

"We must take council as to what is to be done," said Jehuda.

[73]

"May I be permitted to speak a word?" Jekutiel asked.

"Speak," said Jehuda hesitantly, for one never knew what would come from those lips of unwisdom.

"In my opinion," said Jekutiel, "it is to be considered whether, at the end of a hundred and twenty years,* this interloper might not try to occupy the throne."

The word once uttered covered them with an acid sense of shame. But it could no longer be unsaid.

Now Eisik, closest of the followers of Jehuda, perceived that it was his turn to speak.

The fate and story of this Eisik were peculiar.

When he was a child his father had owned a house in a small town. This house had been rented to the Rabbi's brother. For a period this man had been unable to pay the rent. Shortly before a certain New Year he was dispossessed. It is related that the Rabbi, who lived in Lantsut at that time, having heard about the matter two days before New Year, had muttered the words: "There will be a loss." On New Year's Eve, Eisik's father went out to close the outer shutters of the house. He was never seen again. Even in his childhood his son journeyed to see many a *Zaddik* to beg for help in finding his father. All in vain. When, later, the Seer left the seat of the Rabbi Elimelech, an uncle of Eisik had been his chief hasid. This man also, in later days, helped the Rabbi settle in Lublin. At his suggestion the Rabbi took Eisik and his sister Rochele into his house. The girl soon managed the household; the lad studied in the house of study. He never abandoned the hope that some day the Rabbi would tell him the whereabouts of his father. But he never had the courage to ask directly. Whenever the Rabbi addressed him, he answered with eyes cast down. He attached himself to Jehuda Loeb and was the latter's constant companion.

He now turned to Jehuda and raised his slightly crooked

*A euphemism for the time of a man's death.

left shoulder, as was his wont whenever he began to speak. "Will the Rabbi permit me to propose a plan?"

"Speak, Eisik," said Jehuda, and for the first time something that felt almost like warmth tinged his voice.

"It is my opinion," said Eisik, "that one should put the matter before the *Rebbitzin*, our master's wife."

Though no one spoke at first, it was evident that this plan commended itself immediately to all — except Naftali who, when the execution of the plan was being discussed, laughed hoarsely and said, as though by the way: "Don't count on me in this matter."

Eisik was commissioned to speak to the *Rebbitzin*.

THE REBBITZIN

Tila, the *Rebbitzin*, had borne the Rabbi four sons and one daughter. The oldest son, Israel, was about eighteen at this time and had recently been married. He was a solitary soul. His bearing toward his father was so reverential that even when discussion was necessary he always waited to be addressed. He associated very little with the students. He had a household of his own and came into the house of the Seer, accompanied by his wife, only on Sabbaths and holidays. Even in his youth it could have been said of him, as a disciple of the Yehudi did say at a later period, that he was a "walking tractate." The second son, Joseph, was about fourteen. He was shy of bearing and careful to ask the Rabbi's opinion concerning anything he meant to undertake. Of the girlhood of the only daughter, who was about ten at this time, nothing is known, except that she felt closer to Rochele than to her own mother. The third son was a sickly child of six. The youngest was still in his cradle.

Tila was a small woman with delicate limbs and a narrow

little face. An unknown disease seemed to ravage her. There is evidence to show that she thought herself not far from death even when she was being married to the Rabbi. For immediately after the marriage ceremony she asked him to promise her that, when the day came on which she needed his help in the world above, he would not let her wait. She spoke of her illness to no one and answered all questions evasively. Her tranquil bearing and the peace of her countenance had not changed since her marriage. Her aspect had merely grown more delicate, until gradually nearly all the red had faded from her lips. She refused to receive a physician. The Rabbi was always very intent upon learning her desires, in order that each of them might be exactly fulfilled. When she spoke he listened with an entire intensity which he gave to no one else and weighed each of her words so long as she desired to utter them.

When Rochele told her that Eisik desired to consult her and hinted concerning the matter in hand, she refused at first to hear of it. If there was anything to discuss, she said, the Rabbi's return was to be awaited. It was not until Rochele carefully emphasized the fact that there were things which could not very well be put off and which must be communicated to her, seeing that one did not even know when the Rabbi would return, that she gave in and appointed an hour. At the same time she directed that Israel and Joseph should be present.

Israel was on one of his favorite walks. He loved the landscape by the river and was often seen wandering beyond the city and watching the current of the river. Nevertheless he kept the appointment promptly. When Eisik entered, Israel remained in the bay of a window, instead of sitting down with the others. He was as tall as his father, whom all the children resembled, except the third son who was like his mother. But he was slender and his frame was smaller than his father's. He, too, carried his head erect, but his glance was usually melancholy and fixed upon some vague distance.

Joseph's features were somewhat coarser than his brother's. His eyes blinked from time to time, as though the sunlight were too strong for them.

Eisik chose his words carefully. He began by relating the events of the past few days into which he wove details concerning the person and the past life of the troublesome student. He related, for instance, that the fellow had lost the goodwill of his parents-in-law by reason of his unseemly behavior. Thereafter he had wandered like a vagrant from town to town and his abandoned wife had died of grief. It was to be observed that the *Rebbitzin*, who at first had remained tranquil, had wrinkled her delicate forehead over the story of the shirt and had given a slight start when she heard about the woman's death. Eisik thought that the moment had come to take up, however delicately, the chief question. He now addressed himself simultaneously to the mother and the sons. Soon he spoke directly to Israel.

All this while Israel had remained standing by the window. From time to time he had even turned around and glanced at the street. Now, however, just as Eisik was uttering the insinuation contained in the euphemism: "After one hundred and twenty years," Israel approached him swiftly and said: "You will get no decision from me!" With lowered head as was not his custom, but as though he were ashamed of his rapid gestures, he returned to the window.

Eisik raised his left shoulder higher than ever and half turned to Joseph. Joseph neither looked at him nor did he speak. He did not change his demeanor even when Eisik, a little later, turned straight to him and paused for an answer. A shadow of a smile passed over Eisik's face.

"What do the hasidim desire of me?" Tila asked, when he was all through.

"You must warn the Rabbi."

[77]

"Why should I do so?"

"He pays attention to what you say."

Tila's lips seemed to have become even paler.

Painfully she spoke: "I can say nothing but the truth."

"The truth suffices," Eisik observed.

Israel left the window. He looked lovingly at his mother and nodded to his brother and went out.

Silence fell among those who were left in the room.

THE HEART

Meanwhile the Rabbi was visiting his friend Rabbi Israel, the *Maggid*, or Preacher, in Kosnitz.

When Rabbi Elimelech knew himself to be near death, he summoned his favorite disciples to his bedside. They had all come to Lisensk, including the Seer, with whom he had become reconciled a year before. Now they were all assembled, primarily these three: Jaacob Yitzchak, Menahem Mendel of Rymanov, an unobtrusive man with a face like peace itself, and, finally, Israel of Kosnitz, seated by reason of his infirmity and almost paler than the dying man. Elimelech touched his almost breaking eyes with his hands. Then he stretched them out toward the Seer, who at once bent over the dying man, and touched his eyes with them. Next he clutched his head with his hands and then clutched Mendel's head with them. Finally he placed his right hand upon his heart, which had not many beats left, and with that hand he touched the breast of Israel.

Since that time these three had foregathered now and then and their dead master was ever in their midst. These meetings usually took place in Kosnitz, which the *Maggid* left but rarely. He had been born of very aged parents, to whom, as was related, the holy Ba'al-Shem-Tov had prophesied that miracle, and had been sickly from his birth. He had stopped growing early and looked almost like a peaked, narrow-chested boy. Dressed in a coat of rabbit fur, he usually reclined on a couch. When he desired to arise, slippers lined with bear's fur were put on his feet, so that he could stand. He was carried to the synagogue in an invalid's chair. But the moment he arrived there he was transformed. He would get up and walk between the rows of those who were awaiting him and approach the Ark with light and dance-like tread. Then he would sit on a tall stool and pray within an ecstasy of absorption. After the prayer of the Eighteen Benedictions he leaped to the floor, where a fur had been spread out to receive him. There he continued to pray. At times he arose and took a few leaps. When the manservant carried him home in his invalid's chair, he would be as pale as a dying man. But a radiance went out from his pallor.

He was overwhelmingly given to prayer. Prayer is called the service of the heart, and Rabbi Elimelech had given this disciple the heritage of his heart's strength. The thing was thus that he prayed not only at the appointed times. He prayed even as he breathed. He prayed in words and without any words. When he prayed in words he interjected into the liturgical text invocations in the vulgar tongue, even as his heart brought them to his lips. From time to time he would even add a cry of love in Polish, not unlike those cries which one heard from the peasant girls when they accompanied their sweethearts to the fairs and asked of them a present of embroidered ribbons. But he asked for no presents. When he spoke to men, his speech never wholly lost the intonation and the melody of prayer. And one of his menservants reported thus: "He who has seen the Holy *Maggid* sleep knows that he prays even in his dreams."

From near and far came people, Jewish peddlers and Polish princes, beseeching the *Maggid* to pray for them and to advise and to help them out of the illumination of his praying. He

[79]

prayed for them all. One of his prayers that has been handed down to us is: "O Eternal, if Thou wouldst not redeem Israel, then redeem the Goyim!"

On this occasion, too, the two friends sat day by day at Rabbi Israel's bedside and conversed with him. They spoke of things high, of the very highest, but also of the events of the day. Of the high things they spoke as of things which were taking place in the here and now; of earthly happenings they spoke as though these were woven of a heavenly substance. Silences arose among them but did not divide them.

"A wind blows from the west," the Seer once said.

"It is written: Lo, the storm wind of the Lord," Israel added softly in the intonation of prayer.

"The storm is supposed to come from the north," Mendel observed.

"It is written: The storm wind blows according to His command," said Israel almost singing.

They were silent.

After a while the Seer said: "There is a stirring in the depths."

"Suffering is at home in the depths. As it is written: Out of the depths I cry unto Thee, O Lord," Israel replied.

"A great hatred is fermenting in the depths," Mendel said warningly.

"The suffering is even greater than the hatred, as it is written: If thine hater is hungry, satisfy him with bread," said Israel.

Once again there was silence.

"Suffering and hatred — the wielders of power exploit them," said the Seer.

"It is written: The upraised arm will be broken," said Israel.

"The wielders of power walk at the head of the peoples," said Mendel.

"It is written: I have made thee a light unto the peoples," said Israel.

[80]

And again there was silence.

"The fishes of the sea devour each other," Mendel began.

"But Leviathan devours them all," said Israel.

"Is it Gog?" asked Jaacob Yitzchak.

"The name cannot yet be read; it must first be written."

"When will it be written?"

"When the world will be lying in its birth pangs."

"Are these not the birth pangs which are beginning now?"

"Birth pangs or apparent birth pangs, it is not the giver of birth who decides. It is written: we were pregnant and we writhed and what we gave birth to was the wind."

"On what does it depend?"

"On a place being made ready for the child."

"Who is to prepare that place?"

"He who is able."

"How is that place to be prepared?"

Israel sang, "The pure in estate from the vile separate! Melt the mass! Cleanse the ore! Let the dross lie apart!"

"Where shall this thing take place?"

"In the street, in the house, in the heart."

PRAYER

The Seer remained far longer in Kosnitz this time than usual. Menahem Mendel had long left; he remained.

When he was about to say farewell, the *Maggid* caused a chest to be brought to his bedside and took from it a written sheet.

"Our teacher," he said to Jaacob Yitzchak," just before his reconciliation with you, wrote down this prayer which is to be spoken before the liturgy is said. Shortly before his death he entrusted it to me and bade me give it to you at the right hour. The right hour has come."

The Seer took the sheet of paper and went home.

Soon after his arrival in Lublin his wife told him what had taken place. He smiled as he was told the story about the contemplation of the visitors and the performance of the miracle. But he gave a sharp start at the story of the giving away of the shirt. He then reassured his wife; he begged her to be untroubled; he would see to it that all were well.

He went into his study and remained alone there for long. He was about to summon the Yehudi, when he came upon that written sheet which he had brought with him. He opened it and read: ". . . Guard us from all deflections and from all haughtiness, from anger and sudden rage, from dismalness of heart and from evil insinuations and from all other ignoble things and from aught that stains Thy holy and pure service, which is precious to us. Pour out over us Thy holy spirit, that we may cling to Thee and that our desire may be fixed upon Thee . . . Redeem us from envy of our comrades; let no envy arise in our hearts . . . Grant us so to act that all shall see the merits of our comrades and not their lacks, and that we, each one of us, speak with his comrades in the way of veraciousness, which is pleasing in Thy sight . . . Amen. May this be Thy will."

He stood and prayed Rabbi Elimelech's prayer.

Then he summoned the Yehudi.

Young Jaacob Yitzchak's misery was visible upon his face.

Upon the Rabbi's request he related everything that had taken place from the first day on and since then in the realm of his office. He named and characterized the new students who had come to inscribe their names. Together with several older ones they had formed a study group under his leadership. This group was inspired by a great zeal; none desired not to excel. In his characterizations he unintentionally went farther and farther beyond the limitations of even sharp observation. He became aware of this and so, very clearly, of the circumstance that he could not proceed without recounting the incomprehensible, too. And so he did indeed recount it as best he could. He could not keep out of his voice and the play of his countenance the expression of the suffering which the transformation of his being had inflicted upon him. Thereupon he besought the Rabbi passionately to dismiss him from his office, since he was now no longer needed.

"I would have you continue to receive the new students," said the Rabbi, "and to introduce them to our teaching, as you have been doing. It will certainly be easier from now on. Now tell me what else has taken place."

The Yehudi was silent concerning the story of the recovered treasure and several similar incidents which had taken place. But the Rabbi interrupted him and asked after these things, of which he had heard.

"It is true," said the Yehudi in a depressed manner, "that one or two uncanny things did in fact occur. This cannot evidently fail to be so when you are not here and men's desire after the miraculous issues in emptiness. Instead of what they expect, they trick out something which resembles the expected. They use as the substance of this all that happens to come their way. The incidents themselves, however, are so spiritually shabby and absurd that I considered it unfitting to trouble your ears with them."

But the Rabbi did not desist until he had been told all. He listened with interest and some amusement.

Finally the Yehudi had to tell the story of how he gave away the shirt. Now he was not only depressed but painfully embarrassed.

He saw a darkness upon the forehead of the Seer.

"You do right to be angry with me, Rabbi," he said.

"With you, Jaacob Yitzchak?" the Rabbi asked almost astonished. He spoke as though they had been discussing someone else. "I am not angry with you. But can you explain to me why you gave it away?"

"That is just it, Rabbi," said the Yehudi; "I am unable to explain it. I cannot explain it even to myself. An inner compulsion had power over me. And this time I was not able to jump out of the window."

"Was it compassion?" the Rabbi asked.

The Yehudi reflected. "No," he explained; "I cannot really say that. An element of compassion was doubtless present. But it was not the compelling force. Compassion proceeds from the viscera; the wretchedness of a fellow creature inflicts a deep bodily sting; one is sore within. But this . . . what compelled me did not proceed from within me at all. It was exactly as though some power did not desire me to . . ." He could not continue.

The Rabbi pressed him no more. But his face had grown even more somber. "Well, Jaacob Yitzchak," he said, "it was even as it was. Do not grieve about it. We simply do not always succeed in expelling them — those dogs, those insolent ones. Now go to your post."

The Yehudi went into the antechamber, where a paralyzed old woman, who had just been brought from Warsaw, lamented her infirmities. Involuntarily he gazed upon her forehead. A sudden joy ran through him. He saw nothing but the forehead of an old woman. The thing had been taken from him. He turned away. "Blessed be He," he said, "who rolls burdens upon our hearts and then lifts them from us again."

The Seer had remained sitting in a very somber mood. He desired to pray once again the prayer of Rabbi Elimelech. But he could not do so.

GOLDELE IN LUBLIN

One morning Jekutiel came running to the Yehudi with a broad grin on his face. In the inn there had arrived a very fat woman and had told the innkeeper that she was here to have a talk with her son-in-law, Jaacob Yitzchak from Apt.

The Yehudi asked the Rabbi to give him leave to go and went to the inn.

Goldele received him with evil eyes and a smiling mouth. "So there you are, Jaacob Yitzchak," she said.

"Yes, I am here," the Yehudi replied.

Goldele interpreted this agreement as a challenge. "I have had to come all this way to remind you of your duty, Jaacob Yitzchak," she said.

"It takes a long time before a man gets to understand what his duty is," the Yehudi replied. "It is the duties which prevent him from doing so."

That put an end to the woman's patience. "What kind of talk is that again?" she screamed. "Do you know that you have children? Or don't you?"

"I know it," said the Yehudi.

"Do you happen to remember," Goldele continued, "what I wrote you after you had set out on your stupid wanderings?"

"I remember," said the Yehudi. "You wrote me that I was a fool."

"And what else did I write?"

"You wrote me that I wasn't worth having so good a wife and such handsome children."

"And are you worth having had a wife like my poor dear Foegele, may she rest in peace?"

"No, I was not worthy and I am not worthy of her. One is generally unworthy of what one has."

"Very well then," said Goldele. She was disarmed by his agreement and at the same time stung by his incomprehensible explanation of it. "Do you happen to remember what else I wrote you?"

"You wrote me," answered the Yehudi, "that I was to abandon my follies and return to Apt without delay."

"And were they not follies?" she asked.

"No," said the Yehudi.

"What? You still don't see that it was sheer folly suddenly

to get up and run off, all the more so since my good and pious husband, who is now at rest in Paradise, had just become reconciled with you."

"It was no longer possible for me to stay among people."

"Now what kind of business is that again? Weren't you well treated; I mean, couldn't you have had a good time with us?"

"I was well treated."

"Well then," said Goldele in a somewhat subdued tone. "But wasn't it foolish of you to send your wife annually so and so many gulden?"

"It was all that I could earn."

"That's not what I'm talking about. Foegele was taken care of by us, she and her children, in the best way possible! . . . By the way, I was told sometime ago that once, when you had been gone several years, you bought a whole gold ducat's worth of phylacteries. Is that true?"

"Yes. That was toward the end. Rabbi Moshe of Psheworsk, who wrote the book called, *The Light of the Countenance of Moses*, wrote them with his own hands. I saved up toward that for years."

"I don't understand that. And do you remember what I wrote you on that occasion?"

"I remember. You wrote me that a woman needs a husband and children need a father."

"And are you willing to deny that that is so?"

"It is most certainly so," said the Yehudi. Then he added softly, as though to renew the explanation for his own benefit: "He who falls into the hands of the living God is unfit to be either husband or father until God dismisses him."

Goldele had heard only some of his words. "What are you talking about?" she shouted. "Are we not all in God's hands? Anyhow, you didn't come just the same, but wandered about the world year in and year out."

"Yes, I went from village to village."

[86]

"You taught the children of strangers, instead of taking care of your own. And at intervals you vanished completely. For long periods we didn't know where you were. When my husband was in his last illness we tried to get hold of you; you were nowhere to be found. And all of a sudden, without first writing or sending word, there you were again. And you demanded that we shouldn't let anybody come to see you. Wasn't that foolish? Very well, we did even that; we made ourselves a laughing stock and refused to let anybody come in, and I said you were ill. And then, just as suddenly, you were gone again."

"Yes, I had to wander on."

"Wander on! Wander on! What kind of nonsense is that?"

"Mother-in-law," said the Yehudi, and all of a sudden his eyes were brighter and his voice warmer, "have you never heard it said that the *Shechinah* wanders about in exile and that therefore it is becoming for us to wander as exiles and ever again to wander on until we learn that it is enough?"

Goldele was embarrassed, a thing that rarely happened to her. "We don't have to talk about all that," she said in an almost pleading tone. "That's all over and done with. But I've got to remind you of one thing," she continued and her speech was again tinged by reproachfulness, "because you have evidently forgotten it, namely, what happened when, during the year after your last disappearance, my Foegele, may she rest in peace, gave birth to her third child and passed away. All of a sudden you turned up then, so that she could say farewell to you."

"I have forgotten nothing," said the Yehudi.

"And there was something you swore to her," Goldele added.

"When she knew," said the Yehudi very softly — it was evident that he found it quite hard to speak, and yet he directed his words straight at the woman, who was facing him — "that her way was very short now, she asked me, whether

I had liked her a little. Then I said to her, as was most true, that I not only loved her more than myself, which was no great matter, but more than my father and my mother and the friends of my youth and that it was only God whom I could not help loving more. Then she said that if this were indeed so, I was to vow to her to marry no other woman except her sister. 'I will gladly swear to you,' I said, 'that I will not marry again at all.' 'That's not what I mean,' she said. 'I want you to swear to me that you will marry my sister Shoendel Foegele.' This she said exactly as I tell you. She made a mistake and instead of saying 'Shoendel Freude,' she said 'Shoendel Foegele' and did not know it. And so I swore."

"Very well then," said Goldele. "She sent you after me and told me what you had sworn to her. But because Shoendel Freude was but a child then, we didn't mention the matter even after Foegele died. And then you remember how, though with frequent interruptions, you stayed in Apt with your children. Then about six months after Foegele's death I mentioned the matter to you. You said that, when the time was ripe, you would keep your vow." She stopped.

"It is as you say," the Yehudi agreed.

"And now the girl is a grown girl," said Goldele. "But you don't seem to be thinking about your oath."

"I do indeed think about it," said the Yehudi.

"Well, the time is ripe now."

"It is not," said the Yehudi. "The Rabbi of Lublin has imposed a duty upon me and only the command of the Rabbi can release me from it."

Hesitantly the woman said, "After you are married to Shoendel, you could stay for awhile longer in the house of study in Lublin, if that is the right thing to do in your opinion."

"The time has not yet come," said Jaacob Yitzchak.

"Seems to me," she replied, "that some one ought to talk to the Rabbi.

"Take care," cried the Yehudi and his eyes glittered at the woman, who was suddenly abashed, "take care not to grasp the spokes of the racing wheel. You will regret it."

Goldele was more astonished at herself than at anything else. No one had ever spoken in such fashion to her before. Nor would she have permitted anyone else to do so. Not only did she endure it now but she made no further attempt to change her son-in-law's mind. Soon thereafter she departed.

A few hours after she left, Eisik went to see first the hostess at the inn and next the *Rebbitzin*.

EAGLES AND CROWS

Naftali was that one among the disciples with whom the Rabbi preferred to converse and whose opinions concerning the events of the day were most important to him. For Naftali said what happened to occur to him, nor did he afterwards regret having said it. At the same time there was no vanity in him. He often made fun of himself, averring that one should not appear to be wiser than one really was nor silence the inspiration of one's moments. Not that he did not highly value intelligence and wisdom; so much so, in truth, that he once made the Rabbi a strange enough answer. When once the latter admonished him that it is written: "Thou shalt be simple before the Lord, thy God," and not: "Thou shalt be wise before the Lord, thy God," Naftali declared that it needed a great wisdom to be rightly simple in one's commerce with God. At times it annoyed the Rabbi that Naftali never ceased jesting nor spared anyone. Once he demanded of him that he desist from his jesting a whole year. Naftali was unwilling to promise, save on the condition that the Rabbi obligated himself not to remain for more than an hour, as was his frequent habit, in silent prayer and thus delay the cantor and the congregation. The Rabbi, who could not resist Naftali's gay insistence, promised, but broke his promise the very next Sabbath. He observed, moreover, that Naftali by some quip aroused smothered laughter among those about him. He asked him later what he had said.

"I said," Naftali told him, "the Rabbi stands there as though he were thinking of his marriage night."

The Seer smiled. "It is true. As I stood in prayer there appeared before me the soul of a musician beseeching its redemption. The man had played the cymbals at my marriage feast and his soul now sang the melody he had then played to remind me of him."

From now on he ceased trying to change Naftali's ways. He upbraided him from time to time, but always insinuated a conciliatory word, so deeply did he value the unclouded intimacy of their relationship.

Naftali, strong as were the bonds that bound him to Lublin, was in this respect too of a great independence of spirit. After Rabbi Elimelech's death he had first sought out Rabbi Menahem Mendel in Rymanov. Thereafter he had visited the Seer and attached himself to him. Nevertheless he still visited Rabbi Mendel from time to time and stayed with him, even though small vexations would occasionally arise between them. At a much later period he used to give an accounting of these matters.

"When I went to Rabbi Mendel, I had to bring along in my head all the sacred writings. In Lublin, on the other hand, I went with my comrades to the tavern and we drank mead. There are evidently different ways to the goal. One had always to approach Rabbi Mendel with the utmost reverence. The Rabbi of Lublin might scold a little; nevertheless he enjoyed one's jokes. Once Rabbi Mendel came to Lublin and watched us as, according to our custom, we made a merry din and successively danced on the table. He cried out to us: 'Well!' Fear of him overcame us and we were hushed and still. When our Rabbi of Lublin noticed the hush in the room he cried out to us: 'Ho!' Joy welled up in us and we returned to our gaiety with double zeal. Now Rabbi Mendel had to put up with it."

During the winter which followed the arrival of the Yehudi, the Seer bade Naftali give him a report when news of the outer world arrived — news first of the Polish rebellion which spread underground but very perceptibly to Naftali's keen perceptiveness, and, next, at longer intervals, news in such profusion that the hearers had first to arrange and put in order what was told them, of the great tumult in the west of Europe. The Rabbi paid but little attention to the happenings in Poland. On the other hand, all that was told him concerning the events out there in Paris, he received with extraordinarily tense interest, an interest which expressed itself from time to time in brief interjectional remarks which were evidently not addressed to Naftali alone. When the latter described to him, as well as he could on the basis of hearsay, those various and successive characters who made common cause against the old world order and yet fought with each other, the Rabbi would first gaze straight ahead with those inquiring eyes which one knew from his reading of petitions. It seemed at such moments as though all his perceptive powers were concentrated in his eyes. Then, however, a very flame would seem to flare up in his glance and he would shake his head and murmur: "He is not the right one." Naftali, though he was usually unembarrassed by the Seer and well used to surprises from him, yet now occasionally felt a sense of dread under these flaming eyes and this voice with its murmur as of dying thunder.

These reports were naturally often accompanied by conversation concerning the students in Lublin. No one knew

as well as Naftali what went on within the student group —
the stealthy combats, the breaking and the making of peace —
and no one could delineate them as well as he. When he
spoke of these things he would at times hold his hands as
though they were the two balances of a scale and as though
he were meticulously weighing things or characters against
each other. The Rabbi listened benevolently. Now and
then he asked a question; only when the subject was the
Yehudi did his face betray intense interest and sympathy,
not unlike those with which he had just listened to the news
from France. But he never interrupted this part of the
communication by a question. Naftali always spoke of the
Yehudi with emphatic expressions of respect and good will,
yet with an air of reserve.

At the end of the third week in April, on one of the last days
of the Passover, Naftali reported to the Rabbi what had
taken place in Paris toward the end of March and the beginning of April.

"The eagle has had to give up the field to the vultures,"
said the Rabbi. "It is now the turn of the crows."

"Are the crows wholly despicable?" Naftali asked.

"The crows," replied the Rabbi, "are not to be despised.
They are full of life. But they have three questionable charac-
teristics. The first is that no other bird can commune with
them, because its voice is drowned by their screaming. The
second is that they are of the opinion that crows are the only
inhabitants of the world of birds. They think that all birds,
who act as though they belonged to a different species, are
masquerading crows and must be persuaded by being
screamed into silence to reveal their true nature. The third
is that no crow can bear to be alone with itself; a crow which
is separated from the swarm dies of the horror of its loneliness."

"Assuming," Naftali asked now, "that it were possible for
the eagles to live in a single community with the crows,

[92]

would that be less bearable for the eagles than for the crows or contrariwise?"

"I see," said the Rabbi with a merry expression, "that you would like me to answer: it would be less bearable for the eagles. But I share your opinion that it would be harder for the crows."

"And which of the two," Naftali asked, "would feel the greater need of remaining in that single community, the eagles or the crows?"

"The eagles."

"Why is the Rabbi of that opinion?"

"Because the crows live in an original community of their kind. The eagles do not. When, therefore, they make common cause with the crows, it shows that they must have had the desire to form a community with other creatures."

"Yes," Naftali said with a thoughtful air. "It is certainly as you say. Under these circumstances they will have to make various concessions in order to have the crows tolerate them."

The Rabbi laughed. "Not a very happy prospect for the eagles."

"To be sure, it's not a very handsome one," said Naftali. "But how else is a community between species so different to be established?"

"But it will never come to that point!" cried the Rabbi.

"No, no, of course it won't," said Naftali and suddenly his face was crinkled into so many small planes that it looked, not like that of a man slightly above thirty, but like an extremely aged face. "No, it won't come to that point. I merely made that assumption because you said that soon after the end of the eagle the crows will rule; so I supposed that prior to that they must have kept house together."

"They would rule?" asked the Rabbi. "Did I really say they would come to rule?"

Naftali did not answer. He seemed lost in reflection.

After a while he said with a gesture as though the previous subject of their conversation had been dealt with and finished and as though he were now turning to an entirely different one: "The man from Apt is a very precious acquisition. He is a mighty scholar, and yet it would seem as though his true character were hidden behind his zeal for study."

He stopped for a moment; for only now did he remember how similarly the Yehudi had expressed himself concerning the Rabbi and the miraculous. Now he continued: "We know that he was long addicted to mystic study and specula- tion, but later desisted from them. Meir told me that he declined to engage in a conversation concerning the mysteries. Meir considers that peculiar and not calculated to awaken confidence. I am also told that he is given to ecstatic prayer and does not share in the congregational weekday service, because he waits in each instance for the moment in which he can pour his whole soul into the spoken word. Yet one ought not really to say to oneself: 'I'm not in the right mood now;' the hour of prayer demands the appointed praying."

"If it happens to a man," said the Rabbi, "to neglect the precise hour of prayer because of his impassioned love of God, he merits no punishment. Truly, 'great is the infraction of law for God's sake.' Don't forget that we, too, are accustomed to putting off afternoon prayers."

"That is an entirely different matter," Naftali replied. "It happens, because by means of the afternoon prayer, with its similitude to the Divine Tribunal, you have specific inten- tions toward affecting the higher world. For this purpose the congregation needs to be in a state of highest spiritual con- centration. Nor does it happen to our friend from Apt that he neglects the hour of prayer once; again and again he separates himself from the congregation. It is not well that those who are chosen separate themselves from the congrega- tion at the very moment when its unity is strongest."

"The human community," said the Rabbi, "stands in the

[94]

presence of the higher worlds. But in the presence of God himself man stands always like a solitary tree in the wilderness."

Naftali inclined his head. "That is certainly the truth," he said. "Yet when the congregation observes that a place remains empty, its inner solidarity is disturbed. Doubtless the harm done is outweighed by this man's meritorious management of the students. All the more zealous among the young have attached themselves to him, as well as not a few of the old-timers. And in that group all things are well done: the studying is thorough as well as the drinking, and the mood is equally gay during both occupations. I need not tell you about the drinking, and as for our teachings, you will have yourself observed how even more deeply than before they burn in the hearts of these men. Nor are the able ones to be blamed for seeking the company of their equals, since otherwise it will happen that some fool will draw down the discourse of even the best among them to his own level . . . ."

"Naftali," said the Rabbi slowly with an equal stress on every word, "in this case there are neither eagles nor crows. We are, all of us, the errant sons of a single Father, some doubtless a little more foolish than the others, but all so full of failings that the differences among us are no great matter, nor the little more nor the little less, sons and brothers as we are."

Naftali nodded even more emphatically than before. "How very true that is. And yet . . . But you sound exactly as though you reckoned and ranged yourself with the rest."

"How should I not do so?"

The *Zaddik*," said the disciple, "mediates between us and our Father in Heaven."

"Ah, Naftali," the Rabbi cried, "if an angel assured me that I am a *Zaddik*, I wouldn't believe him."

"And I am ready to take oath," Naftali said reproachfully, "that you are a *Zaddik* without imperfection. Doubtless

[95]

we are all brothers. For that very reason it is deplorable to see our confraternity divided, so that a second congregation builds its separate life within the first . . ."

"A second congregation?" the Rabbi asked in a changed voice.

"One need not use that term," Naftali explained.

The Rabbi looked at his watch. Like the putting on of his spectacles this gesture was a symbol that he felt something to be deviating from the natural order of things.

"Accept the petitions in my place today, Naftali," he said.

THE HEAVENLY LETTER

Concerning the Sabbath following Passover an odd circumstance is to be recorded.

In order that this incident be well understood, it must be recalled that the many enemies of the hasidic way held the *Zaddikim* to be hypocrites and frauds and sought, by laying snares for them, to prove that they themselves did not practice the virtues which they extolled. These enemies considered the Seer of Lublin very easy game, since it was obvious that he who praised humility as the highest virtue was a man preeminent for pride. It is not easy to discern the truth that pride and humility dwell well together in a single breast, differing in that respect from pride and arrogance or, above all, pride and vanity, which are hostile each to the other and cannot keep peace.

A man from afar, who had come to visit the Seer, had, as many did, brought his son with him. The Rabbi had been struck by the lad's great, fashionable, burnished buttons on his coat. "He is not one of us," he had said at once. When the lad had been introduced to him he counted off those buttons with his fingers, as children count off objects in their games, and when he had come to the tenth and last he said:

[96]

"Look, that is the way of the Evil Inclination. Today it tells you to do this (and he touched one button), and tomorrow it says, do that (and he touched another), and so it goes on and on until there are no more buttons."

The hearer accepted the monition sullenly. Later one of the hasidim of Lublin observed that the fellow regarded closely the Rabbi's Sabbath garments, which were hanging in the antechamber. But he thought nothing of it.

When the Rabbi returned from the ritual bath on Friday afternoon, the *gabbai* helped him, as was customary, to don his Sabbath garments. As he was putting on the outer coat of white satin, the Rabbi said: "How heavy the coat feels today." He put his hand into a pocket of the coat and drew forth a parchment scroll, sealed with a broad seal that glittered like gold. "Not before the end of the Sabbath," he said and slipped the letter into a drawer. Immediately after the celebration of the entrance of the Sabbath, the hasidim whispered to each other that a message from Heaven had reached the Rabbi. Next morning the message was the sole subject of conversation in the Jews' streets.

At the end of the Sabbath the Seer brought forth the parchment and the hasidim regarded the address and the seal. The seal bore the Name of God. When he observed this the Rabbi put the parchment down and turned away. The Yehudi, who was able to observe his face at this moment, saw about the Rabbi's nose and lips an expression of strong revulsion and distaste. But almost at once he turned back to the hasidim and said: "Open it."

Those who stood near dared not break the seal.

"Do you open it, Hirsch," he said.

Rabbi Hirsch, a man deeply versed in secret lore and familiar with its arcana but also sharp of eye and agile of hand, soon opened the parchment without breaking the seal and unrolled it.

"Read," said the Rabbi.

[97]

Hirsch read. In the letter it was made known to Jaacob Yitzchak, the son of Matel, that he had been chosen as the Messiah. He was to mount a hill near Lublin and blow upon a *shofar* in order to gather in the exiled of Israel and lead them to Jerusalem. Hirsch hung his head. The others remained as though overwhelmed and gazed expectantly upon the Rabbi. Only the Yehudi and Yeshaya, who stood beside him, watched the people who were present one by one. The silence lasted several seconds.

"There is no very far distance from the first button to the last," the Rabbi whispered. Then he called one of the youngest of the students to him.

"Take this rag," he said, "burn it and scatter the ashes on the dung heap."

In the meanwhile the youth who had worn the big buttons had disappeared. In vain did his father seek him in the inn. It was related in later days that he had gone over to the Greek Church and that the Czarist government had appointed him censor for the languages of the Jews. He was said to have borne himself benevolently toward those who had been subjected to his scrutiny by virtue of his office. In his old age, in 1831, he was rumored to have joined the Polish rebellion and to have fled to England after its collapse. There he joined the Mission to the Jews. In the end, however, not long before his death, he was said to have returned to the faith of his fathers.

FAREWELL

Next morning Yeshaya came to the Rabbi and begged leave to return home. For several years he had presided over the rabbinical court and had also been head of the house of study in the Yehudi's native city. His return had been requested repeatedly; he was needed; he had put off the moment again and again. Now it had come. He said that

in the seven months of his being in Lublin he had learned
more regarding the inner character of our teachings than in
all his previous life. He begged to be permitted to return
by the New Year.

Yeshaya was older than the Yehudi by several years. He
had come to that city while the Yehudi was still a child.
Despite the difference in their ages a friendship had arisen
between them; they had pursued their studies in common;
this community had not since ceased. "No one," the younger
of the two would say laughingly to the elder, "can study well
but you and I," whenever once again, quite independently
of each other, they had clarified the meaning of some passage
that had hitherto defied interpretation. Yeshaya had the
face of an ascetic without ever having practiced active
asceticism. In Lublin he had been the most taciturn of all.
Yet, upon being asked, he proved to be better informed than
any concerning what had been said on the subject under
discussion in the course of time. The Rabbi was wont to call
him "my reference shelf." He hated to see him go.

Later the two friends sat on a bench in front of the inn.

"In spite of all, you might better have stayed on," said the
Yehudi.

"You should come with me," Yeshaya replied.

"I must stay," said the Yehudi.

"Have you observed," his friend asked, "how they lay
in wait for a watchword from him?"

"Not all," the Yehudi answered.

"They who did not, acted as though they did."

"We are concerned with the man," the Yehudi said emphatically, "not with the image or reflection of him."

"In a case like this," Yeshaya objected, "one has almost
more dealings with the man's reflection in others than with
himself."

"That is because their faith in him is insatiable," said the
Yehudi.

[99]

"That is hard to avoid if one's faith in a man is great," said Yeshaya.

"Should one on that account avoid faith in any?" the Yehudi asked. "One should be able to believe in him without becoming insatiable."

"I am afraid," said Yeshaya, "men could come to believe in me."

"I am afraid," replied the Yehudi, "of being unworthy of being believed in."

Silence arose between them for a space.

It was Yeshaya who spoke first.

"It goes without saying that I, too, am above all concerned for him. He is a man of great power and I myself would be glad to be called forever 'one of the disciples of the Seer of Lublin.' But I cannot live here, Jaacob Yitzchak, no, not that, nor would I want to be able to do so. Do you know, Jaacob Yitzchak, what it smells of here?"

"I know what you mean."

"Well?"

"You mean: effectiveness is made a conscious goal here."

"That is it."

"But shall one not strive to be effectual, Yeshaya?"

"Ah, you do understand me. Assuredly, so long as God lets us crawl in this mortal dust, it is well that we improve each other's lives a little and even, if you will, each other's souls. And there are some here who have a hidden as well as a manifest power to do this. But it is too much when the little worm rises and with mighty gestures adjures the Heavens, precisely as though the world's redemption depended upon it . . ."

"Perhaps the redemption of the world really depends on us, Yeshaya?"

"On us?"

"Not on our incantations. They probably have power only

upon our own being. Not on anything wherewith we may strive to bring about redemption. Our very striving is the proof of our failure. But when we seek to effect nothing, then and then only we may not be wholly without power."

"That is better; that is possible."

"We do exist, Yeshaya; that is not a delusion. True it is that we are mere creatures, frailer than any other creatures. Not for nothing were we formed of clay. Yet is that not a mighty matter when we think of the Hand of the Potter which kneaded our clay? The imprint of its fingers are visible upon its handiwork. Nor is this all. There is more. He breathed His breath into us, and if we are able to live from within outward as no other created thing may do, it is because His breath enables us to do so. How fair and marvelous it is, Yeshaya, to know at the same time that all images are as naught before Him, yet to be able to speak of Him in images drawn from the image of us, of our mortal being — to be able to do so, to be forced to do so, but also to be permitted to do so, because in His image did He create us! His breath! His countenance! His glance!"

Yeshaya let an interval elapse before he spoke again.

"I love your high enthusiasm," he said, "and yet I dread it too. I cannot but remember how in your boyhood you were often so exhausted by prayer as to seem in a swoon. Yet out of ecstasy all one can draw is a recurrent dying again — never a true life. And therefore I want to tell you another thing before I say farewell. Often now, as in your boyhood, you wait to pray until enthusiasm comes over you. That is not the right way. We do not pray according to the inspiration of the individual heart. We join an ordering of the word of prayer which generations of our fathers organically built. We subordinate ourselves to and within this ordering not as this *I* or this *you*, but as part of that congregation in the act of prayer with which you and I are integrated. What your single heart bids you tell your Creator you can utter in the

[101]

solitariness of your waking at dawn or in your lonely walks. But the order of prayer has its place and its appointed times, which you should respect."

"Do you, too, address that reproach to me, Yeshaya?" the Yehudi cried sadly. "What you say is true. But you also know that it is but a partial truth. What an hundred generations have built up a single generation can ruin. The gathering in which, while the prayers are being droned, a man named Simon thinks of the deal in grain which he is closing and a man named Reuben considers his chance of being elected to the board of directors, is that still your congregation in the act of prayer? The holy Ba'al-Shem-Tov renewed the congregation as such by his fiery doctrine concerning the necessity of right intention; the great *Maggid* of Mesritsh deepened that teaching, yet hardly strengthened the congregation; our Rabbi Elimelech flung his own soul into the fire, as it were, yet he could not prevent the men at prayer from depending upon him. Here in Lublin, today, an ardent spirit doubtless flames from the assembly when the Rabbi stands at its head. When he is not there, the living word is not there either. The word, that it may be a living word, needs *us*. True, it has appointed times and seasons. But those who neglect them and wait do not do so in order to have an easier time. They tarry till they can enter wholly into the spirit of the praying and thus prepare in their aloneness the rebirth of the congregation. When I stand alone before the Lord, I stand there, not as a single soul before its Maker, but as the community of Israel before its God."

"That is not the way to be trodden," said Yeshaya with almost equal sadness. "When you gain disciples — and I know that they will be many and great — the acts of sundry among them will refute you, for they will transform, they must transform your intention into its contrary; the actions of the others will deny you. This particular meaning of yours is not communicable nor can it be handed on."

[102]

"It may be that it will come about as you say, Yeshaya,"
said the Yehudi. "But we dare not spare ourselves. God
marches to His victory by the path of our defeats."

They parted with their friendship unimpaired, but their
mood was one of unconquerable melancholy.

THE ADDRESS TO THE SIXTY

"Behold, it is the litter of Solomon," it is written in the
Song of Songs, "three-score mighty men are about it, of the
mighty men of Israel. They all handle the sword and are
expert in war: every man has his sword upon his thigh,
because of fear in the night."

Rabbi Israel ben Eliezer, the Ba'al-Shem-Tov, said in his
time: "My soul was unwilling to descend into this world,
for it was of the opinion that it would not be able to prevail
against the consuming snakes which exist in this generation."
For that reason sixty heroes, the souls of *Zaddikim*, were given
the soul of the Ba'al-Shem-Tov to protect it. These sixty
were his disciples, through whom his good tidings went forth
among men and renewed the community of Israel. The
greatest of his disciples was Dov Baer, the *Maggid* of Mesritsh,
whose disciple in turn was Rabbi Jaacob Yitzchak, the Seer
of Lublin.

Seven weeks after the Passover, on Shavuot, the feast of
Weeks, the feast of the first fruits and of the revelation of the
Torah, there sat about the Seer's table, having come thither
from near and far, the chosen disciples who had gathered
about him in the space of thirteen years. He counted them
and said: "My sixty heroes."

They had all donned white garments on this day, even
David of Lelov. Only at the foot of the table there sat one,
not known to all, who wore a short, dark coat of Western

European cut. His hair and beard were also trimmed in Western fashion. He was somewhat older than the Yehudi. This was Simcha Bunam, the apothecary. Considering how highly esteemed he was by all the *Zaddikim* whom he sought out, his previous calling had been no less curious than his present one. He had been an exporter of timber to Danzig and had even visited the fair at Leipzig. Thereafter he had devoted himself to the study of pharmacy; he had passed his examinations in Lwow, had received the grade of a Master of that art and, about a year ago, had opened an apothecary's shop in the town of Pshysha. For a long time his devotion had been given to the *Maggid* of Kosnitz. In recent years he had from time to time visited Lublin. Like the Yehudi, he had first been brought here by David of Lelov. The Seer set great hopes upon him. Once he had studied a section alone with him. Then he had said: "Now you are my pupil and I am your teacher." Among those present Naftali alone paid any particular attention to Bunam — an attention similar to that which quicksilver, had it the power to attend, would pay to silver.

It was the interval between the temporary victory of the Polish rebellion and its collapse. To be sure, the Russians had evacuated both Warsaw and Vilna some weeks before. But in the very hour during which the "sixty heroes" were sitting around the table in Lublin, the great little *mujik*, Suvarov, was already drawing up, on the Russo-Turkish frontier, the plan of attack for his beloved bayonets, although he could not yet have had the slightest suspicion that mid-summer would bring him the command to attack. One of the older disciples had a son whom he sought in vain to persuade not to join the Polish rebels, relying upon a saying of the Seer to help him.

The house of study, in which this time, too, the table had been set, was radiantly green, as it always was on this day. Green branches covered the floor and green trees stood against the walls. It was no mere decoration; the Polish forest itself had entered the Jews' *shul*.

The Rabbi, who conversed not only with those nearest him but also with those across the table, used more frugal gestures and a more emphatic voice than at other times. It was as though he had made a decision which was now to be executed. His eyes, too, had a sharper glance than was their wont. No one would have thought that he was near-sighted.

In the course of the meal Bunam whispered to David of Lelov: "Do you know who will be permitted to say grace today? I. Look how the Rabbi regards each one of us. It is an examination which fills one with dread. Who can stand up under it? Neither you nor anyone whom he knows intimately. I am the only one whom he does not know so intimately."

In point of fact, the Rabbi, so soon as he grasped the beaker at the end of the meal, asked at once: "Who will say grace?" And immediately with a smile upon his face, but with inexorable clarity, he passed in review each of those present. The faults and errors of each one, some of them things that had either seemed scarcely to have been noticed or else had long been thought forgotten, were not expressed. What was expressed was always only the ultimate cause of those actions to which a human eye had penetrated and which human lips now translated into words. No one was wounded; no one could be. David of Lelov nodded as though in gratitude; the Yehudi reflected long over each syllable; even the sensitive Naftali laughed as at a good joke and, to the astonishment of all, even the austere Jehuda Loeb of Zakilkov replied to the Seer's smile with a smile, thin though it was, of his own. The end of the address was: "The wise Rabbi Bunam will say grace."

When, later, the Seer began to speak, they were all aware that something had grown ripe for the harvesting. He did

[105]

not speak, as was his custom, from a great depth, but authoritatively and commandingly.

This time, too, he began by an exegesis of a Scriptural saying. It was the introduction to the Ten Commandments, which he had read to the congregation in the middle of morning prayers. Next he proceeded with the significance of the customs of this festival.

"Why," he asked, "do trees cover the walls of this house and of our dwelling houses today? And why do green boughs cover the floors? Because we commemorate the Revelation. But God revealed himself to Israel not in a house but on a mountain, and round about the mountain grew trees and grass. As it is written: 'Neither shall your sheep and your goats nor your cattle seek pasturage in the direction of the mountain.'

"We do not place this greenery round about us in commemoration of a Revelation which took place once upon a time. Revelation *is*; it lives and lasts. It is not something that happened once upon a time and lives now only in our memory. That which has happened happens; it happens *now*. We are not building us an image of something that once was. We, ourselves, create the place of revelation; we, ourselves, wait to be sanctified.

" 'If a man,' the Rabbi of Berdichev once said, 'is worthy of it, he hears on every feast of Weeks the Voice which says: I am the Lord thy God.' If we are worthy thereof, we hear it now and here. If we are prepared to hear, we will hear. How could the Voice deny itself to us? It is addressed to us and seeks us out! 'Where are ye?' the Voice asks. 'Ye, whose God I am? Are ye there? Are ye still there?'

"It is written: 'And Mount Sinai, the whole of it, smoked, because the Lord descended upon it in fire; and the smoke thereof ascended as the smoke of a furnace, and the whole mount quaked greatly.' The world of the peoples is the mountain upon which in this hour the Lord descends in fire, and the mountain begins to smoke; it begins to quake greatly. We, however, stand at the foot of the mountain and behold the first cloud of smoke; we feel the first quaking in our own members. But do we also hear the Voice which speaks to us from the top of the mountain: 'I am the Lord thy God'? If we are prepared to hear it, we shall.

"The other day I was told of an incident that took place in the capital city of the peoples. Four weeks ago the man, to whom all the world bows down, announced that there was a Supreme Being and during this week this Supreme Being is to be magnified through great festivities. And there may be people on earth, perhaps even in our own midst, who rejoice thereat and say: 'Behold, how the godlessness of the peoples is coming to an end!' Yet is this announcement worse than all godlessness. For to the godless the throne of the universe is empty, as are the innermost chambers of their own souls, and they faint after fulfillment and the Merciful will have mercy upon them, even as He has mercy upon those who suffer deprivation for the sake of truth. These others, however, who proclaim the existence of a Supreme Being, place the clownish figment of their thinking upon the throne of the universe; the chamber of their souls, which was built to house the Ever Living, they fill with the machinations of death. Truly, any idol is more living than that Supreme Being. For people who bow down to an idol intend a living thing and bring a living sacrifice. That Supreme Being — who could pray to it and expect it to do unto him that which the living does to the living? And this man, himself, who made the proclamation — himself a messenger of death who affects to bring the message of life; an empty one, who feigns fullness, sterile and hence undisciplined — he will not even be mime enough to address that Supreme Being; were he to do so, the world's laughter would run ahead of the axe which is already being sharpened for him. What would this man with that automaton he proclaims; he tricks him out with power, so that thereby his own power be secured. But when on a morning of terror he forgets to wind up the monstrous toy he has himself invented, it will be the end of both.

"Look you, all this is nothing but the smoke of the mountain of this world. It smokes, because in this hour the Lord descends upon it in fire. He, the Ever Living speaks: 'I am the Lord thy God.' To whom does he address that 'thou'? To him who hears it. Open your ears, hasidim; open your ears, Israel; open your ears, peoples of the world. It is He who leads from servitude to freedom and reveals Himself to the free."

The Rabbi paused. When he spoke again his voice was brighter still and hard as steel.

"The world of the peoples," said he, "is in tumult and agitation. Nor can we desire this thing to cease, for not until the world is broken by conflict do the birth-pangs of the Messiah begin. Redemption is no ready-made gift of God handed down from heaven to earth. The body of this world must travail as in birth and reach the very edge of death before redemption can be born. For the sake of redemption does God permit mortal forces to rebel against Him more and more. But it is not yet inscribed upon any scroll in Heaven at what time the great conflict between light and darkness will enter its final phase. This is a thing which God has placed within the power of his *Zaddikim*, and this it is concerning which we have the saying: 'The *Zaddik* decided and God fulfills.' But why is this so? Because God would have redemption be our own redemption. We ourselves must strive to heighten earth's conflict to the plane of the Messianic birth-pangs. The clouds of smoke about the mount of the world's peoples are still small and transitory ones. Greater and steadier ones will come. We must wait for the hour in which the sign will be given us to influence them in the depths of mystery. We must keep wakeful our inner strength against the hour in which the dark fire will dare to challenge the power of brightness. It is not for us to extinguish; our task is to kindle. It is written: 'The mountains melt before the Lord; that is Sinai.' Wherever the mountains melt and the wonder comes to pass, *there* is Sinai."

When he had finished speaking there was silence. None addressed another as the sixty went their ways.

OUTBREAK

Later on, in the inn, David of Lelov and the Yehudi and Bunam were sitting together. None had yet been able to speak.

Finally Rabbi David raised his voice. For the first time since he had found the home of his spirit in Lublin had all serenity departed from it.

"The path is lost," said he. "Where are we erring? Where shall we turn? There is no return. God take pity on us."

"Have you not taught us, Rabbi David," said the Yehudi, "that when we deem ourselves lost it is a sign that God is about to let his quality of mercy prevail over his quality of exacting judgment? Much or little as we may know concerning God, we do know this: He is no magician. A magician would find no time for exercising mercy."

Vividly Bunam turned to the Yehudi. "You are right, Rabbi," he said. "God is no magician. A magician makes a show of his power even as the peacock spreads his plumage. God keeps *His* power hidden by denial."

"Friends," said David, "let us pray to Him together. This is our heaviest hour. None to come can be heavier. Let us unite and pray."

Of those three was formed a silent ring of praying.

After this prayer they sat silent and at peace.

The *gabbai* came. Rabbi David and Rabbi Jaacob Yitzchak were bidden to come to the Rabbi after a while.

David sent the inquiry whether Rabbi Bunam might come too. An affirmative answer was received.

"What can he have to convey to us?" David asked on the way, "and what argument can we offer?"

"Upon our lips," the Yehudi replied, "there can never be any but this one: that nothing can lead us and the people Israel unto God's power except that we, who have all fallen away from Him, return in repentance unto Him."

"He will answer," Bunam interjected, "that Israel will not repent and return."

The Yehudi looked at him surprised and shocked.

"At this point he *must* say it," Bunam declared.

A little girl came hopping along the street toward them. With all her little heart she was intent upon hopping from cobblestone to cobblestone upon the cobbled street according to a certain order and an exact rhythm. She was too intent to look about her and so her little head suddenly collided with David's knee. It didn't hurt her much, for she only glanced upward a little surprised and reproachful. "Yes," said David, "that wasn't nice of me. Where could my eyes have been?" Out of his capacious pocket he brought forth a bean of the carob-tree.

And now these three faced the Rabbi. He seemed calmer than at table. But on his face a painful tension was visible.

"Be seated," he said with emphatic cordiality.

"What I want to find out," he began, turning to David and the Yehudi, "is just what happened among the students after my discourse at table. It had all the appearance of a sudden falling apart of a well forged chain. I ask you, because I saw you whispering when I was through. Will you tell me what you whispered? Perhaps that might help me to understand what it was that happened among the students."

David of Lelov reflected. "I do not recall having whispered. But I confess I forget such things easily."

"And you, Jaacob Yitzchak?" the Rabbi asked.

"I cannot recall having whispered either. But since you say I did, Rabbi, I must have whispered what I had in mind without being conscious of the act. I certainly did not whisper to anyone."

"And what was in your mind?"

"Rabbi," said the Yehudi, "I dreamed last night that the world was being consumed by fire. I flew through the fire and round about me whirled the fragments of the splintering stars. When I started up out of my dream it seemed to me that a turbid flame was still quivering in my room before it was extinguished. I got up with difficulty. My hands could barely light a candle. To steady myself I opened the Scriptures. Under my eyes were God's words to Baruch, the son of Neriah: 'Behold, what I built I have to raze, what I planted I have to uproot — the whole earth which is mine. And thou, thou desirest a great thing for thyself? Desire it no more.' The words pursued me continuously. Then, this morning, Rabbi, when you were reading the Ten Commandments, it seemed to me at first as though angels were flying through the house in order to hear the words too. But next I had a vision of the conflagration of my dream and throughout the reading of the Commandments I heard the monition: 'Desire it no more.' Later, after the meal, when you spoke of the Revelation, it seemed to me as though I heard the sound of the ram's horn from across Sinai. But thereafter those words: 'Desire it no more' grew strong in my heart again, and when you finished speaking I evidently whispered them to myself."

"What was in your mind while you did so?"

"In my mind? . . . Just those words."

"And did you think of no one at that moment?"

"Oh yes, assuredly. Of us all."

"Of all?"

"Certainly, of all."

"And can you tell me in that case what happened to our chain?"

[111]

"Our chain?"

"In spite of all such minor conflicts as are inevitable among human beings who form a group, Lublin was always at one in the one thing needful. But now it would appear as though somewhere the bond has been loosened."

"The matter on which you question me," the Yehudi replied, "requires some reflection." He pondered in silence. "I can think of no loosening of the bond — until today. There were, for instance, moments of disunity between me and sundry others from the first day on; one such concerned the miraculous. But this disunity has not increased. On the contrary, I am on excellent terms with more than one of the enthusiasts of the miraculous."

"What was the character of that disunity?"

"In the eyes of many of your disciples, Rabbi, the things that happen in the world are of two kinds. Those which they call natural and those which they call miraculous. I, however, and a good many others too, we have more and more reached the conclusion that this distinction does not actually exist. I am unwilling to believe that God confuses our poor understanding with artifices which contradict the course of nature. It seems to me rather that when we say 'nature,' we mean the aspect of creation of all that takes place; when we say 'miracle' we mean the aspect of revelation. On the one hand we mean what is called God's creative hand; on the other hand we mean His pointing finger. The happening, though seen under the two aspects, is the same. The true distinction seems to me to lie in the fact that we often have a deeper awareness of the finger than of the hand. 'Miracle' means our receptivity to the eternal revelation. And as for 'nature,' since it is God's, who would presume to draw its boundaries?"

"You have explained that very clearly, Jaacob Yitzchak. But what did you mean when you said that you could find no loosening of the bond until today? What happened today?"

"Today, Rabbi, I confess that, for the first time, I underwent an experience which severely shook my integration with Lublin. Mine and Rabbi David's, too. And, in all likelihood, Rabbi Bunam's."

Bunam nodded so emphatically that his apothecary's cap slid to one side and some strands of almost blond hair stuck out in every direction.

"And what was that experience?" the *Zaddik* asked.

"Your words, Rabbi, concerning power and redemption. Permit me, Rabbi, to bring forth for you, in the hearing of these comrades, things from the innermost chambers of our minds, in order that I might make the matter quite clear."

"Speak."

"You are to know, Rabbi, that from my childhood on I have been a sayer of the psalms. Whenever in my life anything which surpassed the common norm stirred my heart, whether it was an evil thing or a strangely good thing, a psalm or a few verses of a psalm came to me and helped me to renew peace within myself. This happened to me also in the most difficult period of my wandering life. I had passed several sleepless nights. In a great clarity of consciousness I had been alone with my own misery and the misery of this creature which is man. On such a night very familiar verses came home to me with a new power and significance: 'How long, O Lord, wilt Thou forget me forever? How long wilt Thou hide Thy face from me? How long shall I take counsel in my soul, having sorrowed in my heart all the day?' It came to me: so long as man still deems that there is a counsel for him by virtue of which he can liberate himself, so long he is still far from liberation, so long must he still nourish sorrow in his heart all the day, for so long does the Lord still hide His countenance from him. Not until man despairs of himself and turns to God with the entire force of that despair, even as it is written: 'Abraham knows us not; Thou, O Lord, art our Father' — not until then will help be given him. And

[113]

when that became clear to me and my despairing soul yielded itself utterly and kept nothing from itself — then help came to me. Suddenly I understood a matter concerning which I had reflected for a long time; I knew the hidden meaning of the ritual bath. You abandon yourself, you abandon yourself utterly; thus only you attain possession of yourself. Since then I believe with perfect faith that such is our case and Israel's and man's. Truly does it depend on us; not on our power but on our repentance. Rightly do our sages say that all periods set for the coming of the Messiah have passed by and that his coming depends wholly on our repentance and return. Nor is this an expression of power. It is quite simply that human action for which God waits in order that He may redeem His world. His countenance is not turned away. It is hidden to our eyes because our souls do not face it. Once we turn to Him, the light of His countenance will illuminate us. At times in a waking dream I see the Messiah lift the ram's horn to his lips. Yet he blows no blast. What does he await? Not that we practice incantation over mysterious forces, but simply that we erring children return to our Father."

The Rabbi had listened with a patient bearing. Only for a short while had the first stirring of anger been visible on his face. Now he arose. The disciples, as was natural, arose too. He approached the table which stood between them. Powerfully he placed both hands upon the table, the right hand on the volume of Scripture that lay upon it. It was as though he wanted to register a vow with the holy object in his grasp.

"The men of Israel will not repent," he said. "And yet will the Redeemer come."

A swallow came flying in at the open window and whirred through the room. Blindly it collided with the wall, turned with a last exertion and fell on the table, where it lay still beside the book.

In order that the roof of the spirit should not crash in upon them, Bunam proposed a difficult exegetical problem. The Seer and his disciples sat down and discussed the problem for an hour. All that time David held the swallow in his tender hands. He had filled a little mug with water for the swallow to drink of when it came to.

CONFIRMATION

Late in the evening of the next day young Jaacob Yitzchak and Bunam took a walk among the fields of rye mildly radiant under a crescent moon. It was northeast of the city and they reached an immemorial linden tree which the Yehudi was fond of making the goal of his nocturnal and his morning walks. They sat down under the tree, inhaled its fragrance and contemplated the stars.

"This is the foundation of my faith," said Bunam, "as the verse of Scripture has it: 'Lift up your eyes to the heights and behold Who has created them!' "

"That is a very good foundation," the Yehudi replied. "But we men of Israel had better adhere to the words of Revelation: 'I am the Lord, thy God, who brought thee out of the land of Egypt and out of the house of bondage.' "

"It has been asked again and again," said Bunam, "why the Ten Commandments are introduced thus and do not begin with the words: 'I am the Lord, thy God, who created the heavens and the earth.' "

"It is so," the Yehudi replied, "because in that case man would certainly have thought: 'That is no doubt a sublime God, but He will hardly bother with me and I can't come before Him with my fussy troubles.' For that reason God called out to man: 'I am He who pulled you up out of the very dirt; you can come to Me and lay all your miseries before Me.' "

[115]

"True enough," said Bunam. "But doesn't it seem strange to you that there are times during which it really looks as though God would let us sink deeper and deeper into the dirt and didn't dream of pulling us out?"

"The periods of great trial," the Yehudi replied, "are those of the eclipse of God. It is as though the sun were to grow dark; if one did not know that it is there, one would believe there was no sun any longer. Thus it is in such periods. Something interposes between us and God's countenance, so that it seems as though the world must grow cold, lacking that light. But the truth is that precisely at such a time the great return and repentance which God expects of us becomes possible, in order that the redemption, which He desires for us, be a true self-redemption. We have no awareness of Him; it is dark and cold as though He were not; it seems senseless to turn to Him who, if He is here, will not trouble Himself about us; it seems hopeless to will to penetrate to Him who may, granted that He is, perhaps be the soul of the universe but not our Father. The unimaginable must take place in us to enable us to start on the return to Him. But when the unimaginable does happen, then the great return to God which He awaits is at hand. Despair shatters the prison which imprisons our latent energies. The sources of the primordial depths begin to flow."

They sat in silence. It grew later; the stars gave forth their light and the linden tree its mellow fragrance.

"Nothing grieves me so much," Bunam said at length, "as that our repentance is so listless and so vain. I understand very well how the manicolored world with its thousand charms causes one to lose sight of God. But when one has escaped from this disloyalty and turns back to Him to Whom one is eternally vowed — that even then we do it with such feebleness and self-deceiving confidence; it is this that leaves me inconsolable. I asked myself once how it comes that on the Day of Atonement, though we confess our guilt so many times, no message of forgiveness reaches us. King David had scarcely to say a single time: 'I have sinned,' and at once it was conveyed to him: 'Thus the Lord has taken away thy sin!' It became clear to me that when David said: 'I have sinned against the Lord,' he meant: 'Do with me according to Thy will and I will accept it in love.' But when we say: 'We have sinned,' we think it is proper for God to forgive us. When we go on to say: 'We have betrayed Thee,' we think it is proper for God not only to forgive us but to let all good accrue to us."

"One must not be too hard on men," said the Yehudi, "because they carve themselves images with a glorious and good-natured face and substitute these for God, seeing that it is so cruelly difficult to live in His real presence. And so, when we desire to lead men to God, we must not simply overthrow their idols. In each of these images we must seek to discover what divine quality he who carved it sought, in spite of everything, to delineate. Then tenderly and prudently we must help him to find the way to that quality. Our mission is not to the realms in which dwells the purity of holiness; it is to the unholy that we must pay attention so that it find redemption and become whole."

"One time," said Bunam, "when I was going to Danzig, a timber merchant asked me to take his son along, who was to transact business for him there, and requested me to keep an eye on the young man. One evening I could not find him in our inn. So I strolled along the street until I came to a house from which I heard piano-playing and singing. I went in. When I entered, a song had just been finished and I saw the son of the timber merchant enter an inner door. 'Sing the most beautiful song you know,' I said to the woman who had been singing and I gave her a coin. Thereupon she sang a song so enchanting that none who heard it would want to miss a single tone. No sooner had she begun than that inner door opened again and the young man came back. I approached him. 'You are wanted at the inn,' I said to him. 'Come with me at once.' He came with me without asking who wanted him; nor did he ask when we reached the inn. We played cards for awhile, and then went to bed. Next day he would not budge from my side. That evening I took him to a theater. After coming back I recited a psalm. He asked me to recite another and still another, and in the midst of the reciting he burst into tears. Later on he became a disciple of the *Maggid* of Kosnitz. On that occasion, in that whoring house, I learned that the *Shechinah* can occupy all places, and that it is for us to serve it wherever it is found."

"Tell me more precisely, Rabbi Bunam, what you mean by saying we must serve the *Shechinah* wherever it is found."

"It seems to me I mean thereby just what you mean; it even seems to me that I learned the meaning from you, though I never studied under you. It became clearest to me when I asked myself what was the meaning of that cry of Rebecca: 'Wherefore am I thus?' when the two children struggled together in her womb. For just as one separates silver from lead not otherwise than by melting their alloy in the fire, thus in the glow of that mother womb the ultimate separation of two characters of being took place. This was otherwise than the preparatory separation which took place in that Abraham caused two women to conceive. But Rebecca did not know that the ultimate choosing was at hand and that her womb was the destined oven in which the alloy would be separated into its elements. Our sages relate that when Rebecca in the last months of her pregnancy passed the house of study she felt Jacob being drawn toward it, and when she passed a heathen temple she felt Esau being drawn to it. So she asked: 'Why is it thus with me? I am but a woman, a receiving vessel; how is it that choice and purification take place in me?' "

"You are right in your opinion, Rabbi Bunam," said tne

[118]

Yehudi, "that it is the duty of those who lead to bring forth from each human being the genuine purged of its dross, as God said to Jeremiah. Do not forget, however, that God said this to Jeremiah not concerning that which he was to effect in others but in himself. And do not forget that the problem is not merely that of the purification of one's own character. God promises Jeremiah that, if he fulfills the commandment, he will become His, namely, God's mouth. The language is similar to that in which He speaks to Moses, except that in the latter case the promise is unconditioned. The decision is announced that God will speak through the mouth of Moses. Of Moses, however, it is said that he was meekest of all men on earth. He, the great *Zaddik*, was the root of all souls in Israel and they were his branches. Now it is the order of nature that the branch sucks nourishment from the root; if the branch withers it is to be supposed that the root has taken hurt. So when Moses saw people choosing an ill way, he used to say to himself: 'The fault is in me; I must repent in order that goodness return to them.' He, the meekest of men, placed himself, as it were, beneath all and through his repentance carried them back to God."

While they had been speaking thus and listening to each other, thick clouds had insensibly covered the sky. When they looked up, shivering a little in the sharper wind, no star was visible. But the linden tree stood above them like a tiny sky with its innumerable stars sending out fragrance instead of light.

The Yehudi sighed a deep sigh. "Why do you sigh?" asked Bunam.

"I cannot help thinking," said Jaacob Yitzchak, "how after Moses came the Judges and after the Judges the Prophets and after the Prophets the men of the Great Synagogue. Then came the *Tannaim* and *Amoraim* and so it went on to the time of the admonishers. And when this thing, too, was defiled, and false admonishers multiplied, then arose the *Zaddikim*.

And now I sigh because I see that this thing, too, is at the point of defilement. What will Israel do?"

"Is it not," Bunam replied, "rather the fault of the hasidim than of the *Zaddikim?* It would seem to me that, when the holy Ba'al-Shem-Tov first established Hasidism, the Evil Impulse was much embittered, because it was bound to fear that the hasidim would burn all the evil out of the world with the flames of their sanctification. Then the Evil One hit on a plan. When there were just a few hasidim in a given place he went to them and said: 'You're doing a very fine thing. But how effective can two or three people be? You should at least have the minimum congregation of ten.' And so he added a few of his own adherents. Next they had no money for a synagogue or a Scroll of the Torah or other things. He brought them a rich man from among his minions to bear the expense. And when things were thus arranged he said to himself: 'I have nothing more to worry about; my own people will take care of the rest.' "

"Yes," said the Yehudi, "even as it is written: 'And all the wells which the servants of his father had dug in the days of Abraham, the Philistines stopped them up and filled them with dust.' "

"Once upon a time," said Bunam, "in a simple public house in Warsaw, I heard two Jewish porters at a neighboring table tell each other all kinds of things over their brandy. One of them asked: 'Have you learned the Scripture portion for this week?' 'Yes,' said the other. 'So have I,' said the first one, 'and I find one thing hard to understand. It says there concerning our father Abraham and Abimelech, the king of the Philistines: "They made, these two, a covenant." I asked myself why it says: "These two." That seemed superfluous.' 'A good question,' cried the other. 'But how do you answer that question?' 'I think,' the other answered, 'they made a covenant, but they did not become one; they remained two.' "

[120]

"Granted," replied the Yehudi. "But, be they Philistines or servants of Abraham, hasidim of Satan or true hasidim, how far shall we carry the distinction? Are only the latter to be redeemed and not the former, too? When we say, 'Redemption of the World,' do we mean only the redemption of the good? Does not redemption primarily mean the redeeming of the evil from the evil ones that make them so? If the world is to be forevermore divided between God and Satan, how dare we say that it is God's world? You say: those two were not one. Granted But is that to remain true to the very end of days? And if they are ultimately to become one, when will that becoming one begin? Are we to establish a little realm of the righteous and leave the rest to the Lord? Is it for this that He gave us a mouth which can convey the truth of our heart to an alien heart and a hand which can communicate to the hand of our recalcitrant brother something of the warmth of our very blood? Is it for this that He has made us capable of loving the sons of Satan? All our teaching is false, too, if we refuse to test it by them. Right, we are to fight them for the sake of God, we are to fight inexorably. But we are to fight in order to conquer the citadel for Him, the seven times walled citadel of their soul, and not to engage in a general massacre for the honor of God! And how dare we battle against them, if we do not at the same time battle against ourselves? Are not stubbornness and callousness and sloth and malice to be found among us and not only among them? If we were to forget that, if we were to take the contradiction and, instead of annihilating it, let it cleave to the very depth of the primordial, would we not in the very midst of our combat against Satan have become his followers?"

The wind had done its work. Clouds still towered in the sky. But here and there rifts appeared. It was as though gigantic hammers had hewn breaches in those cloudy towers. Here and there a few shy stars began to show. The two friends looked up and could perceive the place of the crescent moon.

"Rabbi," said Bunam, "in the city of Pshysha, in Radom Street, there is an apothecary shop. Somewhere, not far from there, is a house which awaits you. I do not know that house yet. But I will find it. Come and settle down there and permit me to help you and to be your first disciple."

The Yehudi was deeply stirred but made no answer.

A DREAM

When young Jaacob Yitzchak thought of going to bed at a late hour of the night, he observed the tension of a high state of wakefulness in his whole being. For a moment it seemed senseless to think of sleep. But he knew, too, that he had only to lie down in order to fall asleep without any transition. This thing had been so every night since he had been in Lublin. Formerly the consciousness of the life of the day had clung to him during long hours. "How is it?" he said to himself. "When people will ask me, what I learned in Lublin, I will not be able to put it into words, because it is ineffable. I will be able to give only one answer, namely, that here I learned how to fall asleep. What can that mean? How does it come about that I fall asleep at once? It is so because I yield myself up. I abandon myself as into the arms of a mother. All my resistance is gone in an instant and I yield myself up." Then he remembered how he had had the boldness to tell the rabbi that this abandonment of self was the secret meaning of the ritual bath. "How foolish of me!" he said to himself. "He knows everything himself. I learned it of him. And nevertheless —." He reflected in complete wakefulness and yet could not find the word which ought to have followed that "nevertheless." He realized that it was something decisive, something of deeper import than all the former knowledge of all his life. But he could not find it. So he resigned himself and sitting on his bed spoke the night prayer: "Lord of the world, I forgive everyone who has angered or hurt me or committed a trespass against me ... Let no man be punished on my account. May it be Thy will, O Lord, my God and the God of our fathers, that I do not trespass against Thee and do not arouse Thee to anger ..." He stretched himself out and fell asleep at once.

He slept at ease through the darkness. But in the equivocal interval between darkness and dawn there came to him once more one of his heavy dreams.

He stood, the dreamer, upon the ashes of a dead conflagration and peered into a comfortless gray light. Thence came a man astride upon a buffalo approaching very slowly. The man had on a long black cloak with silvery symbols embroidered upon it and in his hand a spirally twisted staff, which could not conceal the fact that it was a snake. The buffalo stopped and panted as though he had been driven almost to death. When the dreamer beheld this he laughed the buffalo to scorn, and suddenly the buffalo was no longer there. He laughed jeeringly at the snake and thereupon it was no longer there. But when he laughed at the man, who now stood upon the earth, it affected nothing but the man's garment. For when it melted from the man's body, that naked body, which still existed, was made of fire; and when the dreamer sought to laugh again he almost choked and realized that one cannot laugh at fire. Now the man raised his hand and suddenly all was back again, garment and snake and buffalo and in addition there was now a crown on the man's head. It was a real right crown of gold, even as one imagines crowns to be, but the gold was liquid, even though it did not trickle down but remained in place. There was no place for laughter now. The man said something to the buffalo and the buffalo nodded. Thereupon the crowned man waved the snake-

[123]

staff over the dreamer and murmured. The snake spewed forth its venom, but the dreamer blew it easily away. Now the man swung the staff. The snake writhed and was about to wind its coils about the dreamer. But he whistled and the snake desisted. When the man in the black cloak saw this he threw the staff upon the ground. The staff raised itself up and was instantly transformed into a doll in a snow white shift and with naked feet. Its head was the head of a dead woman. But this head spoke.

"It is I," said the head.

"It is you," repeated the dreamer.

"I am Foegele," said the head.

"You are Foegele."

"I am Schoendel Freude."

"You are Schoendel Freude."

"I am Foegele Freude," said the head.

At that the dreamer fell down and the dream arose from him and he was awake. But he dared not believe that he was awake.

THE SHADOW OF ELIMELECH

On the second day of the festival, after morning prayers, David of Lelov took the Yehudi with him to his inn. "I've got to talk to you," he said. But when they were sitting together he was silent for a long time. The Yehudi was accustomed to this in his friend and it never troubled him. David was one of those people who passed magnificently the test of tests, the test of a common silence. This time, however, a special obstacle made itself felt. Finally he started speaking:

"Jaacob Yitzchak, I must now do a thing which I have never tried to do on my own impulse, nor have I often done it when others have urged me to — I must tell about other people. I must do it now, for only so can I make you understand something which it is important for you to understand. When I brought you here, much as I knew, I did not know upon what sea I was launching your little boat. Now that I know it, I must tell you more. It is never easy for me to tell about others, but to tell you about this matter, which you must needs learn, is extraordinarily difficult. The thing itself struggles against being told. Yet it must be done.

"Every great *Zaddik* is commonly called the leader of his generation. What does it mean to be a leader? In order to lead one must know the way. But that does not suffice. In order to lead upon a way which is known to one, one must be ahead upon that very way. Still a third element is required for leadership. One must keep the flock which one leads together. But togetherness is something other than a common following of the foremost. A bellwether is no leader. Togetherness means that each is intimate with the other and each feels lovingkindness for the other. Rabbi Elimelech was a great *Zaddik*. Among his disciples was harmony and mutual understanding. This was true not only of his disciples. Whoever had any dealings with him felt that togetherness in his heart. Recently I met an old woman who long before my time was a maidservant in his house. I asked her what her most vivid recollection of him was. She said: 'I have nothing special to tell you, but what I recall most vividly is this. All week long there was a good deal of conflict in the kitchen, such as is common among maidservants. But on the eve of the Sabbath, after the Rabbi had wished us a Good Sabbath, something came over us which made us embrace one another and made each say to the other: Dear heart, forgive me for what I have done to you during the week.' That was it. He needed not to inspire people with this feeling; they inhaled it in his presence. He kept his flock together by merely being there.

"Our Rabbi was at the head of the disciples who dwelt with Rabbi Elimelech. None of those pre-eminent among them was ever tempted by the notion of disputing this place with him. The *Zaddik* himself who, especially as his years increased, was not fond of attending to matters which could be left to another, was oftener and oftener accustomed to say to people, when a decision was demanded of him: 'Go to Rabbi Itzikel!' It was thus that our Rabbi was generally called.

"In a certain year the feast of the Rejoicing in the Torah came and our Rabbi was missing. This was before I was in Lisensk, but Rabbi Elimelech's son, Eleazar, related to me what happened. He saw how upset his father was and asked him why he was so influenced by the absence of a single disciple, seeing that others, who were present, were not inferior to him. 'You know very well,' said Rabbi Elimelech, 'that annually on this day all my scholars help me to build the Divine Sanctuary. Each carries into it one of the Sacred Utensils. It is his office to bring in the Ark, and when he is not here I can call out to God as often as I will: Arise, O Lord! It is in vain.'

"Now it is known to you, Jaacob Yitzchak, that seven years before his death, that is, seven years before his seventieth year, Rabbi Elimelech underwent a strange change of character. But you probably cannot imagine how great this change was. Not suddenly, but more and more he separated himself from the things of the world; he separated not only his will and his perception, but his whole bodily being. An illumination came over his countenance; his glance glided away from objects and turned within; he walked almost always on tiptoe, which was very curious to behold because he was an even taller man than our Rabbi; from time to time, without any motivation, he raised his arm in a gesture of repudiation. He had always made heavy demands upon his students; his strictness now was inordinate; his words to them were parsimonious and his eyes had an astonished look. Among his disciples there was a group who considered him to be failing with age. In truth, he was greater than ever, only association with human beings was more and more difficult for him; they made him impatient. Rabbi Israel of Kosnitz said: he felt this way because people seemed so awkward to him; for he compared them with the angels whom his own deeds had created and who surrounded him.

"It is not surprising that, under these circumstances, a number of the students attached themselves closely to our Rabbi, who took a friendly interest in each one's person and fortune. A man of ill will, who shall be nameless — he died before his time — gave him the nickname Absalom. He compared him to the son of David who took up his station early in the morning at the gate and flattered and flattered the people who came to lay their affairs before the king. In point of fact, our Rabbi never indulged in such practices.

"Once our Rabbi came home to Lisensk from a journey and related to a comrade that on his way he had seen in the forest two uncommonly great trees, the one broad and powerful, the other slender. The former had grown no more branches near its top but had striven toward heaven with all its power, whereas the less vigorous one stood in full foliage to the top. Soon thereafter he had a long conversation with Rabbi Elimelech. After this he dwelt in Lantsut, which is not far from Lisensk. The story went that in this conversation his teacher empowered him to become the leader of his own congregation. I have good reasons, however, to agree with those who say that on that occasion Rabbi Elimelech had merely bidden him to go to Lantsut and that the authorization in question had been given him later and retroactively, that is to say, a year prior to the death of Rabbi Elimelech.

"On a certain occasion, not long after this conversation, Rabbi Kalman asked me significantly whether I knew what had been the extent of the transformation of the Prophet Elijah during his last days on earth. When I made no answer he said: 'His contemporaries could no longer lay hold of him, as it were, neither could any gain guidance from him for the conduct of life. Then it was that God spoke to Elijah: Their understanding no longer reaches the height of your clarity and sanctitude. Anoint Elisha, therefore, that he may prophesy in your stead. He is a lesser one than you; they will be able to reach him and gain guidance from him in the measure of their understanding.'

"Rabbi Elimelech, at all events, sent to Lantsut all sorts of people with whom he did not care to be troubled. He seemed not to observe the fact that many, especially among the younger students, went to Lantsut without his bidding. I myself, though quite inactively, shared in this turn of affairs. Our Rabbi was wont at that time to pass an occasional Sabbath at Lisensk. He did so, accompanied by his *gabbai*. I had been there for a while and, hearing that he had arrived, I went to his inn to call on him. It was Friday and just before sunset. I greeted him and was about to go, since the hour was not suitable for tarrying. He called me back. 'Rabbi David,' he asked in a loud voice, 'do you know exactly when the Sabbath begins?' 'I know it well,' I replied. 'My very hand tells me.' And I showed him my wrist where the veins were beginning to throb, as they always did at the onset of the Sabbath. 'Well, if you know so well when the Sabbath begins I will tell you a story. A captain's daughter fell in love with a general's son, and, although such a union is against the conventions, the heavenly destiny which led those two was so strong that they were married in defiance of the social convention. Have you listened to my tale?' I nodded. 'Yes,' I said, 'that is the mystery which is discussed in the book *The Fruit of the Tree of Life*: how on common days the upper worlds, in order to purify the fallen powers, espouse those who yearn for them from below, even before the onset of the Sabbath leads to the creation of the Sabbath souls.' The Rabbi embraced me. 'Stay near me,' he said. But I was told that when he came to salute Rabbi Elimelech, the

[128]

latter received him with these words: 'You come here to take my hasidim away from me. Wait, and all will be your heritage.'

"In the period following this, the congregation in Lantsut increased steadily. I took to journeying there, too, and soon it came about that I was there oftener than in Lisensk. You must understand the reason, Jaacob Yitzchak: Rabbi Elimelech no longer had an eye for any. He passed among the students like a thundercloud.

"On the way from Lisensk to Lantsut there is a little town in which a disciple of Rabbi Elimelech was the teacher of children. He, too, was drawn to our Rabbi. Once he spent the Sabbath in Lantsut. Rabbi Elimelech seems to have been conscious of this circumstance. Immediately after the ending of the Sabbath he drove to that little town and appeared in the house of his student and asked after him. The latter's wife answered that her husband had gone out and would soon return. She went forth to meet her husband and tried to persuade him to use some subterfuge, but he refused to tell his teacher anything but the truth. When Rabbi Elimelech asked him where he had been he replied: 'The Rabbi dwells in the seventh firmament whither people like me cannot ascend. But in Lantsut there is a ladder on which one can climb to the very heaven of Lisensk.' 'You think yourself clever!' cried Rabbi Elimelech. 'Away with you.' It is related that the man went into the next room and took to his bed and that he died within the week. Rabbi Elimelech, however, drove onward to Lantsut. In the middle of the night he arrived in our Rabbi's house. No one knows what passed between them. Rumor has it that Rabbi Elimelech made a demand upon our Rabbi which the latter rejected. It was said to have been in the form of an example from the life of Saul, who first would have none of the kingdom and later clung to it in vain. But none overheard the conversation; neither of the participants could bear to report it, and I do

[129]

not believe the rumors concerning it. Much later, however, Rabbi Elimelech's son, Eleazar, recounted to me that upon his return his father had spoken to him of the faithless one and had murmured something to himself that sounded like an imprecation. Eleazar had reminded him of the fact that he himself had bidden students to repair to Lantsut. To which Rabbi Elimelech made a reply which his son had not understood and of which I, too, grasped the meaning only gradually. He said — tears were said to have suffused his eyes: 'But I would still live.' It is not to be assumed that he who had separated himself from all earthly things still clung to the circumstances of mortality. Nor would they have been impinged on by the formation of the congregation in Lantsut. The word 'live' in his mouth must be interpreted as meaning that he still had something to stake on earth and something to fulfill. What that thing was no one knows. But it must have been something contrary to the ideas of our Rabbi and hence rendered questionable by his undertakings. I have heard Rabbi Hirsch, the disciple of our Rabbi, say: 'A teacher like Rabbi Melech has not been known since the days of the *Tannaim* and *Amoraim*. But our Rabbi has better eyes.' I have come to learn since that time that, though eyes are important, they are not the most important things about a man. The important thing is what the eyes seek to see when they exercise their power of vision. And that is not determined by the eyes.

"What is certain is that at that time — all this happened ten years ago — our Rabbi gave up his congregation and journeyed northwestwards along the river San to the town of Rozvadov. There he dwelt for a year. If ever the city is mentioned in his presence he says: 'The Polish word *Rozvadov* signifies: dissolution of marriage.' He found no peace of mind there. He first returned for a brief period to Lantsut. Then he repaired to Lisensk and, as I learned later, received Rabbi Elimelech's forgiveness and authorization. At the same time he told his teacher that he meant to leave that region. And soon thereafter, in fact, he moved to the neighborhood of Lublin. Next year Rabbi Elimelech died. Our Rabbi had to wait seven years near and in Lublin before the community of Lublin, whose leaders were mostly ill-affected toward the hasidic teachings, granted him residential rights and before a benevolent patron presented him, who was living in a cottage at the edge of town, with the land on which his house now stands. That was about a year ago."

Such is the tale which Rabbi David related to the Yehudi on this occasion. It should not be omitted, however, that another version of the legend postpones the gift of the lot and the building of the house to the November following the incidents here narrated. It is well known that at this time Suvarov completed the quelling of the Polish rebellion. Among those who had fallen in the defense of Warsaw was almost the entire Jewish legion. The second version of the legend relates that, when the suburb of Praga went up in flames and Poles and Jews were being massacred, the Seer stood at his window in Lublin and peered into the distance to learn the fate of those he knew in Warsaw. He is said to have told one of the most distinguished Jews of Lublin that the latter's daughter was standing in her room in a flowered negligee and rocking her infant. In gratitude for this information the rich man was said to have given him the building lot. But the other version has been followed here.

OF DEATH AND LIFE

When, on the night after the festival, the Yehudi returned to his inn, he passed a door standing ajar, from behind which he heard psalms being recited by a brittle voice and interrupted by a feeble moaning. He looked in and recognized by the light of the taper a man lying on the bed, whose son, as he knew, had recently been betrothed to a granddaughter of the *Maggid* of Kosnitz. He knew well that this sick man had been dwelling here since the week after Pesach. Repeatedly he had meant to visit the man. Each time he had been told that the patient would see no one but the Rabbi. But on this occasion he could not bear to pass the door. The sick man seemed to be in great pain and no one was with him except a youth, who was evidently his son. The Yehudi asked the latter whether he might not be of some help. The youth burst into tears and uttered no word in reply. At this moment Jaacob Yitzchak observed that the sick man had ceased moaning and seemed with wandering eyes to seek his own. He approached the bed and addressed the man, as though he had long known him, in words which at the same time sought to obtain information and to offer cheer.

"I am about to die," said the man in bed.

In this instant, with a glance of the almost unknown man upon him, the Yehudi became aware of the fact that suddenly the fruit of his sufferings had ripened. "Assuredly you will die," said he, and laughed into the other's eyes, "but not necessarily right away."

"I shall die soon," said the man.

"No mortal can know the time of his death with such exactness," answered the Yehudi. "I know what you mean," he continued, "your limbs and your very entrails feel sore; you are tired to death and you think that any little extra blow, a tug at your shoulder, a cold breath on the back of your neck, is bound to finish you. But all this has only the character of a question addressed to the sufferer, whether he is willing that his end come to him. If he summons his last strength to utter a 'No,' or, rather, if he rouses himself to a beseeching of the Eternal over the head of the Angel who asks the question — then it may well be that the hand which is stretched out toward him falls again."

"Not so," said the man in a beseeching voice, "I know that my hour approaches."

"Whence do you know that?"

"I know it."

"Forget what you think you know," the Yehudi demanded with repressed power, "and turn your face to the Lord of Life."

The sick man was silent. But he who had undertaken to draw him back to life observed that something had come to pass. Those eyes left his own and closed; the lips met tranquilly; the emaciated body seemed for the first time in many days to relax. Minutes passed. The drops of a gentle rain of June pattered against the window panes. The clock on the wall struck the hour. The Yehudi stood still and remained with a gesture of helpfulness where he had been standing. Again the hour struck. The sick man opened his eyes and lips. His glance was lost in the distance. "Blessed art Thou, King of the Universe," he whispered. The remainder of the blessing was not audible.

"Go down into the tap room," said the Yehudi to the man's son, "and ask them to give you a jug of mead." The youth looked at him in dismay and went. "Now we will drink *l'hayyim* — to a good life — to each other," said the Yehudi and put the jug to his lips. The sick man drank a deep draught. Then he drank another and fell asleep at once. A mild perspiration gathered on his forehead. The clock struck two. The Yehudi sat down by the side of the bed and kept this vigil until dawn. By that time it was clear to him that life had gained a victory.

The story of this man was as follows: he was a disciple of the Seer. Yet he came but rarely to Lublin. When the Rabbi had visited Kosnitz the last time this man had been there too. The Rabbi had greeted him and looked at him long and intently. Then he had said: "You must get your soul

[133]

in readiness to die within the year." After Pesach the man came with his son to Lublin and brought his shroud with him. At home he had told neither his wife nor anyone else of the saying of the Rabbi. Nor did anyone in Lublin know about it. He had confided the matter only to his son, after having made him swear not to divulge it. After he had arrived in Lublin he had barely eaten or drunk or slept. He had passed his time in prayer and study. Every evening he went secretly to the Rabbi to beseech his blessing. Otherwise he communicated with none. After a few weeks he was taken ill and since then had been lying in the inn. In the seventh week after the beginning of Pesach the certitude came to him that his end was at hand. On the second day of Shavuot he said to his son: "I must make my preparations."

Early next morning, a little while after the Yehudi had gone to his room, the Rabbi came straight from the ritual bath to look after the sick man.

LEAVE OF ABSENCE

Later that day the Rabbi said to the Yehudi: "You seem to have saved a man who was destined to die. How did you go about it?"

"I have done nothing," answered the Yehudi, "except talk to him encouragingly."

"Encouragingly?"

"Yes. I persuaded him not to let death get the better of him."

The Rabbi's eyes grew wide. "What do you mean by that?"

"What should I mean, Rabbi, other than death and life?"

The Rabbi regarded him attentively. "You look exhausted,

Jaacob Yitzchak," he said. "You have recently done too much and too many different things. You should rest yourself for a while."

"Does that mean," asked the Yehudi, "that you give me leave of absence from my office?"

"That is what I mean," the Rabbi answered. With a smile he added: "I am not letting you go."

"I hope to God that you will never let me go," said the Yehudi. "For I will never leave you, Rabbi, unless you do."

"Once more the Rabbi looked into his eyes. It is related by a disciple that when one looked into the eyes of the holy Yehudi, one was able to peer into his very heart.

On this day, which was a Friday, the early afternoon brought a great restlessness to the Yehudi. He could not bear to stay within the walls of a house, not even of the house of study. In the midst of those who hastened and of those who loitered he walked through the streets which were beginning to gleam with the cleanliness of the Sabbath. He saw everyone and yet no one. He left the Broad Lane with its tall gabled houses and entered Castle Street. He stood a long time beside the Jews' Gate. Thence he walked the whole length of the Tailors' Street which curves around the back of Castle Hill with its coil of houses, adorned with balconies, crazy of stairs, covered with protuberances from cellar to attic. He entered the Butchers' Street, where the Jews' town had begun to be built, and entered the graveyard, which lies beyond. He pronounced the blessing: "Blessed art Thou, O Lord our God, King of the Universe, who hath formed you in judgment and nourished and sustained you in judgment and hath given you death in judgment, and knoweth the number of you all in judgment and will one day recall you to life in judgment. Blessed art Thou, O Lord, who quickenest the dead." Then he climbed up between the bushes on the narrow path between the increasing number of crooked and often splintered headstones. He reached the

[135]

tree-clad top and gazed down on the Franciscan monastery deep in the valley below.

Now he set out on the way back. He passed the community's houses of prayer and study in the Butchers' Street and re-entered the Broad Lane and still felt repelled by the thought of entering at any door and had to begin his wanderings anew. Now he saw with quite other eyes the people who were preparing themselves to leave behind the hardships of the week and enter upon the holy day. "How well it is," he was impelled to consider in his heart, "that I cannot read your ultimate secret and your eternal destiny upon your faces! How well it is that in all my solitariness I am not set above you!" But this reflection did not tranquilize his heart. His restlessness drove him on and on and for awhile he could not even stand still. When he passed, cleaving as it did to the Castle Hill, the little synagogue of the "runners," that is of the wayfaring journeymen furriers, his own wanderings came into his mind. "And am I not still a wanderer?" he asked himself. At once there came to him again the thought of the wandering *Shechinah* as once upon a time — had not someone spoken of the matter that day they sat at the long table?— it had appeared to Rabbi Levi Yitzchak, tarrying with bowed head in the Tanners' Street.

Now suddenly he stood still in front of the furriers' *shul*. His heart stopped beating as he became aware of the fact that all tumult had suddenly ceased and that the street was empty and silent. The sky stood in flames. In the same moment the running furriers came trotting along in the midst of a cloud of furry odor. They filled the street. But each one had thrown over his shoulders a bearskin in place of the customary hare and rabbit pelts, and each one had his *Tefillin* bag in his hand.

"For the love of God, what ails you, brethren?" cried the Yehudi. "Why do you carry your phylacteries? The Sabbath is near and you no longer need them!"

"There is no Sabbath," they murmured. "There is no Sabbath any more."

"The Sabbath is coming now, brethren," he sobbed, "it is coming now!"

The bears danced around him and shook their bags, which rattled as though they held bones. "Never will the Sabbath come again," they growled in chorus and stretched out their necks toward the Yehudi. Under the bears' heads he saw the features of certain of the disciples of Lublin, of Simon Deutsch, Meir, Eisik; he saw the grinning, stupid face of Yekutiel. "Hear, O Israel!" he cried and fell upon the ground.

On the next day, at the "Third Repast," the chair of the Yehudi was empty. When it was quite dark a certain man, sitting wedged in among the crowd which surrounded the table, became aware of the fact that his neighbor, who had just come and whom he could not see, shook like one afflicted with a feverish ague. "Why do you stand here?" he whispered to him. "Go home and lie down." He received no answer and the man thus addressed remained in his place. When the lights were lit the man saw that it was the Yehudi who stood beside him. But now he trembled no more.

BUNAM AND THE SEER

His discourses with Bunam, that rare visitor, were dearer to the Rabbi than even those with Naftali. Naftali brought news of the world into his study; Bunam brought the world itself. It was useless to try to discuss political events with him. He sought at once to translate them into human terms. It was as though he were intent upon scraping off from the simple wooden substance of our life a coat of paint and to do it immediately and thoroughly. So soon as one discoursed with him on the facts of life he was inexhaustible in recollections, stories, examples. Years later, in his old age, he told how he had once had it in mind to write a book. The book was to be called *Adam* and in it should be delineated all that is human. Afterwards and upon reflection he had concluded that it were better not to write the book. But he who heard him turned, as it were, the pages of that unwritten book.

This time the Rabbi had something special in mind when, on that evening after the end of the Sabbath, he issued forth from his door and joined Bunam who was walking up and down the elms, smoking his long pipe of reddish briar wood. He had not summoned Bunam. He did this unheard of thing, that he joined his disciple and walked up and down with him under the trees. In his mouth he had the little meerschaum pipe which he preferred to use out-of-doors. The elm trees were gnarled like cripples. But it was June and their foliage was beautiful.

"Bunam," said the Rabbi, "do you remember how you came to Lublin that first time?"

"How should I fail to remember?" said Bunam. "It was soon after you settled here. I came with Rabbi David and for several days I saw you only from afar and heard you interpret Torah on Friday evening. I did not understand what you were saying. But this much I perceived: that the world to come was within this world at this Rabbi's house. After grace, on your way to your study, you passed me and laid your hands on my shoulders and said to me: 'Bunam, cling to me and the Holy Spirit will come upon you and men will come wayfaring to you in order to hear what you will reveal to them from beyond.' "

"You did not answer me on that day," said the Seer.

"How could I have done so?" said Bunam. "It was so utterly different from that for the sake of which I had come. I am no vessel worthy of the Holy Spirit and I had no desire at all that people should come running to me."

"And yet you returned?"

"Of course I did; I came to stay through New Year and the Day of Atonement; because, after all, I did receive from you what I sought and I was not obliged to accept what you offered me beyond."

"And what was it that you sought?"

"I wanted to learn the extent of the human soul."

"And you found that knowledge here?"

"Yes."

"And what was it that brought you here the next time? It could no longer have been the same purpose."

"It was not."

"You remember my saying before New Year that all who could blow the *shofar* were to tell me so. Do you remember?"

"Yes. And I came to you although I could not blow it."

"Do you remember what I told you then?"

"You said: 'Blowing the *shofar* is a matter of wisdom and not of labor. Therefore the wise Rabbi Bunam should blow it.' "

"And what happened then?"

"Then I went with you to your study and you taught me the spiritual attitude which the blower of the *shofar* should gather within him and assume. Then you took me into the house of study and you said to me: 'Take the ram's horn and practice the attitudes which should accompany its blowing.' Now I had to confess to you that I did not know how to blow it. Whereupon you asked me: 'Then why did you announce your name?' "

"And what answer did you give me?"

"I said: In order to make known to the people what it would desire to hear, Moses let God reveal to him the secret of His Name. Only then did he confess that he was no man of words."

"Was that supposed to be an answer to my question?"

"No."

[139]

"Then give me the answer now."

"The answer, Rabbi, is also the answer to your question: what was it that preoccupied me at that time? I desired to discover how high is the reach of the soul's arm."

"And did you find out?"

"Yes."

"It seems you are always eager to find out something, Bunam."

"Not now. But up to that time it was often so. After I had spent my early youth studying in the Hungarian houses of study all that could be learned there, I decided to acquire all the knowledge which the world had to offer."

"All?"

"The amount conformable to my being; how much, that is, experience alone can teach one in its course."

"According to that I am to you a part of the world and its teaching?"

"Yes, Rabbi. Here is the middle of the world, its central part."

The Rabbi fell silent for a period and smoked his pipe. Then he spoke:

"And do you remember what happened on the day preceding that Day of Atonement?"

"Yes, Rabbi. You summoned me and asked my advice concerning your fur hat which the moths had eaten. You told me that the damage was spreading more and more. Thereupon I advised you to comb out the damaged parts. You answered by quoting the saying: 'He who knows how to read a letter is its carrier, too.' Then I combed out the damaged parts."

"And did you understand?"

"To be sure I understood. I understood that on account of my constant desire to know concerning the nature of the soul, my own soul was threatened with damage. Indeed, much damage had already been done, because I had always

[140]

observed people, instead of associating with them quite simply and getting to see and know them as part of that association. I understood that I must repair the damage which had thus been dealt me, else it would extend more and more. And also, that I must not let any new damage take place. I must associate with people with a simple heart and without ulterior motives. And I have changed in this respect since then. Nor did I become your disciple, Rabbi, when for the first time I studied a section with you, but on the occasion when I helped you repair the damage in your fur hat."

"And are you my disciple, Bunam?"

"I am your disciple, Rabbi, and I shall never cease to be your disciple."

"Yet you did not come for a long time after that occasion."

"True. I had a very hard time. I did not come till next year and even then only after Pesach."

"And when you came I asked you: 'How is it with you, Bunam?' "

"And all that I could answer you was the single word 'bitter.' So bitter was my heart. But you said: 'Then you are helped already, for it is said: A broken and a contrite heart the Lord will not despise.' "

"And were you helped?"

"Yes, I was helped."

"And what do you do now?"

"Now, Rabbi, I compound my medicines and guard my thoughts that they remain unmixed."

"And what is your aim?"

"To cleave to him who needs me, so soon as his need arises. You taught me that, Rabbi: to be where one is needed and to be according to the character of the need."

"We, too, need you here, Bunam."

"I mean, Rabbi: to be ready to serve him who needs me for his purpose."

"We, too, need you, Bunam, for our purpose."

"Rabbi," said Bunam, "my lungs and my mouth could never learn to blow this *shofar*."

While he was saying these things, Bunam, who leaned his back against one of the elm trees, remembered how he had sat four days ago under the great linden tree with the Yehudi. The sky tonight was clear and sown with stars; the moon had grown to be a half-moon. Involuntarily on that occasion the eyes of Bunam had been lifted up to the heavenly lights. Just as instinctively did his lowered glance now brush the countenance of the Rabbi. That countenance was brightly lit, but all color had faded from its cheeks. Never before and never thereafter had anyone seen this change take place in the countenance of the Seer of Lublin.

Now the Rabbi knocked the ashes from his pipe.

THE SECOND PART

NOTATIONS

I SELECT the following material from the recorded notations of a disciple of the Rabbi of Lublin. His name
was Benjamin and he had been born in Lublin and lived
there. He wrote these notations in the summer of 1797. They
have not the character of a diary. They recount in concise
form whatever seemed most important in his recollection.
The passages here communicated are those which bear upon
our specific theme. Rabbi Benjamin writes:

"During the last year the Rabbi's health was much better than during the two preceding years, when he sometimes
seemed very fatigued. He has been more active himself in
teaching, even in teaching the mystic lore which last year
he left almost entirely to Rabbi Meir or else to Rabbi Hirsch,
whenever the latter happened to be in Lublin. His discourses
at table, which seemed for a time merely like brief excerpts
from what he had to say, reassumed their former character.
Repeatedly, and with a special emphasis, he discoursed on
the question of faith in the *Zaddik* and the relationship between the latter and his disciples.

"Twice I took down his words during the night immediately
after he had spoken them. I record them now in this book.
The first time he was interpreting the words of the prophet
Isaiah: Who is there among you that fears the Lord, listens
to the voice of His servant, who walks in darkness where no
light gleams. The Rabbi said: 'Who is there among you
who fears the Lord — who is it that can fear the Lord and
yet be *among you,* that is to say: who can mingle among men

[145]

and guard his communion with them and yet truly give himself up to his Creator, not, therefore, by an act of separation from the creatures, but precisely by fulfilling his devotion to his God in and through them? He can do it *who listens to the voice of His servant*, that is, he who listens to the *Zaddik*, the servant of God, and has faith in him. And why does God call the *Zaddik* His servant? Because the *Zaddik* walks in darkness. He passes through the darkness of the world, through all its lusts and desirousnesses by which it has darkened the countenance of the Lord to its eyes; he goes *where no light gleams*. For to him gleams in the darkness the divine Nothingness, the highest of the potencies which emanate from the ultimate primordial, the 'crown,' which, by reason of its alienation from all substantiality, is also denominated Nothingness . . .'

"Another time the Rabbi was asked after the meaning of the rule that, when on New Year a lamb's head is served, one must say: 'May it be the Will above, that we be like a head and not like a tail.' He interpreted: 'One prays to be the disciple of a true *Zaddik*, who may be called Head; he, too, prays that he gains disciples, who likewise participate in the qualities of the head and remain loyal to him.'

"During this year there came to us, directly or through the reports of Rabbi Naftali, news concerning a prince of armies in the west, Bonaparte by name, who is said to be also called by the name of Apollyon or Napollyon. I had the conversation, which took place on this matter, from Rabbi Naftali's own lips and wrote it down at once. It was on a Friday. The Rabbi had come into the house of study with his pipe in his mouth, as was his custom. It was well known that the gifts of the spirit were measured out to him most richly on that day. Rabbi Naftali told him that this Bonaparte had vanquished the Pope of Rome, and that the latter's emissary, one of the chief among his priests, had thrown himself at the feet of that prince to beseech an easement of the conditions of peace. 'That is the man,' said the Rabbi. Rabbi Naftali was unwilling to explain these words to me. But I told him they were probably to be interpreted in connection with the coming of that Gog, which the Rabbi had announced to us as imminent four years ago. And Rabbi Naftali did not contradict me. He went on to say that he had related to the Rabbi the report that that leader of armies was now standing before the walls of Vienna and that the army of the Emperor of Vienna and of his people was now wavering, even as it is written in the prophet Isaiah: As the trees of the forest waver in the wind. Thereupon he, that is to say, Rabbi Naftali, had heard from the lips of the Rabbi, who seemed to be staring out of the window into the distance beyond, the following words: 'I see him; he is small and gaunt. But he will take on more and more flesh. His legs are short but his head is large.' Rabbi Naftali observed that the man was not a native of the country whose army he was leading, but of an alien island. Whereupon the Rabbi said: 'He is a Sidonian.' Rabbi Naftali insisted that the man came from neither Sidon nor Tyre, but from an island of the west. But the Rabbi repeated that he was a Sidonian, and added: 'He calls himself the lion of the desert. But he is no lion. The sign of the Scorpion is on his forehead. He comes from the Sidonian Islands. He comes from the flood of the abyss. He comes from Abaddon. He loves no one and desires to be loved by all. He wants to turn the world into his booty. He comes from Abaddon.' This is what I heard from the lips of Rabbi Naftali. He told me further that the peoples of the world believed that a great army of the men marked by the Scorpion would arise out of the abyss and lay waste the earth. Their king would be the Angel of the Abyss and would be called Apollyon, which is *Abaddon* in Hebrew, that is to say, 'Forlornness,' 'Ruin.' I attended very carefully to all that was being said and wrote it down immediately thereafter.

"I have not yet related that Rabbi Yehuda Loeb had left us sometime before and had returned to Zakilkow. There was a rumor that this had happened after a long conversation with the Rabbi. He had demanded of the Rabbi that he punish the Yehudi, because the latter had founded a congregation of his own in Pshysha, where he had lived for more than two years. The Rabbi had refused to believe this. The Yehudi had been coming again and again to Lublin. If he had done anything like that he would surely have reported it. When Rabbi Yehuda Loeb repeated his assertion, the Rabbi had said to him: 'You will establish your own congregation before he will establish his. You imagine that you are no longer subject to my power, because you no longer see the Archangel of the Law standing at my side. But you cannot understand that. He, the Yehudi, is subject to no such delusion.' Thereupon Rabbi Yehuda Loeb is said to have turned away in silence and to have left the room. It is reported further that he has been ill-affected ever since then, because the Rabbi had turned over the guidance of the students to the far younger Rabbi Meir.

"As far as the Yehudi is concerned, I have set it down in my previous notations how, after his departure, his opponents formed a solid league, at whose head stood first Rabbi Yehuda Loeb and now Rabbi Simon Deutsch. All practical affairs are in the hands of Rabbi Eisik. It is he who sent spies to Pshysha to find out whether the Yehudi delivers independent interpretative lectures, whether hasidim come to him with petitions and redemption payments and, especially, whether students from Lublin are to be found there and what they are doing. It was no secret that not only Rabbi David and Rabbi Bunam but many others were frequenting the house of the Yehudi. For instance, it was

[148]

established that Rabbi Yissachar Baer, who, to be sure, visits a hundred other *Zaddikim*, is a frequent visitor there. Oddly enough, young Perez, Rabbi Yekutiel's brother, was seen in Pshysha. All the information was put together and submitted to the Rabbi in the right selection and order. This was done chiefly by Rabbi Yekutiel, whom everyone trusted to convey nothing but the truth. In point of fact, nothing was submitted to the Rabbi except the truth. Of course, it was properly prepared, as is customary under the circumstances. Apparently, however, nothing could persuade the Rabbi to undertake any action against the Yehudi, to whom his heart still seems to cling.

"I am bound to add how it came about that Rabbi Simon Deutsch's dislike of the Yehudi, which used to manifest itself by a constant growling in the latter's presence, was intensified to the point of grim hatred. When the Yehudi came here for the first time from Pshysha, not long after he had settled there, he and Rabbi Simon, who was also on his way to Lublin, met at an inn. They breakfasted together. Suddenly Rabbi Simon said: 'I'm going back. I see that the Rabbi is not at home.' The Yehudi contradicted him. After some argument they agreed to go on to Lublin. Rabbi Simon agreed to this in order to break the Yehudi's intolerable opinionatedness. When they entered at the gate of Lublin people who caught sight of them cried out to them that the Rabbi had just left the city to go in another direction. 'Well, did I not have the right vision?' Rabbi Simon asked. 'It is not true,' the Yehudi replied. When they came to the house of the Rabbi they were told that he had, indeed, intended to set out on a journey, but had then put it off. Thereupon Rabbi Simon asked the Yehudi how he had known this thing. 'Because you bragged so with your power of vision,' said the Yehudi. It was on this occasion that Rabbi Simon's dislike turned into towering hate."

[149]

Pshysha is in no way different from the innumerable little Polish-Jewish towns in which there are doubtless far more Poles than Jews, but which create the contrary impression, firstly, because the Jews busy themselves more in the open streets and, secondly, because by their mobility and speaking they mark their presence. Yet it must be added that the proportion of the Jewish population is not small. This was especially evident on Friday when, within the space of a few hours, the little town underwent a complete transformation.

On the main street, called Radomska, which is so called because, if you pursue it and its continuation on the open road, you finally reach the district capital of Radom, there used to be an apothecary's shop. You entered a vaulted room which issued in a lower and darker vault, and to the eye of the beholder it seemed as though this scheme was repeated in the background. A couple of handsome old vessels gleamed above the common merchandise which filled the greater part of the place. Behind the diagonal counter with the scales upon it there were to be seen, in the midst of the jars which contained drugs, sundry bottles filled with different and gaily colored fluids, in which the practiced glance of the customers could at once distinguish mountain-ash spirits from plum brandy, and this in turn from the liquor of the mahaleb cherry. Such customers would occasionally sit at two little side tables. They would drink the apothecary's health and chat with him and occasionally, when trade was slow, play a game of chess with him.

On this particular Friday morning a peasant woman was waiting at the counter for a prescription to be filled. Bunam, who was on excellent terms with the peasants of the region and was often asked for his advice concerning matters unrelated to his profession ("he *knows*," they said of him),

[150]

was asking the woman after the health of her youngest. With his right hand he was completing the prescription, the while he let his left glide over the strings of a guitar which lay on the bench beside him. At that moment a hasid entered. For a while he watched the apothecary with disapproval and surprise. At last he decided to give expression to his feelings.

"Rabbi Bunam," he said, "what you are doing there is very profane!"

"Rabbi Yecheskel," Bunam replied, "you are a fool of a hasid!"

The man went out with anger and resentment in his heart. Later, however, he related that on that night his grandfather appeared to him in vision and gave him a box on the ear and shouted at him: "Don't look after him; his radiance reaches the halls of heaven!"

Not long thereafter Bunam was playing chess with a usurer of evil repute. From his youth on he had been fond of playing chess with people of questionable character. He made each move with a serene devoutness. All the while he would from time to time half sing a little verse, such as: "If forth your steps are led, see that you feel no dread." These sayings of his were always applicable to the stage of the game. But the tone in which they were uttered was such that the partners pricked up their ears. They felt ever more intensely that the thing concerned them deeply. They hated to admit it; they resisted; in the end they were vanquished and conversion conquered their hearts. This time, too, the thing went strangely. Bunam made a false move; his partner took advantage of that and endangered his game. The apothecary begged for permission to revoke the move and the man permitted him to do so. But when the same incident repeated itself the man refused to grant Bunam the favor.

"Once I have let you do this thing," said he, "but now your move must stand."

"Woe to the man," cried the apothecary, "who is so deep in the coil of evil that no prayer helps him to return to good!" Silently the man stared at Bunam, but there was no doubt that a glow had awakened in the ashes of his soul.

Once more Bunam was standing at his counter and twanging his guitar. The door opened and a boy entered who said that the Rabbi begged the apothecary to come to him at once. Bunam was accustomed to being summoned thus. It happened often enough that when the Yehudi met among those who came to him for the healing of their souls what Bunam called a "serious case," he would cry out after a while: "Fetch the apothecary to help me!" It was not true that he accepted either petitions or redemption money. But he turned no one away who came to him for help. This time there seemed to be something special. Bunam called his wife Rivka to come from their dwelling to the shop. She smiled, as she always did, when she looked at him. Her husband seemed always to amuse her anew but also, and in a far higher measure, to delight her. He answered her smile with his own. He seemed to have no objection to amusing her, so long as he delighted her too. He begged her to take his place, gave her certain directions, and went out.

He saw a strange gathering of people in front of the little house on the side street in which the Yehudi lived. Here were gathered the cripples and the paralytics among the Jews of the place, surrounded by their kinsmen and their friends. They were nearly all gesticulating violently and crying out at random. What they evidently desired was admission to the house. When Bunam approached and was recognized from the window, the door was opened for him. But those who desired to crowd in with him were turned away and the latch of the door was shot.

The Yehudi met Bunam in an anteroom. "Advise me what to do, Rabbi Bunam," he said. "Something has taken place which is good in itself. But the consequences for me are wretched. As you know, I paid a visit to my parents in the city of my birth and returned a week ago. I was delayed on the way and had to spend the Sabbath at an inn. When I was about to leave and asked the innkeeper for my reckoning, he refused to accept any money. He said he had liked my way of praying; he had seen the significance of my waiting to pray until my heart was ready to do so; such things were not fit for simple people like himself, but he was glad that there was someone who prayed thus. Under these circumstances he could not bear to let me pay for the little he had done for me. Had I insisted on paying the man would have been hurt. So I asked him whether there was any way in which I could make a return for his friendliness. 'What a good guest can do,' he replied, 'is to bless the master of the house.' His wife, his children, and his servants surrounded him; I blessed them all and entered the carriage and asked the driver to make haste, for my time was short. At that moment the man cried out: 'Ah, the Rabbi forgot to say farewell to our daughter and to bless her.' 'I didn't know you had a daughter,' I said with a touch of irritation. 'Why is she not here? Let her come out at once.' And at that moment she did indeed come forth with uncertain and, as it were, groping feet, very stiff but erect, and approached me and bowed her head for my blessing. And all who were there cried out and sobbed over the miracle. For eleven years the girl had been a helpless paralytic who could not turn from her right side to her left. While they were all busying themselves with the girl who was healed, I jumped into the carriage and drove hastily off. I was sure that no one knew me thereabouts. And now the news of the miracle which I am alleged to have wrought has come here nevertheless, and all the sick and the crippled of our region demand it as their right that I heal them. What am I to do, Rabbi Bunam?"

Bunam nodded to him. Never had he seen his teacher

and friend so perplexed. "You go out to them and tell them the truth, Rabbi," he counseled.

"The truth?" asked the Yehudi doubtfully. "How could they understand it or accept it?"

"Tell it to them in such fashion that they can grasp it and keep hold of it," answered Bunam.

He opened the door and they both went out. Now they observed that, in the meantime, a new difficulty had arisen. To the original group there had been added a number of Polish companions in misery, who stood in a group by themselves.

"Let me deal with these," said Bunam.

Swiftly he approached the Christian group. In firm, clear Polish, for he was a master of many languages, he assured the people that this man was no miracle man. God had simply used him as an involuntary tool because He desired to be a Healer in this case, but that . . .

At this point his hearers interrupted him, not rebelliously, but in the tone of a gentle wail. "The Reverend Rabbi just doesn't *want* to heal us," they lamented. And at once the Jewish group chimed in with a sharper and more demanding tone. The slow, deliberate speech of the peasants blended with the sharp insistent composite idiom of the exile. The distress of mortal man, his pain, his impotence, his boundless hope, condemned to inarticulateness and yet stammering his cry — it was this that overcame the Yehudi. In an instant his perplexity left him. Transformed he stood there in an aura of love.

"My brethren, my brethren," he cried out. "You suffer the suffering of mortality and the *Shechinah* suffers your suffering with you. With you it is lame and stricken and with you it laments your lamentations. I do not know why you suffer; I do not know how help is to be brought you; I do know that redemption will come. The redemption of the *Shechinah* will come. When that comes the woe of man will come to an end and with it your woe. God, the God of the suffering, will bless you. I bless you in His Name. To the becoming One of the Holy One, blessed be He, and His *Shechinah*!"

With a mighty gesture he raised his arms over both Jews and Poles. Together they bowed their heads beneath that blessing. The Jews had not understood his words much better than the Poles. But both groups had perceived the fact that a true word had been uttered, which both received. Slowly but without a shadow of rebelliousness, the crowd dispersed. Only now did Rabbi Jaacob Yitzchak turn around to look for Bunam. He saw that the latter no longer stood at this side. He had gone a few steps forward and stood facing him with head bowed, even as he had taken up his stand to share the blessing in the midst of the sufferers.

TROUBLE WITHIN AND WITHOUT

It is well known that Rabbi Bunam called the Yehudi "the golden ear." This must be rightly understood. It is an error to derive it, as has been done, from an ear with golden grains of wheat which Bunam is said to have seen during his travels in a king's treasury. We do know that Bunam was fond of saying his afternoon prayers out in some open field, and so a legend arose that our archfather Isaac who, as the Scripture tells us, "went out into the field to meditate," appeared to Bunam in the guise of a wanderer and discoursed with him. Often he would stand by the side of ripening fields of wheat and inhale, as it were, the entire "fragrance of the field, which the Lord has blessed." And so when he spoke of a "golden ear," he meant this blessed fullness and ripeness of a field which is manifest in the color of pure gold. And when one considers that from time to time he would break a ripe ear from its stalk and reverently eat the grains of wheat, it is clear that in his praise he meant to include the nourishment which is immanent in this living and burgeoning gold.

Something of his delight in the man to whom, among all his teachers, he felt closest was in that glance with which now, an hour after the incident with the cripples, he watched the Yehudi. The latter, with a tranquil deliberateness, which used not to be his, took long puffs on his pipe and, a little later, just as deliberately ate the little flat cinnamon cookies which Schoendel Freude, much as her husband vexed her, baked as deliciously one time as another. The Rabbi of Ger, a celebrated disciple of Bunam, used to say — as is perfectly obvious from a tradition concerning Bunam — that when the Yehudi smoked his pipe, his soul assumed the attitude of the High Priest at the moment of the incense offering, and when he ate the little cakes his soul was that of the High Priest at the moment of sacrifice.

"Rabbi," Bunam said now, "even though you refuse to accept petitions from people and also to interpret Torah at the Sabbath table, yet you will not be able for much longer to escape your destiny of founding a congregation of your own."

"Are you beginning to say that, too?" the Yehudi replied mournfully. "Is the lie of the slanderers to become truth?"

"Why should you be concerned with the slanderers?"

"I am afraid that I shall be forced to concern myself with them."

"But consider this, Rabbi: if a man comes to you and asks you to direct him, you do not refuse to do so; and when another comes to you and asks you what he is to do to save his soul, you do not refuse your help. Is not the sum of these people who come to you and are received by you and cling to you a congregation in itself?"

"I must seek to fulfill in the case of each who is sent to me that which is delivered to me. But no congregation arises so long as he who is fated to teach and deliver does not desire it to arise."

"A congregation does not arise out of a man's will, but out of his being what he is."

"Yet if he does not will it, the congregation cannot come into being."

"You will be forced to will it."

"Who is going to force me?"

"Who but God Himself, irrespective of the instrumentality."

"It is not His way to use force."

Bunam was afraid of having robbed his friend of his lovely tranquillity of mood. But even in friendship there is a higher law than that of merely sparing one's friend. Softly he said:

"He has spoken: 'I shall be there as He who shall be there.' He is not rigid in the ways of His manifestation. If He desires to lead a man upon His way, He may even manifest Himself under the aspect of force."

"That would be cruel!"

"He is not amiable. He is cruel and gracious. Job testifies to that."

"Did not our sages say: 'Cling to His attributes'? Should we not seek zealously to imitate Him?"

"Yes, to imitate the attribute of mercy, which He reveals to us, not the attribute of judgment whose aspect we cannot bear."

"Bunam, I have learned to know something of the judgment of God, and it was incomprehensible to me even as it was to Job."

"His judgment assumes a gentler form, too. It is a force, then, which does not punish a man, but leads him."

They fell silent. Bunam saw that, though Jaacob Yitzchak was suffering, he had lost no part of his tranquillity.

"There was a time," said the Yehudi after a while, "when I asked myself whether we were really indispensable."

[157]

"Explain that!"

"I mean: whether it is really necessary that there be congregations and leaders of congregations; whether it might not suffice that the sacred writings exist; whether there might not at last arise a generation of true readers in which the living voice would speak to the living heart. And, of course, I came to the conclusion that that is impossible. For one reason, because each true congregation ought to be the beginning of that great congregation of all humanity which will some day arise. And for another reason because, quite simply, people are as they are. And, even more, because God is concerned not only over what we do and do not do, but also over the manner in which we do that which we do. And this thing is not written in the writings."

"Rabbi," said Bunam, "in Danzig, in an inn, sundry merchants asked me why I, who am so well versed in the writings, continue to spend money to travel to *Zaddikim*. What could they teach me in the matter of wisdom or wont which was not written in the books. I tried to explain it to them in every possible way, but they still did not see. One day they invited me to accompany them to the play-house. I declined. When they came back that night they told me that they had witnessed many remarkable things in the theater, the like of which they had never seen before. 'I know those remarkable things, too,' said I. 'I have read the playbill on which are printed the acts and the names of the acting personages.' 'From that,' they replied, 'you cannot possibly have any notion of what we saw with our own eyes.' 'Thus,' I said, 'you now admit that I am right. For the same thing is true concerning the books and the *Zaddikim*.' And so —"

The door opened. There entered a very young woman. She shoved in a wooden cradle out of which gazed the cheery face of a boy child. It was evident that she did not wish to leave the baby alone even for a moment. Except for the

[158]

curving breasts and hips, which had been hers even before her marriage, she could have been called slender; her little head could have been called charming without the big and restless nose which, when she was silent — a rare occurrence, by the way — was her most powerful and expressive feature. When she was excited — and such was her natural condition — and desired to vent her excitement in words, she threw her little head to one side and at the same time opened as wide as possible her pretty gray eyes, with the little brown flecks in them, and her delightfully curved mouth. She did this now immediately upon entering the room.

"Itzikel," she said in a tone which was almost gentle, but in which one could perceive the capacity to change suddenly to a murderous scream, "I want to talk to you and I want to talk to you before Rabbi Bunam, because he is a clever man."

"She heard the beginning of our conversation," Bunam whispered to the Yehudi. "I wonder why she took so long to come in?"

In sterner accents Schoendel continued: "I beg of you to open your ears wide to what I have to say. I insist on being heard. Things can't go on this way!" At once a drop of perspiration gathered above her nose, the certain sign that she was about to give up an ordered form of speech and pour out words like a cataract.

"You of course don't pay attention to anything, Itzikel," she began. "You pay no attention to anything except the dreams which you carry around in you, and you think I don't know. But I know everything. Nothing but dreams, empty dreams, and you forget that you have a wife and you forget that you have a son and you forget everything and you care about nothing except your dreams and you are careful that nothing should happen to them. But we and what is going to become of us, that doesn't concern you. We can go to wrack and ruin, can't we? It's all the same to you. You've got your dreams left, and you don't have to exert yourself even, because people come running to you, crazy about you as they are, and so you'd only have to stretch out your hand. But you, what do you do? You put your hands behind your back; you're far too arrogant to be bothered with them. Oh yes, you show them a friendly face. But in your heart you're arrogant; nobody is as arrogant as you are. I know you and I see through the whole business when you have those far-away eyes — far-away eyes turned to me, just like the far-away eyes you turned on Foegele, my poor, sweet sister. What was her end, I ask you, and what happened to her?"

Jaacob Yitzchak was silent.

"All that doesn't move you the least bit," she went on. "You're so far above it all. You've got your dreams. But I, I never stop remembering how she used to sit there over her embroidery — and you were not there and you never were there — and she didn't want to cry. You think I was too small to know. But I saw how she didn't want to cry, while you were vagabonding around, following your dreams. And that's the very same thing that you want to do to me. But you can't do it to me; I won't stand for it; I won't stop reminding you; you can't get rid of me the way you got rid of her."

Jaacob Yitzchak was silent.

"A human soul could writhe at your very feet," Schoendel cried. "What do you care? You go into your room and you pray. I don't understand how you dare to pray, a man like you. And yet people believe in you; I'll never understand it; they believe in you, of all people; they say you can perform miracles. Why don't you perform the miracle of feeding your wife and child? It's a bit of luck that my good mother sends us something once in a while; otherwise we could die of hunger. All right, you earn a few pennies by teaching. But we can't even use them. You won't let us keep a farthing in the house overnight. Whatever is left at nightfall must be given to the poor. But aren't we poor ourselves? But no, you won't let us keep anything, even if I don't know how I'll get a bit of porridge for the baby next morning. You won't let us, you won't let us!"

She screamed at the top of her voice. Suddenly it failed her. She struggled for breath and then whined softly. The Yehudi looked at her attentively. Then he broke his silence. "Schoendel," said he, "you are saying sinful things. We have a roof over our heads and food and raiment, and provision is being made for Foegele's children, too. What more would you have?"

Bunam looked at him in astonishment.

At the Yehudi's first words the woman had regained her breath and her voice. She added a few more words. But it was evident that she wanted only to bring her speech to a proper close. For soon afterwards, trundling the cradle in front of her a little more violently, she went out through the door and slammed it behind her.

"Rabbi," Bunam asked, "in what respect has this day an advantage over other days? You are not accustomed to answering her at all!"

"Bunam," answered the Yehudi, "did you not observe how it throttled her that her scolding had no power over me? And so I had to let her feel that her words did strike me to the heart. And do they not indeed do so?"

At this moment a soft noise could be heard through the French window, which stood ajar. Bunam immediately leaped through it and seemed to hurtle against some person standing outside, for the Yehudi heard a sharp cry. Before he could do anything his friend re-entered, this time by the door, and drew in by the arm a man unwilling to enter. It was Eisik. Bunam released him. There he stood, having recovered his equilibrium. He even succeeded in raising his right shoulder.

[161]

He turned to the Yehudi and started speaking right away. "I can see, Rabbi, that they have slandered me to you. People evidently told you that I spread evil rumors about you. But that is not true. I did certainly undertake to report how things were going here. But I did that in order to prevent lying reports from reaching our Rabbi. Anybody else would have made a mountain out of a molehill. But I tell only the unadulterated truth. And how great is the power of truth over falsehood!"

"Rabbi Eisik," said the Yehudi, "do me the honor of partaking of the third repast with us tomorrow."

At this third repast something took place which was much discussed afterwards. The Yehudi passed Eisik a piece of herring across the table. Eisik, frightened of the power of the "evil eye," wound his handkerchief quickly around his hand which, he thought, might be in danger of sudden paralysis. He grasped the piece of fish and brought it near his mouth with the intention of feigning to chew and swallow and getting rid of it surreptitiously. At that moment a frightful choking sensation overcame him. In his confusion, though without meaning to do so, he stuck the piece of fish into his mouth and devoured it. At once the choking stopped. But it is told that all during the rest of his rather long life, this thing took place each time that he got ready to eat herring, so that finally he decided to abstain from this favorite dish.

ARMAGEDDON

I communicate in the following pages the further notations made by Rabbi Benjamin of Lublin and dating from
the year 1799.

"At the beginning of the winter the Rabbi, after he had
long seemed under a cloud that went with him wherever he

went, had a conference with Rabbi Naftali. The latter came from the conference with a graver face than was customary. He did not want to tell what had been said, but to my insistent questioning he finally replied: 'Do you not know that Don Isaac Abarbanel interprets Ezekiel's prophecy concerning Gog in the sense that the sons of Edom will first conquer Egypt before they attack Palestine?' 'Well?' said I, not understanding what was at stake. 'Have you not heard,' he cried, 'that Bonaparte is in Egypt?' Now the connection was clear to me. 'But,' I objected, 'Don Isaac avers that Gog is not the name of a person at all!' 'You fool,' he turned upon me, 'what has that to do with it?' But I could not understand why I deserved to be called a fool. Therefore I would not let him go, although he was in haste. I held him by the arm and reminded him of the fact that according to Abarbanel the people called Gog was to fight against Christian nations in Palestine, whereas both Egypt and Palestine were today ruled by the Turk. But this angered him the more. He shook me off and upon leaving said only this: 'Why bother to talk to a man who does not know that Bonaparte is fighting against Christian nations even when he is fighting against the Turks.' But I am of the opinion that he did not refute my objection.

"Soon thereafter the Rabbi sent a messenger to Rabbi Hirsch in Zydatshov asking him to come to Lublin at once. Immediately we all asked what might be the purpose of this invitation, although we knew that there was none among the disciples who equalled Rabbi Hirsch in cabalistic knowledge and in skill in cabalistic magic. I do not wish to be understood as saying that he had ever actually indulged in magical practices. He himself denies ever having done so. When he arrived, the Rabbi shut himself up with him and none of us dared approach the room. Luckily Rochele was busy in the next room, and much later, after Rabbi Hirsch had left, she confided to me she had heard the Rabbi

[163]

say emphatically: 'According to that North may here be interpreted as Northwest.' I inferred at once that what had been meant was the names of evil powers, since it is well known that North signifies the left side. When I communicated this thing to Rabbi Meir he laughed at me and said: 'It is perfectly obvious that an attempt was made to interpret the words that Gog was coming to Palestine from the North as meaning he would come from the Northwest, seeing that in Scripture there is no special word which means Northwest.' In my opinion he had no right to laugh at me, for it is evident that the conversation could not but have been on some aspect of cabalistic practice.

"Generally speaking I think it silly that they refer everything to Bonaparte. What makes them assume that a man like our Rabbi should take so much thought of a coarse creature like that? It is true, of course, that people talk a lot about Bonaparte, even among us. But after all there are other and more important things in the world. I am bound to confess that later on something took place which seemed to confirm Rabbi Meir's opinion. Yet I am certain that in the end I shall be proven to have been in the right.

"Before I report the event which suddenly placed Bonaparte at the center of our attention, I must first touch upon sundry other matters, among them one which frightened us all.

"After the middle of March, a few days before Purim, there came to us to Lublin, after a long absence, Rabbi David of Lelov, the Yehudi, and Rabbi Bunam. They were as merry as though the Purim masquerades were already in full swing. After they had visited the Rabbi, they gave a great feast for all who were willing to come. Rabbi Naftali, who, like myself, had accepted the invitation without hesitating, said to me on the way: 'Why does it say of King Ahasuerus that he prepared a great feast for all his princes and his servants? For those are the identical people. They are his

princes in relation to the masses and his servants in relation
to himself. But the Scripture would imply the following:
Up to the feast they are all princes and servants simultaneously. But under the influence of wine their characters
divide. Some think of themselves only as princes and others
only as servants.' All of us — and many of the hasidim of
Lublin were present — grew very merry. We drank and
drank and sang gay and holy songs and danced. A hasid
of seventy took off his shoes and lifted his caftan and leaped
on the tables and danced between the candles and the glasses
without touching any of either with his feet. In between
stories were told. David told stories of children and Rabbi
Bunam of merchants in Danzig and Leipzig and Rabbi
Naftali told jocular anecdotes of *Zaddikim*. Only the Yehudi
told no stories. But he listened with cheerful countenance.

"Next day the inn swarmed with hasidim of Lublin.
Among them, however, were also sundry enemies of the
Yehudi, whose evident intention it was to spy out whatever
could be reported to the Rabbi against him. In the end they
had so much to tell that the Rabbi is said to have exclaimed:
'Does he come to me to take my people away from me?' The
Yehudi himself seems not to have been aware of these observations and reports. Rabbi Bunam, who took notice of all
these things, had gone on an excursion in the neighborhood
that day. But Rabbi David soon saw how things were and
saw to it that the crowd was reduced in numbers."

(Several years later an addition was made at this point,
as follows: "In the interval Rabbi David told me that
when the Yehudi was informed of the state of affairs on that
occasion, he had been much astonished. Repeatedly he had
thanked Rabbi David for guarding his interests and had
asked him whether he did not have some wish which he,
the Yehudi, could fulfill for him out of gratitude. 'Before
David can bethink himself,' Rabbi David had literally
answered, 'of a wish, he will be ready to put on his little

[165]

shirt.' That is an idiom for dying. Yet on that day the two seemed to have agreed that Rabbi David's son, Moshe, was to marry the second daughter of the Yehudi, the first having been promised long ago, when she should have attained the proper age.")

"It was the day before the fast of Esther. On the evening, after the fast, that is to say, on the eve of Purim, the dreadful thing took place. As the Rabbi was on his way to the house of prayer in order to read the scroll of Esther, his feet suddenly ceased to function. He stood there rigid, unable to move. In vain did they try to support him or to lift him. He had become incomprehensibly heavy. The Yehudi approached intending to carry him, no great matter for a man of his gigantic strength. But the body of the Rabbi had grown even more rigid and the Yehudi could not budge him. Even when others came to his help their efforts were in vain. Then Bunam came along. So soon as the Rabbi saw him he said: 'The wise Bunam is to carry me.' Instantly Bunam did pick him up and carried him into the synagogue. We asked the Rabbi to sit down for a while. He refused. He stood there and opened the scroll. So soon as he began to read the rigidity left him."

(At this point there is a marginal note written in an obviously much older hand: "I would like to interpolate here what I heard many years later from Rabbi Bunam's own lips when he was already blind and Rabbi of Pshysha. He said to a few of us: 'The Rabbi of Lublin had greater and better hasidim than I, but no one knew him as well as I. Once I came into his room and did not find him there. But I heard how his garments whispered to each other and told stories of him.' It seems to me that these words help us to understand why it was Rabbi Bunam who alone was able to carry him on that day.")

"From that day on, a change, which had gradually come into existence, appeared in the behavior of the Rabbi to the

Yehudi. It manifested itself most powerfully in the searching and, as it were, investigating character of the look which he turned upon him.

"It was in the fourth week after these things that the matter took place which I shall now try to relate as best I can.

"Soon after Purim the Yehudi left to go to Apt, in order to visit the children by his first marriage. Rabbi David accompanied him. They intended to return shortly before Pesach, as did Rabbi Bunam, who had gone to Pshysha.

"On the fourth day before Pesach, when all three of them were again on the road to Lublin, the Rabbi gathered about him in the early morning a picked group of his disciples in the synagogue. Several of the older ones had come here for the festival. Among these were Rabbi Yehuda Loeb of Zakilkov and Rabbi Kalman of Cracow. They were all in this assembly. Only a few of the youngest had been asked to come. But I was one of those few.

"In respect to Rabbi Yehuda Loeb, there is something that must be interpolated here. After he had returned to Zakilkov, he had not visited Lublin for a long time. When he turned up at last and the Rabbi greeted him, the latter is said to have said: 'I am told that you have really established a congregation of your own.' To this Yehuda Loeb had merely answered: 'Well? What if I have?' The Rabbi had made no reply. Nor did they seem later to have discussed the matter.

"I cannot entrust to paper all that I know concerning that assembly. There are secrets which may not be recorded in writing. What I dare record is as follows:

"Three days before the meeting, the Rabbi had commanded us to sanctify ourselves during this entire period and to separate ourselves strictly from all mortal preoccupations. Now he called each of us separately to approach him and spoke to each in a whisper. The answers of two among us were evidently not satisfactory, for they were not permitted to remain. Next he bade us form a circle about him in such a fashion that the right hand of each touched the left hand of his neighbor. But we were not to take hold of each other's hands. In the middle of this circle there was a flat desk, on which lay a huge volume that I had never seen before. The book was open. One saw two pages covered with irregular lines and a few drawings. The Rabbi approached the desk and in a commanding voice bade us to conquer all disturbing thoughts and to fix our souls wholly upon the work that was to be accomplished. He gave us directions how we were to deal with every 'attempt at interference,' as he called it, according to its own character. Nothing was to be forcibly repressed; everything was to be absorbed into the spiritual intention of the hour and so transformed by it. Then he mentioned to us special 'intentions,' or *kavonot*, such as even the oldest among us, as I found out later, had never known.

"In immediate connection with this he uttered a verse of the Scriptures. It was a verse from the song of Deborah: 'The kings came and fought; then fought the kings of Canaan, in Taanach by the waters of Megiddo: they took no gain of money. From heaven fought the stars, from their courses they fought against Sisera.' At once in me and probably in all who shared the same memory there awakened that hour, nearly two years ago, when on Shavuot, the feast of Revelation, the Rabbi had quoted at the end of his table discourse a verse from the same song: 'The mountains quaked before the Lord, even yon Sinai.' Thereupon the Rabbi spoke somewhat as follows: 'Don Isaac Abarbanel says, that the occupation of the land of Israel by strange peoples was caused by God in the nature of bait for the hooks that were to catch Gog and Magog, according to the words of Deborah to Barak: "Go, and draw unto Mount Tabor and I will draw unto thee, to the brook Kishon, Sisera the captain of Jabin's army, with his chariots and his multitudes; and I will deliver him into thy hands." For what happened was this, that the Canaanitish kings, when they saw Barak and his men, obviously expecting no danger, tranquilly descending the slopes of Mount Tabor, let themselves be lured to push forward from the pass of Megiddo and the adjoining mountains into the valley of the Kishon and to cross the dry bed of the brook. Now suddenly heaven intervened. A mighty thunder and rain storm set in. The brook overflowed and the clay earth was turned into a marsh and the chariots swirled in confusion, so that they could not withstand the men of Israel who now surprised them not only from the slopes of Tabor but also down the valley from the springs of the Kishon. Such, then — and that is the meaning of Don Isaac — are the peoples who have occupied the land of Israel, namely, a bait thrown out by God in order, as it is written, to strike a hook into the cheeks of Gog and thus to bring him to the mountains of Israel, where he is to fall under the blows of heaven on the open field. And thus it is.'

"These words 'and thus it is,' the Rabbi spoke with such power that we shuddered. 'Thus it is,' he repeated and placed a finger on a passage of the great open book where, as I perceived, there was the drawing of a triangle. But his eyes, of which the pupils were strangely enlarged, did not look upon the page. 'In this very hour,' said he, 'one of his armies is fighting in the valley of Megiddo, which is the valley of Jezreel, on the battlefield of the nations against the horse soldiery and the foot soldiery of all the peoples of the Sultan. The enemy is pressing that army close to the sides of Tabor. I see the contending armies.' We saw them with him, ghostly fighting masses in front of a broad and radiant mountain. 'Himself,' he continued, 'I do not see. But he is not far away.' His glance as he now turned to us seemed veiled. His words beat upon our very hearts. 'This is not yet the real and authentic battle,' said he. 'This is only the bait which he will be able to manage, when he himself is on the scene. Next the heavenly powers will intervene, and then they will need a helper here. But the bait cannot be the helper. That helper can come only from Israel. But it cannot come from the land itself, conquered and desecrated as it is. It must come from those who are preserved in exile. We are the helpers here. Think of the words of Deborah: "Curse ye Meroz, said the angel of the Lord, curse ye bitterly the inhabitants thereof, because they came not to the help of the Lord, to the help of the Lord among the mighty." ' We knew it; truly, we are the helpers. 'Concentrate your souls and arise,' he cried. 'The hour approaches.'

"He looked upon the book and then again raised his eyes, and once more these were the eyes with the enlarged pupils and the tense cornea. 'The man himself,' he repeated, 'I do not see. He had to go upon an errand. He comes from the Sidonian shore. He has gone through the gorges. Now the tall wheat of the fields hides him. There, the field stirs! Wait! Concentrate and wait!' And suddenly he cried out. 'I see nothing more, nothing more at all.'

"His face was dreadfully distorted and his shortsighted eyes, of which the asymmetry was now marked, twitched convulsively. 'Wait,' he cried. 'It must return.' He was in the throes of an enormous effort. We stood unreleased from tension. But after a while he lowered his head. 'It is in vain,' said he. 'An evil influence has penetrated to us.' He went to a bench which stood by a pillar and sat down and rested his head against the pillar. He closed his eyes. It was long before he opened them again. 'Go and find out,' said he, 'who entered the house at that moment.'

"There was no one in the synagogue except ourselves. I and another went over to the dwelling house. In the antechamber we found Rabbi David and the Yehudi. We asked them when they had arrived. The moments coincided. Rabbi David said they had heard that the Rabbi was in the synagogue but had preferred to await him here. I went back and reported to the Rabbi and asked him whether I should summon those two hither. The Rabbi arose and went to the dwelling house. We followed him. He walked by Rabbi David without paying any attention to him. Then he approached the Yehudi and asked: 'What are you doing here?' The Yehudi stared at him but no word passed his lips. The Rabbi retired to his room.

"Later when Rabbi David had found out something of what had happened and now sought to explain it to the Yehudi, I heard the latter say to him: 'I can possess truth only by fighting for it.' It came over me with a kind of dismay that I had never heard any mouth of mortal speak with such clean sincerity. Whatever else this strange man might be, this one thing was revealed to me: that he spoke the truth and that truth was his one and only concern.

"Several months passed until the news came to us that Bonaparte on that occasion, hastening south from the siege of Akko, had won the battle of Mount Tabor. It took another few months until we heard that he had lost the campaign for Egypt and the land of Israel and had returned to Paris. 'So that was only a prelude,' said the Rabbi to Rabbi Naftali. 'The real and important thing is still to come. North is north, after all.' Rabbi Naftali told me that he did not understand what the Rabbi meant by these words. But he had not wanted to ask. I, however, thought that I did have the right clue, seeing that I had listened on that occasion when the Rabbi had said to Rabbi Hirsch: 'Then by north one may understand northwest in this instance.' But since I had not communicated this saying to Rabbi Naftali, neither did I reply to him now. Clearly, however, by 'north' the Rabbi had meant that evil power which had interfered with his action and rendered vain his vision. I am sure, too, that it was really an evil influence. Only I can no longer believe that the Yehudi had anything to do with it and I hope that the Rabbi came to that conclusion too. Of course, I am unable to contribute to the solution of the mystery. How should a man like me dare to attempt it?

"Almost simultaneously with the news of those campaigns there came to us a man from Southern Podolia, who drove a trade with pepper and other wares produced in the lands of the Sultan. He told us that, on the very day on which we had stood about the Rabbi and had seen in vision the beginning of the battle in the valley of Megiddo, there had been issued in Constantinople a proclamation of Bonaparte in which he invited all the Jews of the Turkish and Arabic countries to gather under his banners for the purpose of re-establishing Jerusalem; he had already armed a great many Jews in Syria and this division was threatening the city of Aleppo. When Rabbi Naftali reported this matter to the Rabbi, the latter answered: 'It is not true.' Rabbi Naftali assured him that the man who brought the news was a man to be relied on. But the Rabbi only repeated: 'It cannot be true.' Then he brought the conversation to an end."

(The following is an addition dated toward the end of 1804: "In the years since then Rabbi Naftali has often told me that the Rabbi no longer talks about Bonaparte with him. And when recently Rabbi Naftali departed for a long time, because in addition to the community of Ropshitz, in which he is head of the Rabbinical Court — *Ab Bet Din* — the community of Linsk had fallen to him after the death of his father, I questioned him once more and once more he repeated the assurance that during this entire period the Rabbi had refused to discuss news that came concerning this man. Hence it is exactly as I assumed, namely, that the Rabbi did not permanently concern himself with that vulgar ruffian." These additional sentences were afterwards stricken through.)

I am writing this chronicle on the basis of both written and oral tradition. Wherever the tradition is silent concerning the time of the events, I must seek to determine it according to the facts narrated. But just as, thanks be to God, there are helpers who knew parts of the tradition, which I did not know, so there are also helpers who can reckon better than I. But at times there is nothing that points to any reckoning of time, or it even happens that late narrators arranged events in a wrong order and connection. In such cases I must seek to suppose and to infer according to the content and character of what is related and thus determine in what order of time things may have come to pass. Of this sort are the actions and events which I narrate in the succeeding sections. Thereafter I shall again be on solid ground.

After Succot, the feast of Tabernacles, the Yehudi went to spend the Sabbath in Kosnitz, although he knew that his habit of putting off the time of prayer angered the *Maggid*. Before his departure he said to Bunam: "The holy *Maggid* is the man who has a good right to reprove me, for he is truly prepared for prayer at every moment. Yet for that very reason he is also the one who, when he begins to understand what I want, will understand it entirely."

The *Maggid* had recently needed to lie down less than usual. He used to say, being now around sixty: "I notice that I am getting older from the fact that my health is better." He received the guest in his room with a glance which was estranged at first but grew warmer almost at once. "He did not come alone," he said later on to young Schmelke, the son of Rabbi Yehuda Loeb, of whom I shall tell something further on. "At his right walked the Prince of the Torah and at his left the Burning Fire of Prayer. Never did I see those two together before."

[173]

On the morning of the Sabbath the *Maggid* and his congregation waited to begin praying for the coming of the Yehudi, who arrived a little after the appointed hour. To those who were irritated at this he quoted the verse from the Song of Songs: "This thy stature is like that of Tamar." For he interpreted the word *tamar* not as date palm, but as the name of the daughter-in-law of Judah the son of Jacob. "If," he added interpretatively, "any other woman had been guilty of such impertinence, she would have been punished. But Tamar's intention was directed toward a heavenly decree, and so she went unpunished. But whoever is not like Tamar must not dare to do as she did."

In the course of the third repast, at which Jaacob Yitzchak sat beside the *Maggid*, the latter turned to him and said: "Holy Yehudi, perhaps you could tell me why I experience a greater sanctification and illumination on the second day of Succot, and on all the second days of the three festivals of pilgrimage, than I do on the first? It depresses me to consider it, seeing that the second day is celebrated only in exile."

"For that very reason," the Yehudi answered without reflecting. "When a man and a woman who love each other have a quarrel and then become reconciled the love is more intense. And there is no reconciliation in the world which is equal to that between God and exiled Israel."

"You have given me new life," said the *Maggid*. He drew the head of the Yehudi toward him and kissed him on the forehead.

Next day these two had a long conference. They discussed many things that had come to pass during the last six years. The Yehudi uttered no complaint and reported of each matter so much as was necessary to give the *Maggid* the information he desired. Finally the latter wanted to know more concerning the behavior of Rabbi Yehuda Loeb, whom he knew well from Lisensk and who came to visit him from time to time. Now only did the Yehudi relate something

[174]

which was evidently a source of great pain to him. His son Yerachmiel, who had insisted on learning the watchmaker's trade, had traveled from the dwelling place of the master watchmaker to Pshysha, where he wanted to visit his father. On the way he had stopped at Zakilkov to pass the Sabbath there. The handsome, well-built youth pleased the hasidim in the synagogue, and he was honored by being given a portion of the *sedrah* of the week to read. When he named his own name and the name of his father, Rabbi Yehuda Loeb bade him be turned out of the synagogue.

During the following winter, shortly before Pesach, the *Maggid* invited the Yehudi and Rabbi Yehuda Loeb to spend a Sabbath with him. Yehuda Loeb brought with him his only son Schmelke, who was about eighteen and yet unmarried, shy and of an almost girlish delicacy and wholly wrapped up in thoughts of Torah and of God's service.

On Friday evening the Yehudi and the Rabbi of Zakilkov met at the *Maggid's* table. No greeting passed between them. When the *Maggid* approached the table in order to welcome the Angels of Peace who on this evening gather under the roofs of men, he looked about him and said: "The Angels of Peace are not here; how shall I bid them welcome?" Then he retired to his room. After a while he came back and looked about him and said: "They are not here yet." The same thing happened a third time. Thereupon the Yehudi stretched out his hand across the table to Rabbi Yehuda Loeb and said: "Peace be with you!"

"But only until the close of the Sabbath," the latter announced.

Only now did the *Maggid* pronounce the welcome: "Peace be with you, Messengers of Peace, Messengers of the Most High!"

During the third Sabbath repast the Yehudi, as was his custom, began to chant Psalms. As always they came with such an authentic freshness from his lips as though they were

[175]

the immediate expression of his soul at this moment. One might say that he really *spoke* the Psalms, even when he sang them. When he reached the verse: "He feareth not evil rumor; his heart is armored, he is secure in the Lord," there came from his throat a tone so blithe and trustful, that all eyes were turned on him. The *Maggid* looked at him with a kindly smile, but young Schmelke, whose glance had been fixed on the singer from the first word on, turned toward him a tear-drenched face. Only his father did not look up. Leaning across the table he thrust his thumb between his index and his middle finger, held his hand thus under the nose of Rabbi Jaacob Yitzchak and croaked: "That's what I think of you." The *Maggid* opened his eyes wide. Schmelke closed his own and trembled all over. The Yehudi continued with untroubled voice. "Secure is his heart, he is not afraid until he can look down upon his oppressors."

A saying of the Yehudi, only dimly handed down, may have reference to this incident. It is something like this: "He who thumbs his nose at himself is untroubled even though the whole world does it to him." One of his and Rabbi Bunam's disciples, the reckless and somber Rabbi Mendel of Kozk, adopted this saying in a rather individual version as his own and used it thus: "He who thumbs his nose at himself can afford to do it to the world."

On the way home to Zakilkov the son of Rabbi Yehuda Loeb spoke no word except what was necessary to answer his father's questions, nor did he do so at home. On the next Sabbath, in the course of the third repast, Rabbi Yehuda Loeb explained precisely what kind of a person the Yehudi was. Schmelke held his peace. But when the father said that the *Maggid* would soon find out that he was wasting his benevolence on an unworthy object, the son replied: "Father, the holy *Maggid* told me himself that at the right hand of this man he had seen the Prince of the Torah and on his left hand the Holy Flame of Prayer."

[176]

"Are you ready to defend him?" the father asked angrily. "I will do so to the death," said Schmelke.

"Rabbi Yehuda Loeb snapped his fingers. "Woe unto my son!" he cried. And at that moment he saw upon his son's countenance a foreshadowing of the end. That very night he wrote a letter to the Seer and besought him to change the judgment. Next morning he sent his son with the letter to Lublin. Schmelke repaired to Lublin, laid himself down on a bed in the inn and died. The Seer said of him that, had he been preserved, he would have become a leader in his generation. Rabbi Yehuda Loeb had followed Schmelke; he attended the burial in his Sabbath garments. When he returned to Zakilkov, his wife came forth to meet him and asked after their son.

"I have sent him to the great *Bet Hamidrash*," he replied.

It is related that some months later on the occasion of *Seder*, the consecrated meal which ushers in the feast of Passover, he offered his wife a great surprise on condition that she was not to weep. She gave her promise and suddenly saw their son sitting at the table. Then she burst into tears. "Now you will not ever see him again," said Rabbi Yehuda Loeb.

Since I will have but little more to tell concerning this learned and virtuous man, I may add in this place a thing which — as was the case with the *Seder* incident — was experienced and handed down to us by a rabbi of our time who was familiar with all these matters and, indeed, occupied a rabbinical position in Zakilkov for a period. According to him, Rabbi Yehuda Loeb had deeply lamented the death of the Yehudi and had assured the hasidim who were present that whatever he had said against him had been in the Yehudi's best interests. Had there been no opposition, people would have come in pilgrimage to him even from the lands of the West, and in that case the evil eye would have had power over him.

Sometime after that Sabbath in Kosnitz, the *Maggid*, without having announced his visit, came toward nightfall to Lublin. All night long he sat in the room of the Rabbi. Next morning he left for home. It was many years before they saw each other again. A friend of both, Rabbi Menahem Mendel of Rymanov, was wont to say thereafter: "I am a peasant and guard the windows of two kings' sons, lest each break the other's."

VISITORS

"What, I'm going to let you tell me how to cook noodles?" Schoendel screamed at her mother-in-law, a small delicately built woman, from whom her son seemed to have inherited nothing but his sensitive hands. A few years before, after the death of her husband, she had moved to Pshysha, at the insistence of Jaacob Yitzchak who was devoted to her. "Noodles! In the whole town of Apt there is no one who knows what noodles are as well as my mother! What do you mean? So much flour and so many eggs? Is it a question of flour and eggs? It's the right touch that you must have. If you have that, you can do anything!" She tapped her right hand with her left and looked with satisfaction at her little, plump hands.

The door of the kitchen opened. Yekutiel entered and turned to Schoendel with a question which had evidently been excogitated for the purpose of giving him an excuse to enter the kitchen. He could not bear not examining each room every day. Four months had passed since Yekutiel had come to live in Pshysha. He had at once adopted the custom of, so to speak, passing in review the entire household daily upon one subterfuge or another. He stuck to it with great determination and with a skill with which one would not have credited so simple-minded a person. In order that this matter may be understood I must explain here the character of Yekutiel's famous simple-mindedness.

It is undeniable that he really was simple-minded; but he was more than simple-minded; he was also sly. His slyness was aware of his simple-mindedness, but his simple-mindedness was not aware of his slyness. It was as though a man had one rigid eye and one cross-eyed eye, and the latter could see the former but not the other way around. In this case the world was ignorant of the cross-eyed aspect. People considered Yekutiel as quite simply foolish. Thus it will be remembered that in that first consultation of the opponents of the Yehudi he had been able to formulate the question concerning the danger that might threaten after "a hundred and twenty years." Naftali had not dreamed that the sly Yekutiel here made use of the simple-minded one. Eisik could not have done this. His delight in his own cleverness and in the general recognition of it was too vivid to permit him to pretend to be stupid. Nor would he have equalled Yekutiel in such an undertaking, for the latter did not have to pretend.

When Eisik returned to Lublin and related how the Yehudi had almost caused him to choke by the power of the evil eye, Yekutiel was all ear. Here was a task which was just the right one for simple-mindedness. Yet it took some time before he determined to go to Pshysha. First of all he agreed gladly to Eisik's proposal to take over the job of informing the Rabbi concerning the goings on of the Yehudi and his people, which had hitherto belonged to Eisik. Nor did he even ask why Eisik was willing to get rid of so significant a commission. But when he entered upon this new duty he soon met an unexpected obstacle. This, it should be added, was some time after that nocturnal conversation between the *Maggid* and the Seer, which had ended with the *Maggid's* departure. The assumption of Eisik and of the others that the Rabbi would at once have faith in the word of the simple-minded one did not come true.

[179]

"How am I to believe all this," he replied to a very rich and detailed report, "considering the fact that you yourself neither saw nor heard all this."

Abashed by this rebuff, Yekutiel soon took leave and went to Pshysha with a plan of operations which he communicated to no one. His purpose was executed the more easily because his younger brother, Perez, who had become a disciple of the Yehudi some years before, lived almost steadily in that town now. He figured out how easy it would be to persuade the enthusiastic fool that he, Yekutiel, was remorseful and desired now to share the spiritual blessings of Pshysha. Thus the bridge would be built. It did not, in fact, occur to Perez, who was ever ready to put faith in the words of man, to doubt his brother's sincerity. The next step was to appear before the Yehudi in his brother's company and to convince him of the sincerity of his intentions. What actually happened was regarded by Yekutiel as a strange and unpleasant experience. He had expected one of two reactions. Either — and this he considered most likely — he would be met with confidence, since this vain fellow would consider it quite natural that another man from Lublin submit to his influence and come to Pshysha; or else he would meet distrust, which he meant gradually to overcome by the right use of his simplemindedness. Neither one of these expectations came true. When they appeared before the Yehudi, the latter first turned to Perez with a frank and unembarrassed smile. Then, neither trustfully nor distrustfully, he looked at Yekutiel simply and tranquilly and answered his greeting. The very picture of sincerity — for his simplicity believed in the suggestions of his cunning — the guest explained himself: he had come to see his error and regretted it and desired to study here. The Yehudi simply took no notice of the first two points. In regard to the last he said: "You will not be able to learn anything among us, Rabbi Yekutiel." The supplicant thought that all was lost. But to his astonishment the Yehudi added after a while: "Needless to say, you may stay here as long as you like." Yekutiel thus had the same experience with this man, which Goldele, his mother-in-law, had had with the youth of long ago. You couldn't get at this fellow. Yet he was sure that he would succeed in some way by and by.

Now, to be sure, he had been here all of seventeen weeks and had accomplished nothing worth talking about. What he got by spying and listening was trivial. He whom he was watching was evidently strictly on his guard. Perhaps in the end it would have been better to do as Eisik had done. Well maybe not, when you thought about the bite of herring . . .! At all events he meant to stay over the next Sabbath. On that occasion people were coming from other towns, Rabbi David from Lelov, Rabbi Yeshaya from Pshedbosh, the natal town of the Yehudi, and several others. It might be that if one were properly watchful something hidden might come to the surface.

During the third Sabbath repast there were present a number of *ba'ale batim* from the city. As on all Sabbaths so this time too there was no formal lecture but a conversation concerning both law and life. In the course of this the Yehudi turned to the *ba'ale batim* and exclaimed: "Ah, good people, if one asks one of you why he takes all the trouble he does on earth, each of you would answer: 'In order to raise a son that he might learn Torah and serve God.' And when the son is grown he forgets why his father worked and worried and he, in turn, does the same thing; and if you ask him after the purpose of his own sweat and toil, he will tell you: 'Why, I have to raise up a son for Torah and for good works.' And so it goes from generation to generation. When, I ask you, will we see the appearance of the right son?"

David of Lelov leaned over toward Bunam, who was sitting near him, and whispered to him: "If the Rabbi had heard that, he would no longer consent to listen to any slanderer." But it is well known that the ears of people like Yekutiel can hear more than the tongues of the Davids of this world can utter. Next day Yekutiel returned to Lublin well satisfied. On the very evening of his arrival he officiously told the Seer that, commenting on a lecture of the Yehudi, Rabbi David had said that, had the Rabbi been present, he would have been glad to enroll himself as one of the Yehudi's hasidim. Now it happened that at this very hour the Rabbi had summoned a *melamed* from a nearby village to see him. This man was about to enter when Yekutiel came with great zeal and opened the door. The poor man entered, too. But he was frightened at his own temerity and in his confusion hid behind a wardrobe. Now only did the Rabbi enter the room. When the *melamed* heard Yekutiel give his report he could not restrain himself. He sprang from his hiding place, laid his hand upon the Rabbi's phylacteries which he happened to see lying on the table, and cried out: "I swear that that is a most thoroughgoing lie!" Yekutiel fled like any other simple fool. But the Rabbi questioned the man who was still standing there with his hand on the phylacteries.

"Do you know the people we were talking about?"

"I do not know them and neither do I know the man who just spoke with you," the little teacher answered.

Somewhat amused and not without kindliness, the Rabbi regarded the trembling figure. "Then how were you able to take an oath?" he asked.

"Because I saw and heard that he was lying," the *melamed* answered.

"He who does not know a certain one sees and hears him clearly," said the Rabbi. "Had you not been here, I would have believed him. Not for nothing did Satan preserve him for twenty-eight years so carefully from any temptation of any sin. It has made him too easy to believe."

A few weeks thereafter Schoendel was standing in the room,

while little Asher was sitting on a stool at her feet with a book before him. In a state of livid rage she was polishing knives. She went on polishing them even when they were bright as mirrors. The street door opened and a huge man with a mighty forehead protruding from under his fur hat, a broad reddish face and a long gray beard which contrasted with his thick black eyebrows, entered with powerful tread. Although she had never seen him, Schoendel recognized the Rabbi at once. A knife slid from her hand and fell on the book. The Rabbi bent down, picked it up and put it on the table.

"What is it that you have there?" he asked the six-year-old boy, who had looked up only when the hand of the Seer had touched the book, and who now jumped up quickly.

"It is the prophet Isaiah, Rabbi," answered Asher.

"Then read me from the page that is open before you."

In a level voice the boy read the beginning of the page: "And I have not resisted neither have I drawn back but I have offered my neck to him who would strike it and my cheeks to the angry man, nor have I hidden my face from abuse and contempt."

"Well, well," said the Rabbi, "you have read that well."

Only now did the Rabbi sit down on the chair which she had drawn up for him. "And what are you learning in the Talmud now?" he asked.

"We are studying the tractate *Yoma*, Rabbi," said Asher.

"What does the tractate deal with?"

"It deals with the regulations for the Day of Atonement, Rabbi."

"And what folio have you been studying today?"

"The ninth folio, Rabbi."

"And did you memorize anything on that folio?"

"Yes, I memorized something, Rabbi."

"Repeat it to me."

" 'The second Temple, why was it destroyed, seeing that

[183]

the people busied itself with Torah and with the fulfillment of the commands and with the exercise of benevolence? Because there was unmotivated hatred. Thence we are taught that unmotivated hatred is equal to three sins — to idolatry, to adultery, and to the shedding of blood.' "

"Well, well, you have memorized that well," said the Rabbi. "And why is it said that the latter could be inferred from the former?"

"Because it had been previously said that the first Temple had been destroyed on account of these three sins. Now, however, in the time of the second Temple these three existed no longer. But the unmotivated hatred existed, which did not exist in the time of the first Temple, and so this one thing was as effective as the three others had been together." The Rabbi put on his spectacles and looked hard at the boy.

He remained over the Sabbath and took a good look at everything — at the house and its furnishings, at the people who dwelt in it and at the people who visited it, at the street and at the synagogue. During the Sabbath many more people came than usual and the Rabbi questioned the Yehudi concerning their intentions. Next day he returned home.

Several weeks later a man came to Pshysha who had been in Lublin. He went to the house of the Yehudi and wanted to give him a petition. He said he had first applied to the Rabbi of Lublin, who had sent him hither. The Yehudi refused to accept the petition. Several weeks later, however, the man returned and communicated the express desire of the Rabbi that the Yehudi was to accept the petition. He did so. In the passage which explained the purpose of the petition were written the words: "For the healing of the soul." The Yehudi engaged the petitioner in one of those conversations which do not concern themselves with a specific subject, but the purpose of which is to let your partner know that there are people in the world whom he may trust. And consequently the man soon began to unburden himself.

"I hate my son," said he, "and it is that which has poisoned my soul."

The Yehudi saw at once that neither advice nor instruction would suffice in this instance. To heal the soul of this man it would be necessary to be responsible for him just as though one carried him upon one's shoulders and to carry him thus until he himself could tread his own path. To put it more precisely: one had to take upon oneself that entire hatred without being oneself corrupted by it; one had to transform the passion of hatred, and how could one do that otherwise than by taking it upon oneself? This was, to be sure, a dangerous undertaking. It was clear to the Yehudi that not until now had he been ready to venture upon such a task. And suddenly the insight came to him, that, in spite of all, he had learned from the Rabbi — for where else could he have done so — that for the sake of which he had originally sought him out, namely, the right behavior in the face of evil. To take it on one's own shoulders and to bear it oneself — that is the right thing to do.

On the next Sabbath, during the third repast, he gave his first interpretative lecture, which centered in the words of Isaiah. "Hearken unto me, O house of Jacob, and all the remnant of the house of Israel, that have been borne by me from their birth, that have been carried from the womb; and even to old age I am he, and even to hoar hairs will I carry you: I have made and I will bear; yea I will carry, and will deliver."

"God is our prototype," said the Yehudi.

Therewith the congregation of Pshysha was founded.

Tila, the *Rebbitzin*, lay at the point of death.

For many years everybody had thought that this thing might come to pass on any day, so fragile was she and yet so calm. Yet now, when it was about to be, it seemed an incomprehensible thing. People went about with tense faces, as though they had to unriddle a mystery which hovered in the air, and when two met they looked into each other's astonished eyes. Only the Rabbi had also on this occasion his very special expressions, which were a part of the incomprehensible circumstances. Among the hasidim two opinions prevailed. Some said it was beyond all question that the Rabbi had long known the period of his wife's dying to the very day, and had even written it down in the notations concerning future events which he continuously wrote. It is even told that such a notation was found in his posthumous manuscripts. Others declared that this was, indeed, true, but that the foreseen time had by no means arrived, and that, consequently, there were two possibilities: either, contrary to all appearances, the *Rebbitzin* was not going to die at all at present, or else, extraordinary as this must seem, an evil influence had intervened and was hastening her end.

Meanwhile Tila lay on her deathbed, remote from all the processes of the world of awareness, and murmured fragmentary, indistinct sounds to herself. Only her son Israel who, though as usual he stood by the window, comprehended every sound she made, only he understood that his mother's spirit dwelt in the places and times of her girlhood and murmured from thence into this alien room. She sat up now and with her hands stroked the back of her head and down over the nape of the neck, as though she were carefully combing the long, long hair which had been hers in her girlhood and which had been cut off prior to her wedding according to the prescription of the law. She stretched herself out again

[186]

and lay still for a while. Then in a changed, lamenting voice she began once more to speak coherently. Again none of those about her except Israel understood that she was experiencing her wedding over again, incident by incident, and uttered all that which on that original occasion had arisen in her heart. She moved her feet under the covers, rhythmically one after the other, as though she thought she was walking. She stopped. Now, thought Israel, she comes to the house of her husband. Suddenly she moved her arm and gently contracted her hand as though she were placing it upon some object. But almost immediately she opened it again with a cry.

"The door knob is burning," she cried; "it burns." Her head, which while she uttered that cry she had lifted from the pillows, fell suddenly back.

"That is the end," Israel said to himself. "The end must be like that."

The Rabbi refused to accept consolation. With a shaking of his head he rebuffed anyone who came to offer it. Hence no more attempts were made. But a friend of his happened to be in Lublin at that time. This friend went to him and asked him why he refused to be consoled.

"How can I permit myself to be consoled," said the Rabbi, "seeing that it says in the Talmud that a man whose first wife dies could be compared to one in whose days the Temple was destroyed."

"Once upon a time," the man answered, "I heard you yourself interpret that very passage as follows: 'Everyone in whose days the Temple is not rebuilt is to be compared to him in whose days it was destroyed.' And you interpreted it further: 'Just as in those days the anger of God, though directed against the people, was moderated by the destruction of the Sanctuary of wood and stone, even so the Divine anger is moderated whenever a man suffers as keenly over the fact that the Temple was not rebuilt in his days as though it had been destroyed in them.' Now you are indeed the faithful shepherd of all Israel. This thing having happened to you, it is certain that your suffering moderates God's attribute of judging."

"You have consoled me," said the Rabbi.

Among those who in those days came to Lublin, in order to speak comfortable words to the Rabbi, was also the Yehudi who, indeed, since the founding of his own congregation, came oftener to seek out his teacher than he had been doing. Concerning this meeting of the two a matter is related, to the understanding of which I would like to add something here. Since Eisik's experience with the bite of herring, the enemies of the Yehudi were convinced that he had the power of the evil eye. Moreover, since that little *melamed* had given evidence against Yekutiel and had then completely vanished, they were equally certain that none other than the Yehudi had managed by a trick of evil magic to place him behind the wardrobe. But granting that he had always possessed the power of the evil eye, whence and how had he acquired the gifts of a magician? They had an answer to that, too.

You are to know that among the disciples of the Seer there was one in a nearby city, Ittamar by name, who was known far and wide as a person of singular goodness. In his earlier years he had been a veritable merchant prince and had got a considerable fortune. But he gave gifts to the poor in such measure that his possessions dwindled. Now he sold all he had in order to be able to continue to provide, at least, the Sabbath needs of those whom he was supporting. To this man the Rabbi once confided the secret of the conquest of enemies. He confided it to him alone because his goodness was such that one could be sure he would make no unrighteous use of it. Now out of his abundant goodness he had indicated it, if not exactly confided it, to the Yehudi too. And now one saw what the latter did with it.

One other thing must be preliminarily mentioned in this

place, namely, that the Rabbi himself, as unimpeachable reports bear witness, believed in the power of the evil eye, not only as exerted by men, but even by angels. During repasts, at which the presence of an evil eye was to be feared, he would give the order to pronounce a "whisper" of exorcism, in order to render the evil vain. This will help us to understand why he was ever at all inclined to give credence to the rumors circulating concerning the evil gifts of the Yehudi. Many, to be sure, will not understand how it was possible for a man of the Rabbi's intellectual powers to entertain such beliefs. But it is my task to relate what happened and not to make it understandable.

When the Yehudi went to see the Rabbi in order to speak consolingly to him during the seven days of mourning, the latter said: "She spoke against you."

"I scarcely knew that," said the Yehudi.

"And what did you do when you heard of her illness?"

"Nothing!"

"Perhaps you did, after all?"

"Ah, well, I recited Psalms."

"And you call that nothing?"

"What should I have done?"

"You should have been angry at her," cried the Rabbi, "for then her bowl on the balance of the scale might have risen."

"Am I capable of that?" answered the Yehudi.

The Rabbi looked into his eyes with an even more sharply searching look than he had done on that day when he gave him leave to go and had looked into his eyes and through the eyes had gazed into his heart. Then he turned aside and with lightly bowed head murmured into his beard: "Truly, the Yehudi doesn't know what anger is."

Sometime thereafter the Rabbi wrote to one of his familiar friends, a distinguished member of the Lemberg community who never engaged in the most trivial undertaking without

[189]

consulting him. He informed him that he was minded to marry the man's sister-in-law, a virgin named Beile. Soon thereafter he dispatched Naftali of Ropshitz and Simon Deutsch to the city of Brody where Beile and her two sisters lived with their brother. He bade them go into the house where these people dwelt and go straightway into the kitchen. There they would find the three virgins. They were to ask her who stood in the middle to be his wife, for God had destined her for him. And so it came to pass.

There is connected with this courtship an anecdote which, to be sure, in my judgment bears the stamp of having been maliciously invented by the opponents of the hasidic way of life. Oddly enough, however, it is recorded in hasidic documents otherwise reliable in character. Consequently I reproduce it here, though with all proper and necessary caution. According to this story the girl in question who, as was well known, was quite a personable woman who would not look ill even beside a husband like the Rabbi, was no longer in her first youth. Many and favorable matches for her had been proposed to her brother-in-law. In each instance the latter had consulted the Rabbi, who had always given the same reply, namely, that this was not yet the right thing for her. When the girl threatened to become impatient at a moment when a very favorable marriage alliance was offered her, the Rabbi had dissuaded her with the words that something much greater was in store for her. This is said to have taken place shortly before Tila's death.

In the period between the courtship and the wedding, it is related that Beile was accused before the Rabbi of having been seen in Lemberg in gay and modish Western garb. The Rabbi had approached the window and wiped the dew from the pane in the middle and had gazed out for a while. He had then given a precise description of the garments which the girl was wearing at that very hour and had added: "It is beyond all criticism."

[190]

But when Beile crossed the threshold of the house in the Broad Lane in Lublin and put her hand on the door knob, she started violently back and shook her fingers. "The door knob is fiery hot," she complained. Someone else opened the door for her.

Later on she discussed this incident with Rochele, who had been married for some time but who continued to look after the Rabbi's household and now introduced the new wife to its ways. Both agreed that nothing but witchcraft could account for this thing and that it was to be ascribed, said Rochele, to a very questionable man from Pshysha who had been among the wedding guests. He was known as the Yehudi, because his name and the Rabbi's were identical, wherefore he could neither be called nor addressed by it.

Beile received this information with an evil expression upon her half-open lips, yet not without a tickling of her vanity.

From this time on the attacks undertaken against the Yehudi for the Rabbi's benefit were once more orderly and coherent, as they had not been during the period just preceding. Beile mastered the art of listening to stories and even more the art of lending to stories the desired form and the appropriate intention.

THE CHILD

A year had passed since the wedding and Beile showed no sign of the blessing of motherhood. Weeping she besought her husband to pray that children be given them. All he answered was this: "Only he may pray for children who has none." Seeing that her beseeching was in vain she visited her brother in Brody and persuaded him to return to Lublin to plead for her with the Rabbi. The brother brought as a gift a bottle of very precious wine in order that the Rabbi might fill the Sabbath beaker with it on Friday night. Curiously enough the Seer, when he saw the unopened bottle, refused to use the wine for the act of consecration. Thereupon the hasidim examined the bottle and found out that it did in truth contain not wine but pale mead. This circumstance was evidently to be ascribed to the error of a servant. Yet the incident did not seem of good omen to Beile's brother. Nevertheless he sought out the Rabbi at the end of the Sabbath. The latter knew at once that the man had a matter to take up with him and asked what it might be.

"My prayer to you is," said the man, "that you help me to know what I am."

"Well, I can tell you that," answered the Rabbi, "you are a pious and learned man."

"That isn't what I mean," the brother-in-law objected. "I want to know it in the sense in which one knows a thing which one actually sees with one's own eyes. And how am I going to get to know it? I will if my sister bears the Rabbi a son. For our sages tell us that the majority of sons resemble the mother's brother in character. If God grant me the grace, I will discover what I am through the walk and conversation of the boy."

The Rabbi was softened by this plea and confided to him that the only thing to do was for him and his sister to repair to Kosnitz. None but the *Maggid* could help her. When now those two placed their case before the *Maggid*, he bade the brother to leave the room and spoke with the woman alone. He finally advised her that on Friday night, during prayers, she should approach the Rabbi at a specific moment and tug him by the *tallit*. He would turn to see who it was, whereupon she was to say: "I want to bear you a son."

The woman was about to thank him and to take her leave, but he was not ready to let her go.

"The thing will work only," he added, "if there is peace between you two and the whole world."

Beile asked him just what he meant by these words.

"Is there no one," he asked, "to whom you are unjust?"
She was silent. "Is there no one," he continued, "against
whom you speak evil?"

She could not but confess that now and then she made
some slight insinuations against the Yehudi to the Rabbi;
but she begged the holy *Maggid* not to believe that she was
unjust; she merely repeated what reliable people had asserted,
and that the man was not to be trusted was clear enough
from the circumstance that on her very wedding day he had
bewitched the knob on her husband's door. Hadn't she
actually burned her hand?

"You are a very foolish woman," said the *Maggid*. "If
you marry a man like the Rabbi of Lublin you may expect
the door knob of his house to burn you when you enter.
As for your reliable witnesses, they are slanderers. If you do
not promise the Rabbi of Pshysha to utter no more slanders
against him, you will bear no child."

There was nothing left for Beile to do but follow this order
on the occasion of the Yehudi's next visit in Lublin. She
approached him and softly besought him to forgive her. The
Yehudi looked at her in surprise.

"Since I am not angry with you," said he, "how am I
able to forgive you?"

"From now on," she replied, "I will neither speak evil
of you nor listen to evil concerning you."

"Well, that is a praiseworthy resolution," said he and
could not help smiling.

"So there is peace," she asked, "between myself and you?"

"So far as lies in me," he assured her, "there is peace
between me and all men." He was still smiling. This was
on a Friday evening so that later on she carried out the
Maggid's other direction too. It was not many weeks before
she recognized that she was pregnant.

The *Maggid* came from Kosnitz to be present at the boy's
circumcision and was given the honor of being the godfather.

The Rabbi asked the *Maggid* to let him know what name should be given to the boy. The *Maggid* replied: "Shalom," that is to say, Peace. And so the boy was called. After the ceremony the Rabbi and the *Maggid* withdrew and conferred. "I foresee no long life for this child," said the Rabbi.

The *Maggid* was irritated; his glance was deeply reproachful. But all he said was this: "In hours of joy one should rejoice."

From that time on Beile and the child were asked to sit opposite the Rabbi. If the boy laughed when the hasidim came to say farewell, they felt that grace was with them; when he wept, it was no time of grace.

THE BEAKER

For some time Naftali had been the official rabbi and head of the Rabbinical Court in the city of Ropshitz. Nevertheless he continued to spend a considerable part of the year in Lublin. After the death of his father, the famous Rabbi of Linsk, that congregation, too, sought to acquire his leadership. After long negotiations an agreement was made according to which he was to function in both towns. From that time on he had, of course, to limit his visits to Lublin.

When he came to make his decision, he declared to his comrades that before he left Lublin this time he would drink from the beaker which the Rabbi used on Friday evening to make *Kiddush*, and from which none other was ever permitted to drink.

Soon thereafter, also on a Friday, a peasant came to Lublin with a sack of onions, which he meant to sell to the Rabbi for the Sabbath repast. At this time onions had somehow disappeared from the market. Naftali lay in wait for the man and bought his entire store. Next he asked him where he had got his coat. When he was told that the coat was of pure wool and had been made by a Jew and that, therefore, he himself could wear it without offending against the command not to wear garments woven of two kinds of material, he bought the man's coat and hat, too. Disguised as a peasant and with artfully distorted face, the sack of onions over his shoulder, he arrived at the Rabbi's house and demanded in Polish to speak to him. He had onions for sale, but was willing to turn them over only to the Rabbi in person. For the sake of the Sabbath meal the Rabbi received him. The visitor looked about him in the room, as though he had never been here before. For the onions he asked only one half of the current price, with the proviso, that he be given a large glass of brandy in order to slake his great thirst. All the beakers which were profferred he declared to be too small. "That is the right one," said he and pointed to the Rabbi's *Kiddush* cup. If he couldn't have that one, he would take his onions home again. He lifted the sack, which he had put on the floor and slung it over his shoulder. For the honor of the Sabbath the Rabbi finally consented. Swiftly but in a loud tone of voice Naftali pronounced the blessing ". . . by whose word all things came into being," and drank. The Rabbi made a wry mouth. Finally he decided that it was best to laugh.

KOSNITZ IN 1805

Not far from Kosnitz on the road to Lublin there is situated Pulavy, both the little town and the estate being the hereditary seat of the Princes Czartoryski. At the time of this tale the castle was still to such a degree the center of life in the place that every house was connected with it in some way by either heredity or fate. It goes without saying that every Jew, too, whether in the capacity of lessor or broker or purveyor, was equally interested in the prosperity of the princely family. The Czartoryskis, kinsmen of the Jagellonian royal family, who had acquired genuine merit in the reformation of the Polish state, were broad-minded and just men who wanted seriously to be Europeans. They were never very popular; their ways did not permit this. But everyone, who got really to know one of them, at once gained confidence in the entire family. In 1787 the seventeen-year-old Prince Adam was returning home after a carnival which he had enjoyed in the provincial capital. This was in spring, about six months after his return from that visit to Germany during which he had heard Goethe read his *Iphigenie* to a circle of intimate friends. On the way back to Pulavy a quaint idea but one still in the spirit of the carnival occurred to him. At home, not from his parents, but from the servants in the house, he had repeatedly heard stories about a wonder-working rabbi who lived in Kosnitz and to whom repaired in crowds not only peasants but even members of the Polish nobility in order to receive advice and direction in the lesser and larger affairs of their existence. This thing occurred to him because he was meditating on a love affair which had arisen in the provincial capital and, half jestingly and half with true passion, the desire suddenly overcame him to know what the end of that matter would be. Acting on the impulse he left his carriage in a village just before Kosnitz; he disguised himself as a peasant lad and proceeded on foot to Kosnitz. He went straight to the house of the *Maggid* who, as he was told, had but recently returned home from a journey. (It had been from the deathbed of the Rabbi Elimelech.) When the *gabbai* asked him after his name, he said he was "Woipek, the son of the woman Shascha" and said he had come to ask for a "healing of a malady of the heart." He was admitted. The *Maggid* sat alone in a small room. Before him on the table lay his *tallit* and upon it were placed his *tefillin*. To his own astonishment Adam was taken aback

[196]

by that fragile figure with its pale face. He repented of his frivolous impulse, but it was too late. The *Maggid*, having sent the *gabbai* out of the room, was already speaking to him.

"Sit down facing me," he said in a pure although somewhat cumbersome Polish.

Adam sat down. He did not know why, but his shoulders trembled. The *Maggid* looked into his eyes. Adam tried to endure that glance. He could not and lowered his eyes at once.

"Adam, son of Jesabel!" the *Maggid* said. (Isabel was, in fact, the name of the young prince's mother. She had been a Countess Fleming and known for the beauty of her eyes.) "Adam, son of Jesabel," said the *Maggid*, "clowning does not befit you; abstain from it." Adam felt the blood rise to his face. "Try to remember, Prince," said the *Maggid*, "what you really desire to know." Adam felt how the carnival adventure, which had just been burning him as at the core of a flame, dwindled to ashes. Nothing loomed in his consciousness now but the disintegration of his unhappy country. He dared once more to raise his eyes to the *Maggid*, who answered his glance in friendly fashion. "Are you now thinking of what you would really like to know?" asked Rabbi Israel.

"I am now thinking of it, Reverend Rabbi," Adam answered.

"Fix your whole soul upon it for still a little while," the *Maggid* continued. For some seconds complete silence reigned in the room.

"Is it possible," the prince could not help reflecting, "that I sit here before this little Jew as though he were the Pythia of the Delphic Oracle?" But at once another thought arose and replaced this one. "And how was it," he thought, "in the story of that baldhead Elisha, of whom it is written: 'When the minstrel played, the hand of the Lord came upon him?'" And he thought, too, not even a minstrel is needed. And once more the *Maggid* began to speak without looking at him.

"There is one about to come," he said, "who desires to rule over all that is under the vault of heaven. He whistles to the nations that they hasten hither to erect him his throne. He whistles to you, too. He assures you that he will help you. But ye, believe him not! He is not thinking of you. He thinks of nothing but the throne. But the throne will crash and the man will fall to the ground and he will be carried away." The *Maggid* fell silent.

"And how about us?" the prince asked.

The *Maggid* hesitated before he answered. Then he said: "I know no more. At the right hour you will come back and question me again. Perhaps I shall know more then." Once more he was silent, but in such a way that it was clear that he would speak again. Finally he said with great emphasis: "It is written: 'Have no reliance upon the easy givers.'" Quite intentionally he translated the passage thus and not as customary, the "nobles" or, the "princes." The *Maggid* had spoken the words of the Psalmist in an almost singing tone. Adam Czartoryski was sure that he would never forget these words. He bowed and went.

In the autumn of 1805 the Czar Alexander was paying a visit in Pulavy to the parents of his friend, Prince Adam Czartoryski, whom he had made the confidant of his far-reaching plans and the actual leader of the foreign policies of the Russian state. Adam and the representatives of the high Polish nobility, who were among his intimates and who were assembled here, expected from day to day that the Czar, in accordance with certain conversations which he had had with the prince, would proclaim the re-establishment of the kingdom of Poland and that he would proceed to Warsaw to have himself proclaimed king of Poland and thus give the signal for the war of liberation against Prussia. But despite the prayers of Czartoryski, Alexander put off the decision again and again. Suddenly he left, taking the prince with him, but promising to come back. His first stop was at Kosnitz. Here he received an emissary of the king of Prussia and sent the latter a letter in which he lamented the sufferings which his heart had had to undergo during recent weeks, that is to say, during the negotiations with the Polish nobility.

It was on a Sabbath, three days after the feast of Tabernacles. While the Czar was conferring with the Prussian general, Adam Czartoryski went to the house of the *Maggid*, whose permission to call he had first obtained. When he saw him again face to face at the end of eighteen years, it seemed to him that the *Maggid*, despite his gray hair, had not changed. "And I, look what I have become," he thought to himself. It was a fact that only his lofty forehead, although furrowed, had preserved the clearness of his youth. From the hollows of his eyes to his chin disillusion had graven its marks.

The *Maggid* was resting on a sofa. He started to arise to return the prince's greeting, but the latter begged him in an almost dismayed tone to remain where he was.

"I have been expecting Your Excellency," said the *Maggid*.

"The hour of my question is here," Czartoryski declared, "but I need scarcely formulate it, especially seeing that I dare not speak quite explicitly."

"No word is needed, Your Excellency," the *Maggid* agreed.

"Do not call me Excellency," Czartoryski besought him, "Call me Adam or Prince Adam."

"I know, Prince Adam," said the *Maggid*, "what is the great love of your life. But it is not granted you to express that great love with all the frankness it demands. Jacob loved Rachel with a great love and when he had served for her seven years, they gave him Leah. To be sure, he knew that he had but to serve another seven years to get his true

[199]

love after all. You, Prince Adam, have consciously served for Leah, because you dared to hope that you would be able to serve for Rachel thereafter. But now the promised one has not been given to you and you ask: whither does the way lead?" He stopped. "The way leads through thorn and briar, Prince Adam," he went on, "and it is not yet possible to say where its end will be. Do not depend upon the apparently generous, who bury you under their dreams. You must now cease your wooing of Leah; soon you will yourself recognize the necessity and proclaim it. So soon as you will have begun to do so, there will come the man who desires to rule all that is under the skyey vault and whom you know now and he will act as though it were in his power to give you Rachel. But it is neither in his power nor in the power of others who nurse the same delusion. Whatever he undertakes will crash with his fall; what the others undertake is mere destruction. In truth, however, the men in power, who will divide Poland among themselves, have no power over it. No one has power over it but God and the country itself."

"Itself?" cried the prince. "How can that be? This wretched, violated, splintered people?"

"No earthly potentate," said the *Maggid*, "has power over the soul of a people, unless that people chooses to give him that power. And only power over the soul is veritable power. It was for this reason that Isaiah warned the people of Judah against making an alliance with Assyria against Egypt or with Egypt against Assyria."

"Yet how," Czartoryski asked, "can a land like mine, partitioned among three great powers, fight to regain its freedom unless it comes to an understanding with one of them? Other measures have been tried; they failed and were bound to fail."

The *Maggid* said: "God leads a people from slavery to freedom when it is ready to exchange the service of the mighty against His service. All else which men commonly call freedom is illusory and deceptive. The peoples, who determine that nothing shall intervene between them and the rulership of God, they alone are able, as our prayers have it, 'to establish a Covenant in order that His will be done' unto the beginning of His kingdom on earth."

"But, Reverend Rabbi," the prince asked again, "how can a people enter the service of God? How can a whole people do that?"

"No one can wholly serve God," Rabbi Israel replied, "except a people. For the service of God means just this, and all individual justice can supply but the single stones toward a structure. A people alone can build justice. This is the meaning of Isaiah when he said: Intertwine not your destiny with the injustice of the mighty but build up justice with your own lives. Then will the love of the peoples rush toward you and you will become a blessing in the midst of the earth."

"But how can an oppressed people, unable to determine the foundation of its own existence, conceivably build the structure of justice?"

"Every man who lives among men, though he be a slave, has the choice between justice toward them and injustice. Nor is it impossible for any people, even though it be sorely subjected to an alien will, to build up that twofold justice: justice among its own members and justice with its neighbors. The measure in which it can do so fluctuates. But the measure of your ability is precisely the measure of God's demand upon you. Not more — nor less."

"Ah, Reverend Rabbi," Czartoryski lamented, "we consume ourselves in our efforts to make this land, so torn asunder and so atomized, whole and free, and you demand of us that already we build a structure of justice. It is fearfully difficult to introduce an element of justice if only into the relationships between the various groups of our population according to their different ways and desires. How many antitheses and

[201]

contradictions have we seen arising. Far be it from me to accuse those only who differ from me; assuredly we, too, bear a burden of guilt. But things being now as they are, what shall we strive for and where shall we begin? In this confused coil I see no thread that may be grasped in order that the confusion be disentangled. Certainly specific rights may be granted. But how would that change the nature of the existence of the whole?"

A smile flitted across the *Maggid's* face. When the prince saw this smile he suddenly understood something that he had not understood hitherto. He thought to himself: "If the holy men of this people can still smile thus today, then Israel is a reality, then it is true that God purposes something with and through them . . ." There was a pain in his heart; he wanted to recall the words he had spoken. But already the *Maggid* began to reply to them.

"We, at all events," he said, "do not demand what the world calls rights. All that we need is that the people Israel have the right to arrange its life according to the directions of its God. Long, long ago God scattered us over all the earth because we had failed in an earthly task, and since then He purifies us in the fires of suffering. You He has partitioned among your enemies. But you are permitted, unlike us, to continue to dwell together. Nevertheless, you are beginning, even as we do, to perceive that in the lives of peoples there is a mystery of suffering which is allied to the mystery of the Messiah. In the depth of suffering the return to good is born and this return it is which evokes redemption. Now this return is the beginning of justice of which redemption is the completion. You tell me, Prince Adam, that you can find no thread. You can see none so long as you are willing to try nothing less than the disentanglement of the whole. The beginning and the beginning alone is placed into the hands of men. But it *is* placed in them. Simply make a beginning and at once you will see all about you, in the very

[202]

circle of your personal activity, all kinds of threads. You will have to grasp but a single one of them and it will be, if God wills it, the right one. Others will do even as you have done and what will come to pass, will come to pass."

The head of the *Maggid* had sunk back upon the pillows. His eyes were closed. It was a little while before he opened them again and regarded his visitor almost with surprise. Adam approached him and bowed down. "Bless me, Holy Rabbi," he begged. The *Maggid* leaned over him. "The Lord bless you, Adam, son of Jesabel," he said, "on your long and difficult way."

The prince had been accompanied by his huge, brown Great Dane, who had at once lain down at the *Maggid's* feet. The *Maggid* who had his own special way with animals (it is told that no mosquito dared sting him) gave the dog a friendly nod as he now arose to follow his master.

Next day the Czar, accompanied by Czartoryski and the Prussian general, left Kosnitz. Several nobles, among them Prince Joseph Poniatowski, the nephew of the last kings of Poland and a kinsman of the Czartoryskis, came to meet him from the direction of Warsaw. But they received from him no word of promise or presage. Without stopping at Warsaw, Alexander accompanied by Czartoryski, proceeded to Berlin. Two weeks later the treaty of Potsdam was signed and the two monarchs swore eternal friendship on the grave of Frederick the Great. A month later Prussia started to prepare for war against Napoleon, and still a month later there took place the battle of Austerlitz.

After the prince's visit Rabbi Israel sank into a state of exhaustion which lasted to the end of the week. His life seemed in danger, for no one had ever seen him so bereft of strength. On Friday there arrived two hasidim from Pshysha with a message that the holy Yehudi had sent them hither to sing the songs of the entrance of the Sabbath to the Holy *Maggid* on this evening. For the Yehudi held songs and singers in highest esteem in his congregation, and these two were his best singers. Their arrival was announced to the *Maggid* and he ordered that the men were to sing that evening. When he heard the first notes he raised himself up and his face grew radiant. Soon he breathed with easier rhythm. His forehead waxed cooler and he felt new strength suffuse his body. In the end he looked up like one awakening and whispered: "The holy Yehudi saw in the gleaming mirror that I had made my way through all worlds save for the world of melody in which I was not. And so he sent me two messengers to lead me back through that world."

CHILDREN GO, CHILDREN STAY

What follows is once more taken from the memorabilia set down by Rabbi Benjamin during the summer of 1807.

"Since last winter, when the Emperor Napoleon was in Warsaw, such was the tumult of events that I made no entry in this book. However, it is not my intention to recount the events of the war which stirred everyone, with the probable exception of the Rabbi, very deeply. I say: with the probable exception of the Rabbi. I must add that none of us nowadays is in a position to say what his attitude to Napoleon is; but no one observed the slightest excitement in him. When one of us in some connection which I do not recall emphasized at Hanukkah the circumstance that, after the leader of the Polish legions, General Dombrowski, had arrived in Warsaw, one could look forward to Napoleon's early arrival there, the Rabbi looked at the speaker deprecatorily and said: 'Seven years ago, when he was at Megiddo, he was very near us; now he is far away.' Nevertheless we had the feeling from time to time that the events had a special significance for him. I remember that, several days later, during a table discourse on the Sabbath of Hanukkah, he spoke these words: 'When we light the Hanukkah lights, why do we pronounce this blessing: "Blessed art Thou, O Lord our God, King of the universe, Who performedst miracles for our fathers' sake in those days, at this time"? The days spoken of are far days, the days differ, but the time is this very time — the time in which God creates miracles is never a past time but always this present time. Therefore, immediately afterwards, we pronounce this blessing: "Blessed art Thou, O Lord our God, King of the universe, Who hast kept us in life and preserved us and hast permitted us to reach this time." We are grateful not for that which happened once upon a time nor for those other days, but for this time which is now.' And suddenly he raised his arms high and exclaimed: 'I thank thee, *Ribbono shel 'olam*, for this time.'

"Now I must recount a painful matter, which took place in the spring. Or, rather, there is something that must first be told.

"We could not help observing that the *Rebbitzin* who, during the first year of her marriage had taken a violent share in the slanders against the holy Yehudi, ceased from this during the second year and refused to lend her ear to gossip. I was especially happy when I ascertained this, because since I, myself, have been going to Pshysha, I know what a wretched coil of lies the gossip is. However, I also know this: the fact that the Rabbi continues to listen to it, continues to strike the Yehudi to the very heart. Why is this so? It is so because among all the disciples none is so deeply the Rabbi's disciple as he, himself, even though he spent only a short time without any interruption here. There is no one among us all who has so keen an insight into the Rabbi as he. And finally, it is so, because he, whenever he criticizes any opinion or attitude of the Rabbi — a thing which he does but rarely and with the greatest reserve — does so strangely enough in the name of the Rabbi himself.

[205]

When, thus, he seems to oppose him, in ultimate reality he sides with him. So, as I have said, for several years we heard no angry word from the *Rebbitzin* against the Yehudi. If anyone spoke against him in her presence she broke off the conversation.

"Then, suddenly, during last winter, her behavior changed again. As far as I may be permitted to have an opinion, the thing came to pass as follows. On a certain occasion the Yehudi came to Lublin for the blessing of the New Moon. He asked to be announced to the Rabbi. It appeared later that his message had never been delivered. Under the impression that his visit had been announced and that he was welcome, he walked through the open door into the Rabbi's room. The Rabbi sat without a book in his hand facing the *Rebbitzin* and Shalom. The Rabbi was wholly absorbed in the boy and did not observe the Yehudi. The latter withdrew at once. He sent no further word, but appeared only when the Rabbi, apprised of his arrival, sent for him. I do not know why this incident vexed the *Rebbitzin*. But the fact remains that from then on she once more shared in conversations unfavorable to the Yehudi.

"Soon thereafter the child fell ill. While several of us were with the Rabbi in his study, the mother came rushing in and, oblivious of our presence, besought him to pray for the life of the child. From her despair one would have thought that the boy was dying. The Rabbi regarded her with a somber glance. It seemed for a while as though he could not bear to speak. Then he said softly: 'You know to whom you must turn.' And now a strange thing happened. The *Rebbitzin* approached me at once and besought me to accompany her to Pshysha in this very hour. This confirmed me in the opinion that the Rabbi, too, was aware of the holy Yehudi's power of prayer. When we arrived in the latter's house the woman threw herself at his feet and stammered inarticulate sounds. But it was evident that he knew at once what had happened.

His face, which he turned to her, was suffused with tears. The tears leaped from his eyes. She did not see them; she was beside herself. 'Help!' she cried. The Yehudi bent over until his head almost touched his knees. 'Enough! It is enough!' I heard him moan. The woman seemed to think he desired her to speak no more. She bit her lips until they bled. But he had not addressed her at all. Finally he bade her arise and go home. 'I will pray without ceasing,' said he amid sobs. Then he embraced me. 'Benjamin,' said he, 'how little does man avail!' We drove home. When we entered the house of the Rabbi the child was dying.

"Some weeks later, when I was in Pshysha, Asher, the Yehudi's son, who was almost twelve now, fell ill. At first it did not seem a serious illness. Then, however, he got worse and the mother ran about like a madwoman and howled. Once she burst into her husband's study while we were discussing a problem of the Law. She reminded me of Beile on that other occasion. She screamed: 'This is their vengeance!' The Yehudi, though himself deeply concerned over his son, drew himself up and looked upon her, not angrily, but rather with a mixture of pity and astonishment, as though he were amazed that such a thing could be. He said: 'Don't go to pieces!' Then he took her by the hand and gently led her out.

"Now she hit upon another idea. But let me first put in a matter which I have not yet touched upon. It is well known that the Yehudi is accustomed to give away any money he has beyond what is necessary at the immediate moment. In spite of this, the woman succeeded in the course of the years and without his knowledge in saving up a considerable amount of money. Some of this she got from her mother in the form of gifts and some of it she got from her husband behind his back. When she had enough, she caused a house to be built in secret. When it was finished last autumn, she commissioned a few of his disciples to take him there and show him the house and reveal to him the fact that it was his own and that he was to dwell in it henceforth. For a while he stared at the building without quite understanding. Then he gave a bitter laugh. Never had we heard him laugh thus. 'It is written,' said he: ' "House and monies are a heritage from fathers but from the Lord Himself is a wise woman." How could a man like me, who is busy serving God, earn himself house and land? Therefore the Lord sends him a wise wife who builds him a house.' When now the boy lay ill and his fever rose, Schoendel declared she would give all her movable possessions to the poor, for it is said that thus one could save the life of a child. The Yehudi was well contented. But when this did not avail she came to him and asked what more she could do. 'Why don't you sell the windows and give the money to the poor?' he said with a disconsolate smile.

"In the succeeding days things went worse and worse with the boy. And now something extraordinary happened. I explained before, that, during several years, Rabbi Yissachar Baer used to come to Lublin and also to Kosnitz and also to Pshysha and used to divide his visits in such a way that he arrived at the Seer's a month before the New Year until the end of the Days of Penitence. From there he goes to the *Maggid* and then again, after some time, to the Yehudi. Now it happened that, just at the period when the boy Asher was so very ill, he felt an overwhelming desire to go to Pshysha at once, although this was not the time of his regular visits. When the wagon of the peasant who was taking him as a matter of pure kindness (for he was very poor) was crossing a hill from which one could see the little town in the valley below, he heard from there the weeping of the child. The sound seemed to come from the house of his teacher, yet that was really impossible. It was even stranger that he seemed to hear the child calling him. When he entered the house of the Yehudi, the latter took him by the hand and led him

[208]

to the bedside of the moaning boy. On the floor the woman was crouching. 'I am at the end of my strength,' he said. 'I can pray no more. It is not by accident that you have come; take him upon yourself and you will surely give him back to me healed.' He lifted the woman from the floor and left the room with her. In the first moment Rabbi Yissachar Baer was — he told me this himself — more dismayed than he had ever been before in his life. Never had he practiced healing, never even attempted to influence another's physical condition. He had never supposed himself the possessor of any special power, all the more since he was very obscure in Lublin. So soon, however, as that was expected of him which he believed without any doubt to be within the power of his teachers, also of the Yehudi, although the latter refuse to recognize it, he dared no longer to doubt. In an instant his dismay was conquered and his whole soul was aflame with the necessity of accomplishing what had been demanded of him. And he brought it about. What means he took no one on earth save himself ever knew."

(An addendum many years later: "When I recently visited Rabbi Yissachar Baer in Radoshitz, who in the years between has become the most famous among the wonder-working men of this generation, he confessed to me that he owed his later rise to that hour long ago.")

"The boy had recovered. But he was still so weak that he could hardly walk. His father did not wait until the end of his convalescence, but took him along to Kosnitz. I know not what he discussed with the holy *Maggid*. It could not have been the boy's illness. That lay in the past. But I have a suspicion that he wanted to arrange that for a period, as he desired, Asher was to be separated from his mother. At all events, the *Maggid* took the boy into his house during the whole year preceding his maturity in the sense of the Torah, that is, until he became a *Bar Mitzvah*, a son of the law. He shared his room with him and took him every morning to the ritual bath. The *Rebbitzin* did not object, because she regarded it as the operation of a counter-magic.

"Since the death of little Shalom the relationship between Lublin and Pshysha had assumed a curious form. Even during the years preceding this the situation seemed to be such that, whenever the Yehudi came to Lublin, his first encounter with the Rabbi established peace between them. So soon as he left, however, the slanderers regained the upper hand. Now another and very strange element was added to the situation. Whenever the adversaries hastened to the Rabbi with their accusations and he agreed with them and scolded at the Yehudi, they knew as a matter of experience that they had failed completely. But when he said: 'Such a man! What a pity,' then they could be certain that they had aroused hatred in his heart anew.

"In some way, which is not quite clear to me, I suspect a connection between this matter and something which took place just the other day. Unexpectedly the Rabbi turned to Rabbi Meir, who to common knowledge was one of the leaders of the opposition to the Yehudi from the beginning, and said to him that he was to pray for a long life for the Yehudi. Sometime thereafter Meir came to Lublin from Stabnitz, where he was rabbi of the congregation, and sat near the Rabbi at the Sabbath table. The latter leaned in his direction and asked him whether he had been praying that the Yehudi should live long. Meir answered that, since the Rabbi had issued the command, he had prayed that prayer every day. 'Good, good,' said the Rabbi. I would very much like to know what that signifies. Why does the Rabbi command such a prayer? Does it signify that he causes prayers to be prayed against his own anger? But why in the world does he select Meir? Nothing but riddles!

"I myself in my own person have experienced the Rabbi's indulgence as well as his anger. That I had been favorably inclined toward the Yehudi for many a year — this he knew since it had come to be, and even at times teased me about it in conversation. Nor did he send me on fewer errands than formerly. For instance, he once sent me in a particularly important matter to Rabbi Hirsch in Zydatshov, although the latter belonged to the opponents of the Yehudi. This trip, by the way, was rendered unforgettable to me by a thing which that extraordinary man said to me, namely, this: 'I am now an empty vessel; soon I must visit Lublin again in order to be filled.' Once the Rabbi even asked me, why I had not recently gone to Pshysha. In accordance with the truth I answered: 'Because I can't afford the trip.' He gave me the wherewithal, though no one ever knew. Unfortunately, although only to exalt the Rabbi, I confided this matter to a comrade, and the enemies of the Yehudi went so far as to make it a cause of reproach against the Rabbi.

"But now the following took place just a few weeks ago. It was on a Friday evening. Later on I learned that on that very day peace negotiations were being conducted between the Czar Alexander and Napoleon. After grace the Rabbi said: 'Tomorrow morning at the stroke of seven you are all to pray in company.' He went to his study, but came back to the table and said: 'You too, Benjamin.' He knew that in recent years I had been praying later. Next morning everybody hurried and they took me along. I wrapped myself in my praying-shawl. At breakfast the Rabbi asked: 'Did you all pray together?' They said: 'Yes.' He asked: 'Benjamin, too?' They answered: 'Yes.' But the second son of the Rabbi, Rabbi Joseph, said: 'It does not seem to me that he prayed.' Now the Rabbi called upon me and asked: 'Did you pray with your comrades?' I answered: 'No.' He was silent for a space. Then he said: 'I excuse you.'

"In my heart I thanked God because I knew that, had he not excused me, nothing would have been left of me. If anyone were to ask me, why I had not joined in the praying, I could not answer the question. Why did I not, especially since I was bound to remember a saying of the Rabbi: if ever all of us just once would recite a single prayer in complete spiritual communion with him and with each other, something very lofty would be attained thereby. Why did I not pray, despite all that? I cannot tell. All that I know is that on that occasion something kept me from praying with such power, as though a human life were to be saved by what I did or did not. And now, a few days ago, the Rabbi, accompanied by his son Israel, accosted me as he walked by. 'Benjamin,' said he, 'guard yourself; a time will come when all will shun you.' I summoned all my courage and asked: 'Rabbi, do you mean that shunning by men which God, too, shares, or do you mean that loneliness among men in which God visits the lonely one?' He did not answer. He frowned and went upon his way. Rabbi Israel did not follow him. He stayed with me and took my hand and accompanied me to my house.

"Since I have determined to record everything which I learned concerning the relationship between those two men, our Rabbi and the holy Yehudi, I will not omit an alleged event, which has been repeated hereabouts. To me it seems highly improbable; indeed I cannot give it any credence, seeing that it corresponds to the character and way of neither man. If, nevertheless, I insert it here, my chief reason is that almost more than any real event it shows how the situation developed — a situation characterized by the fact that it gave rise to a rumor of this kind and that the rumor was circulated as truth.

"When the Yehudi was here the time before the last and the Rabbi communicated to him over and over again and ever more emphatically the assertions of the slanderers, he is said to have become so passionately indignant that he rushed up to the Ark, which stood in the Rabbi's house, and to have sworn that all was lies and deception. This is said to have

[212]

allayed the wrath of the Rabbi and to have caused compassion to enter his heart. When the slanderers, headed by Rabbi Simon Deutsch, came back, he turned them away and based himself upon the oath of the Yehudi. Then it was Rabbi Simon who approached the holy Ark and swore that it was he who spoke the truth. So when the Yehudi returned, the Rabbi is said to have confronted him with the oath of his opponents. The Yehudi, according to the story, had been silent for a space. Then he had said: 'There is only one thing that I can think of. If those people speak the truth it means that I think evil of you. And our sages have said that he who thinks evil of his teacher is like one who thinks evil of the *Shechinah* itself. But it is well known that he who thinks evil of the *Shechinah* — his prayers are not accepted by Heaven for the space of forty days. Let the Rabbi with his clear vision gaze into Heaven and see whether my prayers are accepted.' The Rabbi is said to have leaned back his head and closed his eyes for a while. Then he declared: 'It is, as you say. But your power is so great that it is possible that I am misled even by Heaven.' "

THE LANGUAGE OF THE BIRDS

I would that I could illustrate by some concrete thing what Pshysha was. I would I could lift my index finger and point to it, even as on an antique gorgeous raiment one points out the faded pattern. But nothing is left. What is it that Pshysha was? Well, a dwelling place of the spirit. But what does that word signify? What can it mean in an age which calls every facile babbler a representative of the spirit and which at bottom seems to have no choice except to see in the life of the spirit either a highly developed means of combat or of amusement? Very well; but I confess that

I still have faith in the spirit which hovers over the creatures germinating in the waters, even as the eagle hovers above his nest; that is to say I still believe in the existence both of the "waters" and of the wide-winged bird above them. Only where this is so, do I say that the spirit is and do I see it. So let me call Pshysha, in spite of all, a dwelling place of the spirit.

A greater surprise than even that visit of the Rabbi seven years before — if perhaps not for the Yehudi himself, yet surely for his friends and disciples — was it when there came into his house Meir, doubtless the man of soberest passion in the circle of his foes. To him and also to his older brother, Mordecai, in whom however the smoldering glow of feeling never flamed into passion, to these two the Yehudi seemed to be an alien element which had penetrated the sanctuary and was boldly in revolt against the whole realm of mystery: against the sacred majesty of that high man who stands in the middle of the world, against his covenant with the higher powers, against his influence upon the blendings of the spheres of heaven, against his combat with the demonic forces. Meir's passionate wrath and Mordecai's calm rejection had finally led to a point where these two even avoided any personal communication with the man they hated. When, years ago, the Yehudi could find no lodging in the crowded Jewish quarters of Lublin and caused the brothers to be asked to shelter him briefly in their rooms, they had sent his messenger packing with rude refusals and even the gentle Mordecai had gone so far as to exclaim: "What does that mean, 'the Yehudi'? I, too, am a *Yehudi*."

It is evident how hard it must have been for Meir to do the Rabbi's bidding and to pray that the Yehudi enjoy a long life. And now he himself arrived. He did not in so many words try to effect a reconciliation, but in his changed countenance the desire for reconciliation could be clearly read. What had happened? In Pshysha no one ever learned. The Yehudi himself probably did not care to know. But through the group of people who were close to Mordecai (it cannot be said that he had any actual disciples), something has been preserved, it is not much, but enough to give us a present idea of the incident.

The two brothers, who, despite the difference between them, were very close to one another, had had, not for the first time, the same dream during the same night. In this dream they saw once again that goblin-like creature, Jaacob Yitzchak, son of the woman Matel, by name like the Rabbi himself who, for a whole long year had so deeply disturbed the whole body of the disciples and the master too. Meir had recognized him at once as one sent by the demons. Since his disappearance no news of him had reached Lublin. In their dream they saw him in far more devilish guise — with the tusks of a wild boar and the wings of a bat. They saw the Rabbi and all his disciples make for him with long, pointed, iron staves in their hands. Yet they could not drive him away. He expanded upwards and downwards; about his head was wrapped a stormcloud and his feet were invisibly buried in the darkness of the abyss. But now appeared a broad-shouldered man, who raised his strong unweaponed hands against the monster and forced him to flee. With violent fright each of the brothers at once recognized this man to be the Yehudi. And next — at this same point both hesitated to go on as they were recounting and comparing their dreams — now all the disciples led by them, by Mordecai and Meir, turned against the victor. They surrounded him with their staves; and suddenly the staves of Mordecai and Meir had turned into axes with which they hewed off the two hands of the Yehudi. Morning found Mordecai so shamed and weakened by his dream that he could not get up nor immediately set out for Pshysha, as he felt it to be his duty, being the older of the two. Meir went in his stead.

The days he spent in Pshysha were quite different than he had expected them to be. He felt no trace of hostility anywhere. The Yehudi treated him with equable kindliness and everyone else received him in friendly fashion. At first this was more difficult to bear than the harshest resistance would have been. But gradually he himself began to feel unembarrassed in this atmosphere without reserve or guile.

When the time came for him to bid the Yehudi farewell, he decided to his own surprise to submit a question to him, which had long tormented him, but especially since the time of his dream.

"How does it happen," he asked, "that men who have measurably become masters over the impulse to sin, yet permit themselves to be misled by whispered suggestions of the Evil Spirit, not so far as to sin crassly, but yet so far as to entertain false opinions and to be guilty of false actions?"

"One thing is certain," the Yehudi answered, "that if a man pronounces but one time with all his might the words: 'Hear, O Israel, the Lord our God, the Lord is One!' the Evil Spirit ought wholly to despair of ever winning that man's soul. For anyone who truly acknowledges his Creator to be the only Power in the universe, cannot be subjected to any other, since he perceives every other to be but delusions and frauds. What, then, is the device of the Evil Spirit? He shows to each the high levels he can reach and lets him reach them. Then is that man's mind fixed upon the levels; then he is no longer devoted to God alone, even though he thinks he is. The power which alone he does not perceive to be either delusion or fraud comes in the end to be himself and his striving from level to level. I tell you this, Rabbi Meir, because in my early years I was subject to this very danger. It was at the very time when I came to Lublin. In Lublin I learned to recognize the delusion of the levels. And what is a man to do who is thus tempted to protect himself from the snare of the fowler? He goes into the lonely forest and stands there and cries out until the levels and grades are taken from him again."

[216]

When the Yehudi had finished speaking they said farewell. On the way home, Meir, rocked in the wagon that bore him, fell into a gentle slumber. When he was suddenly awakened the wagon was being driven through a forest, in the trees of which birds of all kinds trilled their melodies. And when he listened carefully, lo, he understood what they were singing. Dismayed he sprang from the wagon and ran into the forest and prayed and did not cease praying until the voices of the birds brought no more to his ear than they had always done before. With tears he thanked God. He looked around; the wagon was waiting nearby; he got into it; the horses pulled. Soon he nodded again until the drover stopped at an inn and awakened him. He never knew whether the miracle had happened to him dreaming or waking. Nor did he ask. But the great change had come over him in that hour.

On a later occasion the Yehudi was taking a walk with his disciple Perez. This man could listen like none other, for his ears were deeply bound up with his soul, so that he heard nothing through the ear which his soul did not absorb. They crossed a meadow on which pasturing cattle lowed, while a flock of gabbling geese climbed up out of a brook that flowed through it.

"If one could but understand all this speaking!" cried Perez.

"If you reach a point," the Yehudi observed, "at which you can grasp to the ultimate depth what you yourself are speaking, then you will learn to understand the speech of all creatures. For though there are many languages, the speech of all creatures is one."

And on still another occasion he said to Yissachar Baer: "If you wish it, I can teach you to understand the speech of birds and of other animals."

And the other answered: "If this is to be my portion I will reach the knowledge alone."

[217]

"That is the very answer," said the Yehudi, "which I hoped you would give me. But have you reached the point of knowing whether that speech is a speech of words or of gestures?"

"I think," Yissachar Baer answered, "that all aboriginal speech is to be understood at that point where word and gesture are still inextricably blended."

"I see that you know what is most important," said the Yehudi.

There we have, as handed down to us, three apparently quite separate expressions on the same subject addressed to three really different people. The three observations are not different. They merge into a single one. That was Pshysha.

There was another disciple who as a matter of self-mortification had embraced silence and would utter no words except those of the law and of prayer. The Yehudi watched him for a period. Then he summoned him. As the man was approaching the city of Pshysha toward evening, he saw the Yehudi cross the meadows with several disciples. He leaped from the wagon and ran to meet him and saluted him.

"Young man," the Yehudi said to him, "how is it that in the eternal world of truth I see no word that comes from you?"

"Rabbi," the other said to justify himself, "to what end shall I speak idly? Is it not more profitable only to study and to pray?"

"If you do that," said the Yehudi, "no word from you yourself enters the world of truth. He who does nothing but learn and pray does not even learn and pray, for he slays the word in his own soul. What does it mean — to speak idly? You can say idly whatever you like; you can say it veraciously, too . . . and now I will have a pipe and some tobacco prepared for you against the night. Come to me after evening prayer and I will teach you how to speak."

They sat together through the night; when morning came the man's apprenticeship was over.

That was Pshysha.

This, too, is taken from the notations of Rabbi Benjamin of Lublin. It belongs to the spring of 1809.

"Great is the Rabbi of Lublin. Undoubtedly there are many aspects of his character as well as certain actions of his which do not seem intelligible. Once in a while one is tempted to rebel because one cannot help believing that one, oneself, has some small modicum of understanding. But finally one submits, without changing one's own opinion, to the enormous forcefulness which the Creator has bestowed upon this being of flesh and blood.

"In recent years the Rabbi made some extremely curious observations. Thus, on a certain occasion, in the course of an impassioned speech, he fixed prophetically the day and hour of the coming of the Messiah. When he was asked about this later on, he said he did not remember having said any such thing. Another time, when the calculation concerning the beginning of the last age was being discussed, he used the following similitude. A son observes something in his father which strikes him as an impropriety. Can he have the boldness to reproach him with it? What he can do is this. He can say: 'Father, is it not a fact that there is such and such a passage in the Torah?' And so it is with the *Zaddikim* of those generations who would hasten the redemption of man. In a verse of Scripture they find an indication that the Messiah will come in such and such a year. Then they show this verse to our Father and say: 'Father, is it not a fact that there is such and such a passage in the Torah?'

"From this angle we may also understand a saying of his which we heard from his lips about a year ago and which I have not yet recorded. But I must preliminarily say something concerning what gave rise to it.

"It is known that Rabbi Menahem Mendel, sometime after he had settled in Rymanov, for some inexplicable reason

[219]

went back to the city of Prystyk where his father-in-law lived. More than a year ago, however, he returned with his family to Rymanov, and now only did his true leadership of the congregation begin. That leadership was severe, as was to be expected. Not only are all members of the congregation closely supervised as to their absolute honesty, so that, for instance, on the last day of every month the measures and weights in all Jewish shops are tested, but also emphatic limitations are placed upon an even moderate delight in worldly things. Among other regulations, Rabbi Menahem Mendel had forbidden the employment of musicians at weddings. He paid very strict attention to the raiment of his people. The men got off easily; they were merely forbidden to wear collars and a few things like that. His regulations concerning the garments of women were more precise; he subjected women, too, to specific other limitations. They were not to milk cows without supervision, nor extend their walks beyond the limits of the town, nor sit in the streets on Sabbaths and holidays, and so forth. Girls were not to wear bangs nor have their hair curled; married women were not to have silver embroidery on their headkerchiefs when they went out, nor were either to wear modish sandals nor German shifts nor gay and adorned frocks. Tailors who made modish garments were punished. Rabbi Menahem Mendel based his regulations upon the sermon which the prophet Isaiah preached against the anklets and the crescents and the pendants and the chains and the mufflers and the headtires and the ankle chains and the sashes of the haughty and mincing daughters of Zion.

"Rabbi Menahem Mendel was not content to publish these regulations in the district of Rymanov. He sent messengers abroad in the land who were to publish his protestations. When one of these came to Lublin, the message he brought vexed our Rabbi. 'The daughters of Israel are to wear adornments,' said he, 'especially now when the time of great rejoicing approaches.'

"Undoubtedly the hope of redemption is hardly less strong in the heart of Rabbi Menahem Mendel than it is in that of our Rabbi. But while our Rabbi's mind is ever fixed upon the hope that the light hidden within the darkness will pierce the obstacle that holds it back, all of Rabbi Menahem Mendel's expectations and plans are determined by his certainty that the powers of darkness are bound to win an initial victory before at the core of the darkness the burgeoning of the germ of light can take place. That secret light, according to him, must be kept in utter purity. At the same time the power of evil must rise to its highest point until its all-obliterating cruelty is faced by nothing else on earth than that pure light in its grace-given powerlessness. Then and only then will the Divine Light incline to it and bestow upon it the gift of action. Thus did I hear this doctrine from the mouth of our Rabbi Hirsch, who occasionally goes to Rymanov. There his namesake, Rabbi Hirsch, the "servitor," confided it to him. It is known that the latter has long administered the house of Rabbi Menahem Mendel and is one of the great exponents of the hasidic way. He heard it directly from his teacher. Next time I was in Pshysha I told the holy Yehudi about this. He did not answer one word. Later I talked about the matter with Rabbi Bunam and Rabbi Perez. Rabbi Bunam said: 'It is written: He has put an end to the darkness. God alone decides how far in any period the province of the darkness may extend.' But Rabbi Perez looked into my eyes with his own gleaming ones and added: 'The light is pure so long as it does not concern itself with its own self.'

"But there is something in connection with this belief of Rabbi Menahem Mendel, which must be mentioned here. Like our own Rabbi he means by these ideas to refer to the influence of the *Zaddikim* on the course of events. Like our Rabbi he, too, thinks that it is the duty of the *Zaddikim* to make Napoleon into Gog. Yet his meaning and our Rabbi's meaning are not identical. He interprets it as praying and taking spiritual risks that Napoleon may be the universal victor.

"Now I must relate a matter which took place in the spring of this year. It partakes of the marvelous. The son of a future generation who reads these memoirs may perhaps have difficulty in believing that such things were. Therefore I shall name the names of my witnesses who are trustworthy men. One of them is Rabbi Naftali of Ropshitz who, when I was his guest this summer, related to me what he had seen with his own eyes. The other is Rabbi Shelomo, the grandson of Rabbi Elimelech, a friend of mine for long years. He related to me his share in the events when he brought back to our Rabbi, who had dispatched him to Rymanov, the answer of Rabbi Menahem Mendel.

"First of all, let me recall the fact that faith in the significance of the first night of Pesach for the coming of redemption has always been very deeply rooted in the soul of Rabbi Menahem Mendel. I have been told that he was a great wanderer in his youth and wandered as far as the land of Spain. There he celebrated Pesach in a subterranean cavern with a Marrano. As they were sitting together so great a light suddenly fell into the cavern that they were frightened, and at the same moment the beaker of wine that had been filled and set aside as the custom is, for the prophet Elijah wandering on earth, rose high in air, as though someone were putting it to his lips. Then it sank back upon the table, and it was empty. Since that day Rabbi Menahem Mendel often pointed out the fact that Elijah in the guise of a herald of redemption would appear on that very night on which once upon a time Israel was liberated from Egypt.

"On the day before Pesach of this year Rabbi Menahem

[222]

Mendel, surrounded by his faithful ones, was busy in the early morning with the preparation of the unleavened bread. Rabbi Naftali stood beside him as he pushed the flat-cakes into the oven. And each time he murmured in his pertinacious way: 'We'll shove them on to Vienna; we'll shove them on to Vienna!' Rabbi Naftali barely understood the words. So soon as he thought he had done so, he interrupted Rabbi Menahem Mendel and cried out: 'How can the unclean have any share in the preparation of that which is clean!' And instantly he fled from the rabbi's wrath. Some weeks later he found out that on the day prior to that Napoleon had begun to start his army on the march toward Austria, and again several weeks later, that Napoleon in the meantime had entered Vienna, at the very period when at his command Prince Joseph Poniatowski led his Polish troops into Lublin.

"Immediately after Pesach, Rabbi Naftali had gone to Kosnitz and had related this incident to the *Maggid*, of whom he knew that he was a passionate opponent of Napoleon. The *Maggid* had made no reply. Naftali returned to Lublin and reported to our Rabbi. At once the latter sent to the city of Mogielnica, where Rabbi Jacob the son of Rabbi Elimelech lived, and summoned the latter's son, Rabbi Shelomo, to come to him. Upon his arrival he bade him go to Rymanov with a personal message from him to Rabbi Menahem Mendel. The message was worded as follows: 'It is written: *And sons of the Highest are ye all*. It may not be that the sons of the Highest work at cross purposes. To me, as to you, it is a sign from God that he has let this man wax so mighty. Like yourself I have felt it to be my duty to work with might and main to the end that he become that Gog concerning whom prophecy speaks. But it is given to no man to know in what manner the triumphs and the defeats of this man are allied to redemption. It is not for us to be partisan on one side or the other. This was not always my opinion; I have recognized my error. Our only aim must be to see to it that the density of happenings does not thin out, but become greater and greater. This is our common task. Each one may cultivate a special feeling in his heart; the work must be common to us all. Let us make a covenant toward this common effort.' When Rabbi Menahem Mendel had received the message he bade the messenger to repeat the following answer for him: 'It shall be as you propose; for it is known to all that the Holy Spirit rests on you. I cannot change what is in my heart. But I will drop my plans and do nothing more except in agreement with you.'

"For what I have to say next I can adduce no witness, but I have it from one to whom it was communicated by the person most concerned. This person is the third son of the Rabbi, named Zvi, who has been a soldier in the Austrian army since the beginning of the year. When he came to bid his father farewell, the latter said: 'When you see the Emperor Napoleon, you are to greet him for me.' The youth did not understand these words but dared not ask for an explanation. When Napoleon reviewed the Austrian regiments stationed in Vienna, he was there. The troops stopped and he found himself facing the Emperor. Napoleon summoned him and commanded that he be asked who he was. Not venturing, of course, to give the message, he replied: 'I am the son of the Rabbi of Lublin.' Napoleon laughed. 'Tell him,' said he, 'to tell his father from me that I am not afraid of him.'

"Yet it was but a week later, on the first day of Shavuot, the feast of the Revelation, that, on an island in the Danube, Napoleon suffered his first defeat.

"Soon thereafter the Russians occupied Lublin. They were said to be Napoleon's allies, but no one believed this. The Rabbi went to meet them and observed them for many minutes. I see no unfruitful one among them,' said he."

The little incident, which I must report in this section, took place soon after the return of Rabbi Shelomo of Rymanov to Lublin. I do not find it mentioned in the memoirs of Rabbi Benjamin. To make it quite clear I must go back a great ways.

Several years before this, approximately at the time when Prince Czartoryski visited the *Maggid*, a new student had appeared at the court of the Seer. His name, too, was Mendel. He was eighteen, thick set and of noticeably dark complexion. His black eyes were never seen to change their expression.

He had two passions which were, in fact, but one: to discover truth and to communicate it. The first determined the nature of his life work, the second his relationship to his fellowmen. He threw himself upon the study of the Law as a great beast upon its prey, and from his childhood on he was greatly hated. Far later, when he was already the far-famed and bitterly criticized Rabbi of Kozk, he once came on a visit to his little native city. There he visited the *melamed* who had once taught him his *Aleph Bet* and who had also read with him the five books of the Torah. The teacher who had taught him later he did not visit. When the latter met him he asked whether he was ashamed of him. He answered: "You taught me things that admit of a reply; for one interpretation says one thing and another says another. But he taught me that true lore which is unanswerable and which therefore stayed by me. Hence it was my duty to pay him a special respect."

When he was a boy he would have nothing to do with the hasidic way. For a long time he was of the opinion that it might deflect him from his studies. He was so devoted to study that he would sometimes stand for hours with a talmudic folio volume, bound in wooden boards with heavy copper clasps, in his hands, without thinking of sitting down.

In his home town there was an old man who used to tell the young people stories about *Zaddikim*. "He told stories and I listened to him," the Rabbi of Kozk said later on. "He mingled truth with untruth. I marked and remembered the truth. And thus I became a hasid."

He came to Lublin first when he was fifteen. The Seer had given the following commission to a man who came from Mendel's town: "Somewhere in your town there glows a sacred spark. Find him who bears it and bring him to me." The man watched carefully the behavior of several lads; he thought of Mendel last of all, for the boy had the reputation of being slightly "cracked." Finally it occurred to him that he might find out something by spending the night in a corner of the house of study. After midnight he saw Mendel there studying with one foot on the floor and the other against a wooden bench. This happened several nights in succession. Finally, one night, the watcher coughed. So soon as Mendel knew that there was someone else in the place he went over to the oven and clapped his hands and acted with deliberate clownishness. But the man said to him: "Don't try to deceive me. The Rabbi of Lublin sends for you. You must go to him."

In Lublin, on the way to the Rabbi, Mendel saw in a shop a little knife which pleased him, and so he bought it. When he stood before the Seer, the latter said to him: "Did you come here to buy a little knife?"

Mendel looked into his face. "I have not come to admire the gifts of the spirit," he answered.

Soon thereafter Mendel's father appeared in Lublin to fetch him home. "Why do you abandon the way of your fathers and make common cause with the hasidim!" he cried.

"In the song by the Red Sea," said Mendel, "it says first: 'This is my God, I praise Him,' and only thereafter 'The God of my fathers, I exalt Him.' "

[226]

The father was unwilling to admit the force of this argument.

When Mendel was eighteen and was married and living in the city of Tomashov in the house of his father-in-law, he begged for permission to go for a week to Lublin. The permission was granted and he was also given enough money for a week. He stayed in Lublin more than six months. In the succeeding years he returned a couple of times, but never remained long.

Shortly after the Rabbi had sent that message to Rymanov, Mendel came on one of his visits to Lublin. He was seen walking about in a somber mood and not speaking to anyone. When he came to see the Rabbi and handed him his petition, the Rabbi said to him: "Your way is the way of melancholy. It is not a good way. Leave it."

Bitterly Mendel turned to go. "It is my way," he said from between his teeth.

In the House of Study he found a youth of his own age who kept pacing up and down.

"What plans are you turning over in your mind?" he asked.

"What concern is it of yours?" the other said.

"It is my concern," said Mendel, "because, like myself, you are planning to go to Pshysha to the Yehudi."

The other admitted and told him how badly worried he was as to the countenance with which he was to appear before the Rabbi to ask for leave of absence, seeing that the Rabbi would know concerning his intention at once. Mendel proposed that they were to leave together and were not to say goodbye to the Rabbi at all. Upon this they agreed. But first they wanted to spend another week in Lublin.

On the day after the messenger had returned from Rymanov, the Rabbi was discussing with his disciples the coming of the Messiah and addressed questions to them. When it was Mendel's turn he said: "So far as I understand two things must occur, one among us and one between heaven and earth. What must occur among us human beings is something which each one's soul tells him and there is no need to speak of it at length. But what is to take place between heaven and earth is known to none and one cannot discuss it at all. During many generations each generation has sought to bring about the coming of the Messiah. All failed. It seems to me that he will come when one ceased to occupy oneself with the question."

The Rabbi listened in silence but with unconsenting eyes.

On the journey to Pshysha, Mendel fell ill. Upon arrival he had to go to bed. His comrade ran to the Yehudi and besought him to remember Mendel in his prayers. "Did you leave Lublin without the Rabbi's permission?" the Yehudi asked. When he was told that it was so, he went along to the inn.

"Determine," he said to Mendel, "to return to Lublin as soon as you are well and ask for leave of absence."

Mendel shook his head. "I have never," he replied, "repented me of the truth."

The Yehudi looked at him a long time. "If you cling so pertinaciously to your own insight," he said at length, "you will recover without going." And so it came to pass.

But when Mendel came to the Yehudi after his recovery, the Yehudi said: "It is well for a man in his youth to bear a yoke." At that a readiness for true service suffused the young man's being.

VISION

In the middle of the night the Yehudi started up violently from his sleep. Since Schoendel was nursing her second boy-child, he slept in a little room alone. The window which had been left ajar the night before was wide open, although there had been no breath of wind. A voice cried: "Lift your eyes on high!" He approached the window and looked up. Neither moon nor any star was visible. The darkness was impenetrable. Suddenly there arose a cleaving tone, the long drawn blast of a heavenly *shofar*, and on the instant the darkness was dispersed. Red udders exuded the milk-white light of origin. The drops fell into a pool brilliantly illuminated from an unknown source. The pool's rim was greenishly iridescent. The Yehudi no longer stood at the window but at the edge of the pool. The milky radiance pierced his eyes. A movement took place in the white liquid. A wave arose and curved and took on a form which became the form of a body. The Yehudi beheld a woman swathed from her head to her ankles in a black veil. Only her feet were naked and through the shallow water in which they stood it could be seen that dust, as from long wayfaring on an open road, covered them. But they also bore bleeding wounds.

The woman spoke: "I am weary unto death, for ye have hunted me down. I am sick unto death, for ye have tormented me. I am shamed, for ye have denied me. Ye are the tyrant, who keep me in exile.

"When ye are hostile to each other, ye hunt me down. When ye plot evil against each other, ye torment me. When ye slander each other, ye deny me. Each of you exiles his comrades and so together ye exile me.

"And thou thyself, Jaacob Yitzchak, dost thou mind how thou meantest to follow me and estrangedst thyself from me the more? One cannot love me and abandon the created being. I am in truth with you. Dream not that my forehead radiates heavenly beams. The glory has remained above. My face is that of the created being."

She raised the veil from her face and he recognized the face.

She said: "When shall I find rest? When may I go home? Will you help me, Jaacob Yitzchak? Will you help me only a little?"

And already the form had vanished. Nor was the pool any longer to be seen.

The Yehudi found himself back at his window. A voice cried: "Approach me and my redemptiqn will approach." The darkness was dispersed. With a great reddish circle about it the white moon soared up the sky. At her two sides hovered two winged beings, fire-hued the wings of the one, ice-white those of the other. They floated down to earth and toward the Yehudi.

"Thou shalt prophesy," said the one.

"Thou shalt die," said the other.

THE ANSWER OF THE YEHUDI

On the following Sabbath, a little more than a week since the messenger had returned from Rymanov to Lublin, the Yehudi assembled his disciples about him, from the oldest and first, Bunam, to the youngest and last, Mendel. Not as in Lublin did they sit at a long table with the Rabbi at the head. The benches stood at random, and somewhere on one of them the teacher occupied a temporary seat, so that, despite the deep seriousness of his leadership, the picture presented was one of an uncomplicated and familiar comradeship.

The Yehudi addressed them thus.

"It is written: 'In loftiness and magnificence hast Thou clothed Thyself.' All the loftiness and magnificence which we take for God's Being is nothing but His raiment. He clothes Himself therein in order to approach His creature. The extreme of Divine Majesty which we may perceive is nought but a self-degradation of God for our sake.

"But after two ways He did truly clothe Himself in servitude. The one way is this, that He has apportioned to the

[230]

world His *Shechinah*, His 'indwelling,' and has permitted His *Shechinah* to enter into the process of history and to share the contradictions and sufferings of the world, and has sent His *Shechinah* into exile with man and with Israel. It is written: 'In all its distress is He distressed.' The *Shechinah* is not inviolable by stripes and wounds; it has identified itself wholly with our fate, our misery, our very guilt. When we sin, it experiences our sinfulness as something that happens to it. It shares not only our shame but also the disgraces which we would not acknowledge as such; these it tastes in all their shamefulness.

"And the other way is this, that He has placed the redemption of His world in the power of our return to good. It is written: 'Turn back, O sons, who have turned away and I will heal your turnings away.' God would make perfect His creation not otherwise than by our help. He will not reveal His kingdom until we have established it. He will not assume the crown of the kings of the world until He can receive it from our hands. He will not be reunited with His *Shechinah* until we bring it to Him as a gift. With dusty and bleeding feet He permits His *Shechinah* to tread the road of earth because we do not take pity upon it.

"For this reason all calculations concerning the end of time are false and all attempts to calculate it to bring nearer the coming of the Messiah must fail. In truth all such things deflect us from the one thing needful, which is this, to reunite Him and the *Shechinah* by virtue of our return to good.

"Truly there is a mystery here. But he who knows it cannot make it known, and he who feigns to make it known proves thereby that he knows it not.

"And truly there is a miracle here. But he who would perform it will surely fail; only he who does not attempt it dare hope to have a share in it.

"Redemption is at the door. It depends only and alone upon our return to good, our *teshuvah*."

[231]

After the Yehudi had spoken, his disciples sat there for a long while without desiring to make any comment. Only Mendel said by and by: "Now I understand something which I never understood before."

"And what is that?" asked the teacher.

Mendel answered: "It is the words of Bileam: 'The Lord His God is with him and the shout of the King is among them.' "

"And how do you interpret the words?" asked the Yehudi.

"God," said Mendel, "is with us, wherever we are and however we are constituted. But the dawn of His kingdom can arise only among us, only in Israel, when and not before there exists this 'in,' this place within us."

DAVID OF LELOV INTERPOSES

For many years it had become a custom for the scattered hasidim who adhered to Rabbi David, and who in spite of his great reserve were many, to set out for Lelov prior to Shavuot, to assemble about a mile outside of the little town and then to proceed on foot, headed by a few musicians. When they reached the little forest just before Lelov, the musicians would begin to beat their cymbals and to play on their little fiddles, so that they could be heard in the town. The hasidim would then sing to that accompaniment and thus they all proceeded to Rabbi David's house. Here they would stand, playing and singing, until Rabbi David came into the yard. By that time it was usually after sundown. The people surrounded him with long, lit wax tapers in their hands and he interpreted Scripture with radiant countenance. Thereafter there was more playing and singing and afterwards they danced, and this would often go on until dawn. Finally the Rabbi would address to them the greeting of peace, whereafter they all drank *l'hayyim*, "to life," and with rejoicing they conducted him back to his door. In the morning they all prayed together. Then there was a meal at the Rabbi's, frugal but delicious. Then they all mounted long wagons, in which they stood up packed close, and so they proceeded to spend Shavuot in Lublin. They put their money together and made Rabbi David their cashier.

In recent years the tumult of war had again and again prevented this journey and each time Rabbi David had had to tell his hasidim, as he had told the Seer fifteen years previously, the story of the long table which extended from Lublin to Lelov. This time, however, after Prince Ponia-towski had gone southward from Lublin to conquer Galicia, a curious mood had come over everyone. Not as though anyone considered the situation to have become stabilized. They had suffered too often even to imagine such a thing. But, although no one knew why, there arose a general need to gather in crowds. Not only had a great procession of hasidim come to Lelov — without any previous agreement, and as a matter of course, all the wagons were assembled early in the morning, and this train, preceded by the wagon of Rabbi David, set out on the way to Lublin.

Although three years had gone by since his sixtieth birth-day, David of Lelov had almost no gray hairs and his large serene face was smoother and less furrowed. And despite the fact that he was as always a man of exceeding modesty and given to laughing and jesting, yet had his appearance attained a princely impressiveness. There were youths who in all seriousness said of him: "David, the King of Israel, lives and endures."

On the Sabbath which in this year immediately preceded the feast of Revelation, and during the third meal, the hasidim, including those who had come with their leader from Lelov as well as sundry from Pshysha with their leader, sat and stood about the tables in the house of study of the Seer. Also Yeshaya had come from Pshedbosh. David of Lelov observed his teacher from time to time. Nothing that had happened in all the years had changed the attitude to him in his heart. He was often amazed; he never passed judgment. To this day, had they come to him and said, the Seer is awe-inspiring, he would have answered that that was, in fact, the man's true nature. The years, of course, had taught him more concerning the nature of a man. At this moment too, sitting at the table, he regarded the Rabbi with a certain astonishment. He noticed that the eyes of the Rabbi, too, were fixed in a certain direction. Unswervingly they sought out the Yehudi. David could not interpret the expression of those eyes; he would have been tempted to say that they had none. Now they left the face of the Yehudi, not turning to another object, but gazing into unimaginable heights and depths. And now at last it seemed to David that they did assume an expression. What was it? He dared hardly trust his impression, and yet, and yet, thus had a boy once looked whom he had caught in the act of tearing out the brilliant wings of a butterfly. What had he, David, done on that occasion to prevent the wretched deed? He remembered well. He had uttered the shrill cry of the hawk, for the throat of David could imitate the cries of all the beasts he knew, and the boy had been startled and the cruel hand had been opened and the captive had flown. And on the instant David of Lelov struck his fist upon the Sabbath table. A wine bottle crashed to the floor.

The Seer started up. "Who did that?" he asked.

"It was I, David, the son of Isai," replied Rabbi David.

The Seer was taken aback but said no word. Only a little later he turned to David and asked with a smile upon his reluctant lips: "Was your father's name Isai?"

"My father?" said David, as though awakened from a dream, "no, Shelomo; Shelomo was the name of my father, may he rest in peace."

Nothing more that was noteworthy took place during this meal. Later on Bunam asked David why he had beaten the table with his fist. He explained: "I saw the Rabbi seeking the hall of my friend among the halls of the firmament, in order to rob him of the gifts of the spirit. So I had to shock him and drag him back to earth. It will have sufficed. No man undertakes a thing like that twice."

"But why," asked Bunam, "did you tell him that your father's name was Isai?"

"If only I knew that myself," said David and laughed.

"And do you realize that you violated the Sabbath?"

"Of course I did. But when life is in danger the law of the Sabbath is transcended. And did not the holy Ba'al-Shem-Tov say, that when *Zaddikim* descended from their proper spiritual level, it was a kind of death?" The two days of Shavuot also passed without anything remarkable. In an elaborate discourse at table the Seer treated of the signs which God reveals to man through history.

When, on the morning after the festival, the friends came to say farewell to the Rabbi, he received them in his old friendly spirit. They sat with him for a while. Then he turned to the Yehudi and said: "You know how your opponents beset me. And you know equally well that I love you and take pleasure in our community of spirit. But once upon a time, when I had the same experience in relation to my own teacher, Rabbi Elimelech, it was borne in upon me that there is no way of checking the power of hatred. And so I left Rabbi Elimelech and removed to another part of the land. And so I advise you in all kindness to come to Lublin no more." The Yehudi fell silent. Thereupon he said farewell to the Rabbi.

As they were going out Bunam asked him: "What will you do?" And David asked him: "Would it not, indeed, be for the best that you come here no more?"

But the Yehudi answered: "The Rabbi did not receive

from Rabbi Elimelech what I received from him. His influence has permeated me and can be separated from me no more. If the need arises to bear witness for God without respecting any man, I must oppose his word and his action. But no mortal power can separate me from him; only death can do that." Then he added softly: "Moreover the hour is late."

The friends said no more.

THE WOMAN AT THE CRADLE

Several months thereafter Schoendel was sitting one day beside the cradle of little Nehemya and was rocking him. The Yehudi had locked himself into the adjoining room, as was his custom from time to time when he wanted to be undisturbed. Suddenly the child awoke and began to wail at the top of its voice. In vain did the mother try to soothe it playfully and with caresses. It wailed all the more, not after the manner of a child, but like an adult who despairs of all consolation.

The door opened and Jaacob Yitzchak asked: "Schoendel, do you know why he weeps?"

Dismayed by this strange question she gave no answer.

"I will tell you the reason," he continued. "His voice as he weeps is the voice of an orphan." He went back to his room and locked the door behind him. Schoendel sat in confusion by the side of the cradle. But since she was accustomed to her husband's strange behavior, she attributed no special importance to it. The child had ceased weeping for a while. Now it raised its wailing voice; again and again she tried to soothe it, but in vain.

Once more the Yehudi entered and once more he asked: "Schoendel, do you know why he weeps now?"

She shrugged her shoulders.

"He weeps," said he, "because all his life long men will persecute him and he will be forced to drink the cup of this groundless hatred to the very dregs."

And once again the boy raised his wailing voice and once again the Yehudi asked his question.

"Oh, leave me alone!" Schoendel hissed.

But he was not to be deterred. "He weeps," he said, "because his sons, too, will be persecuted." He went into his room and closed the door behind him. Instantly the child ceased weeping and fell asleep.

This anecdote as here handed down was related by Schoendel herself.

MOURNING AND CONSOLATION

On an autumn day the news came to Pshysha from afar that the beloved of the people, Rabbi Levi Yitzchak of Berdichev, had died. They mourned for him together. It was not the mourning of individuals; they mourned him out of the depth of their community with each other, even as they had loved him out of that depth.

When they were sitting together in the evening one of them said: "It seems to me that concerning every matter which moves our community or weighs upon it a story can be derived from the life of Rabbi Levi Yitzchak, may his merit be our protection."

"Let us put that to the test," one of them proposed. "Let us mention one subject after the other and whoever knows a pertinent story from the life of the Rabbi of Berdichev, let him tell it."

They all agreed.

And this was the first saying that was said:

[237]

"Why is so much hostility directed against the hasidim of Pshysha?"

Bunam arose and related:

"During the period when in many places the enemies of the hasidic way carried on a veritable feud against Rabbi Levi Yitzchak on account of his way of serving, and inflicted whatever injury they could upon him, sundry thoughtful men wrote to Rabbi Elimelech and asked of him whence those people got their insolence. His reply was: 'Why are you surprised? It has ever been thus in Israel. Woe unto our souls! Were it not so, no people in the world could ever have succeeded in imposing a yoke on us!' "

Now came the second saying:

"No one tries to understand why we do not begin to pray until our souls are prepared for prayer."

Mendel arose and related:

"They told the Berdichever that a certain *hazzan* had become hoarse. He summoned the man to him and asked him: 'How did you happen to become hoarse?' 'It happened,' he answered, 'because I prayed before the reading stand.' 'Quite right,' said the Rabbi. 'When a man prays before the reading stand he gets hoarse; but he who prays before the living God does not get hoarse.' "

Thus, in succession, they proposed questions and told anecdotes.

Finally Moshe, the son of David of Lelov, who was visiting the city with his wife, the daughter of the Yehudi, spoke as follows:

"There are many who seek to interpret the things that are now coming to pass in the world. They assure us that these things are the birth pangs of the Messiah or something comparable. But we say that it is not given us to know whether this be so or not. Those others are of the opinion that we should try to exert mystic influences in order that the shape of things be such as it should be. But we here do not believe that we have any duty except to turn to God with our whole being and to seek to establish His kingdom by a communal life of justice, of love, of consecration. Those others reproach us for interfering with their plans. But we have recognized the facts that all those plans of theirs turn us aside from the one thing that God demands of us. What can we learn concerning this matter from the life of the Holy Rabbi of Berdichev?"

It was the Yehudi who related now:

"When Rabbi Levi Yitzchak recited the *Haggadah* at the *Seder* celebration and came to the passage concerning the four sons and to the passage concerning the fourth son who 'knew not how to ask,' he was wont to say: 'He who does not know how to ask is none other than I, Levi Yitzchak of Berdichev. I know not how to ask Thee, Lord of the universe, and if I did know how, I would yet not be able to bring myself to ask. How could I venture to ask Thee why everything happens as it does happen, why we are driven from one exile to another, and why our adversaries torment us thus! But in the *Haggadah* the father of the son who does not know how to ask is commanded: "Do thou reveal it to him!" And the *Haggadah* refers to Scripture in which it is written: "And thou shalt proclaim it to thy son." And am I not, *Ribbono shel 'olam*, Thy child? Yet I do not beseech Thee to reveal to me the mysteries of Thy way; I could not endure them. But this I pray Thee to reveal to me, deeply and clearly, what this thing that now happens means to me, what it demands of me, and what Thou, Master of the universe, wouldst communicate to me through it. Ah, I would not know why I suffer, only whether I suffer for Thy sake!' "

Everywhere Pshysha was the subject of conversation, above all, in those families from which sons or young husbands went, against the will of their elders, to learn of the Holy Yehudi. And now it became unmistakable that Pshysha was in a state of conflict with the rest of the hasidic world. This conflict originated often enough within a community in the form of a question of education. Next it would extend beyond the communal border and be transformed into widespread attack. Two instances which occurred in the spring and summer of the succeeding year will teach us something of its character.

Rabbi Baruch, the grandson of the Ba'al-Shem-Tov, used to be not a little emphatic about his assurance that he was incomparably superior to all the *Zaddikim* of his time. He said that he was called and chosen to be the supervisor of them all. His behavior was in accordance with his belief. He told everybody that the originator of all mystic teaching in the early talmudic ages, namely, Rabbi Simon ben Yohai, had appeared to him in vision and confirmed the fact that he was the "perfect human being."

"After my death," he once said, "the *Zaddikim* will bar the gates of Paradise against me. What will I do then? I will sit me down beside the gates and interpret the *Book of Radiance* in such a manner that the vital power will suffuse all worlds and the *Zaddikim* will open the gates in order to come out and listen to me. Then will I enter into Paradise and bar the gates and the *Zaddikim* will remain without."

On a certain occasion a disciple of Rabbi Baruch was in Pshysha and sat with the Yehudi at the latter's table. The Yehudi turned to him and said: "Greet your master from me in the words of Koheleth, the Preacher, which is Solomon: 'At the end of a matter the whole is heard.' In the end of things all the levels and all mystic lore and all miraculous

[240]

practices count for nothing; only the whole counts. And what is this whole? It is life in its simplicity. 'For this,' as the Preacher says further on, 'is the whole man.' We are bidden to be human, only human and nothing other than human — simple human beings, simple Jews. I will give this world and the world to come for a little Jewishness."

Soon thereafter a hasid from Lublin brought the Yehudi a letter from the Seer. The latter had visited Rabbi Baruch a long time ago and since that time had felt no friendship for him. In the letter it was written: "You did right."

The Yehudi reflected a long time before he understood to what the words referred. Then he wrote in answer: "I said nothing but what I learned of you, Rabbi. There was a time when you expected redemption to take place in a certain year with great confidence. When the year was over you said to me: 'All the simple people had experienced an entire return to good; there was no obstacle to redemption within them. The obstacle came from the higher men. By reason of their elevated qualities they could not attain to humility and therefore not to entire conversion.' "

When the Rabbi of Lublin read these words, he could not recall ever having said anything like this. It seemed to him that the Yehudi had once asked him whether this thing were not so and that he had answered in the affirmative, since he did indeed esteem humility beyond all other virtues. But, then, it was well known that the Yehudi quoted in his teacher's name not only what he had been taught by him but to whatever the teacher had merely given his assent.

The other example is an anecdote which in later years Rabbi Bunam was fond of telling his new students, that they might understand the character of his master's teaching.

"One morning the Holy Yehudi instructed me and several other hasidim to undertake a short journey. But he told us neither goal nor aim. I asked no questions, but gathered the people together and we left the town. Toward noon we

reached a village and entered the inn which was leased by
a Jew. I sat down alone in the anteroom. The others went
in and out and asked questions concerning the meat which
was to be served them. They wanted to know whether the
animal had been free from blemish and whether the *shohet*
had been a proper person and whether the salting and wash-
ing of the meat had been done thoroughly. At that there
arose a man in tattered garments, who had been sitting near
the oven in the host's room and who still held his wanderers'
staff in his hand. He spoke thus: 'Oh, ye hasidim! Ye make
a great to-do whether a thing is pure enough to enter your
mouths. But you are less concerned over the purity of that
which proceeds from your mouths.' I went nearer to look
more closely at the man. But he had already vanished, as
is the custom of Elijah upon his wanderings, as soon as his
work is done. We all understood to what end our teacher
had set our feet upon the way, and we returned to Pshysha."

MESSAGES

On a November day of that same year Rabbi Benjamin
made the following entry into his book:

"Since that time, three years and several months ago,
when the Rabbi rebuked me, I have not been privileged to
serve him as a scrivener, as was the case before, because he
took pleasure in my handwriting. But late yesterday evening
I was summoned to his presence; there was something to be
written.

"When I entered the Rabbi's room he was sitting at a
table on which three candles were burning. It was obvious
that he did not see me. His two hands lay on the table. I
looked upon them and was frightened, for they were trembling. I had never seen this thing happen to him before. The

[242]

two hands lay there and trembled continually. Suddenly the Rabbi himself looked upon his hands. In that instant the hands ceased trembling and lay still. Only now did he see that I was standing by his side. He stared at me for long, as though he did not recognize me. Then he pointed to two large white sheets of paper which lay ready on a little side table; he gave me a freshly trimmed nib and bade me to write first on the one sheet and next on the other sheet what he would dictate to me.

"On the first sheet I wrote somewhat as follows:

'To (here he bade me leave space for a very long name) in the North.

'The Emperor of the North is to be told in his dream:

'The hour has come in which you must publicly part company with the man who will render of no avail all your plans once he has obtained the mastery of the seas. Only in conflict with him can you achieve the goal which you have set yourself: to establish the continental hegemony of your empire, to unite the nations who have kinship with your own, to reconstitute the dignity of the peoples and of the throne, to cause to re-arise under your protection justice which has been overthrown. At his side you will shrivel and fade; in opposition to him you will be lord of the future.'

"On the second page I wrote somewhat as follows:

'To (again he bade me leave space for a very long name) in the West.

'The Sidonian, the captain of armies, now ruler of the West, is to be told in his dream:

'The hour has come when you must curb the pretensions of the man who calls himself your friend and yet stirs up the lands against you. You cannot gain the mastery of the seas until he will no longer dare to conspire against you with your enemies. Your great dream of a renewal of the East under the shadow of your hand cannot be fulfilled as long as your rival plots against you in the mask of an ally. Even the work which you have completed must be protected against his onslaughts. If you do not do this your empire will crumble after your death.'

"When I had done writing the Rabbi took the sheets from me and read them. Then he himself took up a pen, dipped it in other ink and wrote the names into the spaces I had left for them. Next he dried the sheets above the candle that stood in the middle and folded them. Now he bade me take the first sheet and burn it in the flame of the candle at the right and to gather the ashes in a pewter bowl ready for that purpose. When I had done this, he bade me take the second sheet and burn it in the flame of the candle that stood at the left and to gather the ashes in a copper bowl. Both of the bowls had covers. Then he said to me: 'Take the pewter bowl in your right hand and the copper bowl in your left and go through the door which I will open for you and go through the gate which I will open for you and go out into the street.'

"I said: 'And where do I go then, Rabbi, and what am I to do?'

" 'I am going with you,' he said.

"We went out. In front of the housedoor the Rabbi stood still for a little while. By the bright moonlight I saw that he turned his head abruptly to the right and to the left. 'Where is the East?' he asked suddenly.

" 'Did not the Rabbi recite his evening prayers?' I asked in astonishment. For I could not interpret his words otherwise than that he wanted to turn to the East in prayer.

" 'Show me!' he cried out impatiently.

"I showed him. Now he preceded me, but not toward the East; he went Northwest. I followed him. He walked quickly but with a shuffling and uneven gait. We left the city behind us and went in a northwesterly direction to the pool of Tshechov. Here he stopped and I stopped too. He leaned over the water.

" 'Benjamin!' he cried, as though he did not see me.

" 'Here I am, Rabbi,' said I.

" 'Benjamin,' he said, 'put the two bowls on the ground.'

"I did so.

" 'Take the bowl of pewter,' he went on, 'and pour the ashes into the water!' I did that, too.

"In the next moment the Rabbi slid on the slippery bank and would have fallen, had I not held him up. Again he stared at me for a while.

" 'Where is the East?' he asked me again.

"I was so confused by what had happened that I had to reflect for a moment before I could point in the right direction.

" 'Take the two bowls, the full one and the empty one,' said he.

"Now he went ahead of me toward the South until we came to the Cracow suburb. At this point he turned westward and we walked on till we came to a great gray stone all overgrown by moss. Here he stopped and so did I. He bent forward and laid one hand on the moist moss and left it there for a while. I observed that it trembled again but this time he paid no attention. He drew himself up.

" 'Benjamin,' he said, 'put the two bowls on the ground.'

"I followed his bidding.

" 'Take the copper bowl,' he said, 'and strew the ashes on the stone.'

"I obeyed. The air had been quite calm until now. But at this moment a sudden whirlwind arose and carried the ashes away. The Rabbi shivered.

" 'Benjamin,' he said, 'take the two bowls and let us go.'

"He preceded me on the way to his house. Sometimes his tread was steady, then it shuffled again. We entered his house and his room. I put the bowls back in their place, as he told me.

" 'You are to know, Benjamin,' said the Rabbi calmly,

[245]

'that from this hour on you share the secret and must reveal to no one what you have experienced and what you have done.'

"I said farewell and left. I do not feel that I have betrayed the secret by writing of it here, since I will give this book to no man to read."

THE GREAT JOURNEY

From that night on, in which the Yehudi had experienced the visitation of the *Shechinah* and of the two Winged Ones, a new expression had entered his speech. It was this: "Redemption is at hand." But he never omitted to precede or to follow the saying with the cry: "Return!" or: "It depends merely on our *teshuvah*, our return to good!" How is this to be interpreted? Now, as before, he was opposed to any determination of the last days. Yet he averred that redemption was at hand. He proclaimed the immediacy of redemption and yet declared at the same time that it was dependent upon our return to good. These two things are to be understood only within a mystic entirety, but this true mystery man can reveal not otherwise than through his own life and death. My own poor contribution to a right interpretation is the following: an hour dawns in which the redemption of the world is near; all that is needed is that we grasp this hour. But it cannot be grasped otherwise than by virtue of that entire turning of the human being from the way of man to the way of God, which we call *teshuvah*.

Yet there was another cry which, since that night, came ever and again from the lips of the Yehudi, which seems opposed to that. "Return," cried he, "return hastily, for the time is short and there is no leisure for new transformations, for redemption is at hand." The contradiction is an apparent one only. In their profound imperfection and alienation from God, men were not to console themselves with the hope that future wanderings of their souls might bring them to perfection. The time is short and the decision is to be made now. When he spoke thus, the Yehudi spoke concerning the troubles and the need of the individual human souls, whom he addressed, even though at the same time he spoke to many. It is furthermore to be considered that the words "the time is short" had another very special meaning for the man who spoke them and thought them since that night.

And now I must give an account of the strange journey, which he undertook during the summer after those messages had been sent out by the Rabbi of Lublin.

In the previous spring he visited once again the *Maggid* of Kosnitz. Seeing him, the Yehudi said to himself: "Now he looks like an aged angel — if angels could age. We imagine the faces of the angels to be smooth. But those who are messengers to the earth may not have smooth faces; surely they partake of our lacks, and *our* sorrows may dig furrows into *their* countenances too. And he?"

At the same moment the *Maggid* said to him: "You are to know, Holy Yehudi, that I now stand before God, in readiness like a messenger boy. But there is an anger, which I cannot eradicate from my heart."

After a while he spoke again: "Now comes the turning point."

He guessed at once, that the Yehudi took these words in the Messianic sense, and so he added: "There is much talk now of the birth-pangs of the Messiah. I don't talk about it any more. If there is a matter of which one can know nothing, silence is more seemly."

' He paused a moment and then continued: "I speak of that wicked man. It is being said that he is Gog or may become so. I know nothing of it and desire to have no dealings with it. God alone knows whether the time is ripe. It seems to me that the time is not ripe. At all events, it is not for us to render what is wicked even stronger than it is; rather is it our duty to oppose it. When a dragon like this one slays the peoples and poisons their souls, we should cry out to him: You will fall! And now he turns hither. Once again he would exploit the nation in whose midst we live by flattering hopes which he cannot fulfill. But this time the people will refuse to be exploited by him again; it will not yield to his flattery, and this will bring him to grief. Many men from this land of Poland will go with him; I know the individuals who will join him, but the people itself will not yield. Faith in him is dead. Among all nations there are masses who no longer believe in him. This means that the turning point of his destiny is upon him."

After a while he spoke again: "We must put an end to all the efforts on our side to check the downfall of this wicked man, else all that we have built up here will crash with his downfall. And whosoever in his thoughts and in his intentions attributes more weight to that wicked man than he has, every such one seeks to delay his fall. And he who does so will fall with his falling. And we will all fall, for we are all bound to each other. The work of the Holy Ba'al-Shem-Tov will fall, if his disciples deny him. For he came to conquer the evil in men's souls; but he who seeks to inspire this man with power helps to make mightier the evil in the human soul and in the world."

Again he was silent; he seemed weary of speaking; but soon it was as though new strength flowed into him. He continued: "The Rabbi of Lublin will not voluntarily desist from his plan. He must be made to know that his friends are not prepared to accompany him on that last and decisive stretch of road. Concerning me he knows it now. But I can do no more than tell him the truth. Perhaps you others can effect more than I. Do you go to Rymanov and tell Rabbi Menahem Mendel there what is to be said."

Doubtfully the Yehudi looked at him, but he could not contradict him. He perceived that between him and this small, seventy-year-old man with the face of an angel aged by suffering who faced him, there was an understanding deeper than any words of man could formulate.

"Are you willing to go on that journey?" the *Maggid* asked.

"I am willing," he answered.

"God bless you, my son," said the *Maggid*.

"There is still another monition that I would give you on your path," he added later, "but I do not know whether you will accept it. It is written: 'Return ye to Me and I will turn Me to you.' The prophet warns those who return to God, that their striving is not to limit itself to the setting straight of their own soul or the root of their soul; for this is still in the realm of the service of the self. True service is to return to God for the sake of the exile of the *Shechinah* and the exile of the community of Israel. Therefore it is said: 'Turn ye to Me' — turn ye not to your own rectification, but to rectification for My sake. Then I, too, will rectify your soul and mind and vital strength, 'and I will turn Me to you.'"

"I can well accept that," said the Yehudi, "only I must be permitted not to renounce showing people, as well as I can, the path they seek to pursue of themselves and for their own sake."

Sometime after his return from Kosnitz the Yehudi prepared himself for the journey to Rymanov. This journey was a strange one to him. The wanderings of his youth had been necessary, just because they had no set goal, but had been errings about. His later journeys to his teachers and others that he had undertaken had always had a significant aim. Now he went on a journey, a far one according to his notions, to this town in western Galicia, on an errand which he could not concretely grasp. Yet the way itself was goal enough to him. He was accompanied by Bunam, Perez and Yerachmiel. They did not travel straight through, but loitered in town after town. It has been justly observed that this journey became a triumphant procession and demonstrated, as hardly anything had yet done, that this movement toward a more living piety, which is called the hasidic movement, had taken deep hold upon the people. We must not fail to add what was most important in the journey to the Yehudi himself. His heart was less inclined to triumph than it had ever been. To him every Jewish community through which he passed was a Pshysha in which he felt he should accomplish in the few days or hours something comparable to what he had accomplished in his congregation in the course of seventeen years. And he succeeded in doing so. Wherever he came there arose a great Messianic yearning and a great willingness to repent. His spoken words had this effect, but his silence had it, too; his passionate insistence had it, but also his reserve. Generations later there was to be found in those places not only the recollection (unbroken till yesterday), but also the living trace of those days. Yet he himself was not satisfied. "True, I stir people," he said to Bunam, "but I cannot actually take them on my shoulder. The hour is late. And there are so many. I ought to be able to send out messengers. But even if I could do so, people would not listen to them as they do to me. Why not? Because they are not 'famous'? Ah, what a pitiful thing is this thing called fame! How well do I understand the Holy *Maggid* of Mesritsh, who, when he became known in the world, besought God to announce to him by what sin he had become thus guilty!"

They stopped in Ropshitz, too. Rabbi Naftali, now a very well known man, not only went to meet the Yehudi many miles, but commanded his followers strictly to show himself no kind of reverence during the presence of this guest, to whom he desired to be wholly subordinated. What moved him thereto has been handed down to us. It will be remembered that Rabbi Naftali's understanding and his wit did

[250]

not prevent him from seeing the whole of existence as circling about miracle and counter-miracle — if we were not speaking of such saintly people, we would be tempted to say magic and counter-magic. It had been experienced in Lublin and heard said from Pshysha, that the Yehudi was the counterforce. In the meantime he had grown ever more powerful; now he was evidently faring forth into the world in order to bring his old adversaries to an accounting. For the accomplishment of such an object it is obviously necessary that the victim offer a point of attack. This was to be avoided at any cost. Naftali did not so much as dare to enter his own house without having obtained the Yehudi's permission. He behaved as though he were one of the Yehudi's hasidim and were a guest with him here. The Yehudi did not understand this astonishing demeanor. Before continuing his journey he paid a visit to Naftali's mother and conversed with her concerning the various interests of the establishment. Naftali listened in some anxiety, lest his mother by one of her answers offer the point of attack. But all went well and the guests took their leave. Naftali said that he himself intended to proceed to Rymanov next day. Since he did not intend to stop anywhere he would in all likelihood be there ahead of them.

When they approached Rymanov the Yehudi's carriage could scarcely pass. The road was cluttered with the vehicles of those who had come to see him from near and far and with the people on foot who had come out of the town to bid him welcome. The walls and roofs of the town were thronged. The six-year-old son of Rabbi Menahem Mendel came running to his father and cried: "The Messiah has come!" This austere man, who was offended by the least disorder, could not but regard this tumult as a kind of insurrection which symbolized the subversive character of the age. Looking out of the window he expressed his irritation frankly. But then he, too, left the house and went to meet the guests. He welcomed them with the restrained friendliness characteristic of him. His true opinion was mirrored in the demeanor of Rabbi Hirsch, his "servitor." The latter, who had started life as a journeyman tailor but had then taken to study, had now for long served the Rabbi admirably, had studied under him like no other and was later, as is well known, to be his successor. He stood at the door of Rabbi Menahem Mendel's house. When the guests passed there he greeted the Yehudi before his master's eyes as condescendingly as though the latter had been a drover.

Later in the day Rabbi Menahem Mendel sent a messenger to the inn and bade the guests dine with him. When the messenger had departed Bunam said to the Yehudi: "You have sometimes said, Rabbi, that in a difficult case which puzzles the physician you send for me, in order to get the opinion of the apothecary. Now I want you to listen carefully to what the apothecary tells you. Assuredly in comparison to the physician he is but what a clerk is to the head of the house. But they told me in Germany that a clerk who, from his vantage point, has mastered many business details, is often a better judge of what will profit and what will not than the head of the house. Therefore listen to me! At table he would invite you to interpret Scripture. Take my advice and utter not even half a word! This is not the right business for you!"

The Yehudi was a little surprised at Bunam's insistence, but he understood it well enough. If Rabbi Menahem Mendel were to attribute but little weight to his words of interpretation, he would rebelliously blame him for having uttered things false and impertinent; were he to choose to regard them as weighty, he would be rebelliously angry with him for having ventured to speak more elevatedly than became him. The Yehudi understood that "Lublin" was here, too. Undoubtedly the *Maggid* had known that too, and yet he had sent him here.

At table all things happened as Bunam had foretold. But the Yehudi did not explain his refusal to speak by assigning an empty pretext. He said: "I cannot speak words of instruction at your table, for I see well that you harbor a grudge in your heart against me."

Rabbi Menahem Mendel looked at him in surprise, but the tension went out of his features. "It is true," said he, "that I cannot forgive you for the way in which you have acted toward our teacher, the Rabbi of Lublin."

"What action is it," asked the Yehudi, "which you cannot forgive?"

"You rebelled against him," said Rabbi Menahem Mendel, "and took his disciples away from him and criticized him arrogantly."

"Who is it that bears witness against me?" asked the Yehudi.

Rabbi Mendel looked about among those at the table. There sat three or four of the men who were well known to be opponents of the Yehudi. But upon the countenance of none was there a readiness to speak. Yissachar Baer, who was present, too, opened his lips. But Rabbi Mendel waved him aside and looked at those others. At last he fixed Naftali with his glance.

"Rabbi Naftali is to bear witness," he said.

Naftali started. Now the thing he had feared had come about. At the very next moment a thing happened to him for which he was wholly unprepared — one of those things which he, being an admirer of the miraculous, had from his youth up counted among the high evidences of the Divine Presence, although it had never occurred to him that such a thing could be experienced by him. He felt a mighty pressure rising from his very marrow into his head. And this pressure was a command, inarticulate but unmistakable: "the truth!" And next the actual words were formulated in his brain: "I must speak the truth; I must no longer be afraid,

[253]

but speak the truth." And now, when clarity of thought, passionately suffused by that inner command, returned to him, he was suddenly aware that the truth was something altogether different from what, through all these years, he had told the Rabbi of Lublin as a matter of course. Something quite different? Nay: the very contrary! If he had anything to fear now it would be from the other side, not from the Yehudi. But all fear had departed from him. A great sense of freedom entered into him. It was quite different from the freedom of his independent reason, of which he had been so proud, because it was his own. This new freedom poured itself into him and yet it was himself, it was his own self that was free.

He raised his head — this whole process had lasted but an instant — and said: "According to my knowledge the Rabbi of Pshysha has incurred no guilt toward the Rabbi of Lublin."

He chanced to look at Bunam who was sitting opposite him and saw the latter's big, yellowish eyes with their declining power of vision fixed upon him. He lowered his head. There was complete silence in the room. Rabbi Menahem Mendel also made no comment. After a while they began to speak of other things.

After dinner the Yehudi asked for permission to return to his inn. His followers, at the request of Rabbi Mendel, remained a while longer. "Did you mark him well?" he asked those about him, when the guest had gone, "Like Rabbi Zeira, exactly like Rabbi Zeira!" The hasidim naturally knew what he meant, namely, that the soul of that talmudic master, who had gone from Babylon to Palestine and fasted an hundred fasts in order to forget the teachings of the Babylonian houses of study, had reappeared on earth in the person of the Yehudi. But what was it that was common to those two? Yissachar Baer remembered how he had once entered the room of the Yehudi and found him almost stripped leaning over the flaming fire of the chimney. He seemed almost disembodied in that hour. And was it not related of Rabbi Zeira, that he sat on a burning oven and was not burned until he was disturbed. Naftali remembered another anecdote: how Rabbi Zeira permitted a malicious butcher from among those who had returned from Babylon to beat him, when he had desired to buy something of him, without cursing him or so much as reproving him, in the opinion that such was the custom. The disciples from Pshysha thought still other thoughts. Was it not handed down that Rabbi Zeira had had the friendliest relations with a gang of wild and ungovernable oafs, who dwelt in that neighborhood, in order to persuade them to repent? Was it not this which was taught and practiced by the Yehudi? Was one not to take the evil upon one's own shoulders?

Next day the Yehudi had a conference with Rabbi Menahem Mendel. "The great conflagration," he said, "of which for some time we have been seeing the reflection in the circle of the heavens, now approaches us. And you, you and the Rabbi of Lublin, think only of fanning its flame. What is to become of us? The other peoples can seek to protect themselves; we stand, as it were, bound and an easy prey to that burning, which our leaders seek to intensify."

"It were well," cried Rabbi Mendel, "that Jewish blood flow until one can wade therein up to the knees from Prystyk to Rymanov, if thereby our exile be brought to an end and our redemption dawn."

"But supposing," said the Yehudi, "that this fire is nothing but a fire of destruction? God can kindle such a fire and blow upon it, too, and know what He does. But we? What gives us the right to wish the evil an increase of power and lend it such increase, if we may? Who tells us whom we serve thereby, the Redeemer or the adversary? Who dare be bold enough to speak today in the words of the prophet: 'The word of the Eternal came unto me'?"

"Redemption, you say," the Yehudi continued. "Do you not see under your very eyes immeasurable possibilities of serving the cause of redemption? Behold, Rabbi, how in front of you a great tree grows heavenward out of the dark depth of the earth. It is covered with young foliage, each leaf is a soul from among Israel, thousands of souls, tens of thousands, and each soul waits for you, Rabbi, to set it to rights, in order that the tree may grow into the realm of redemption!"

"It is too late in time," said Rabbi Mendel, "to think of the individual soul."

The Yehudi replied: "Never will a work of man have a good issue if we do not think of the souls whom it is given us to help, and of the life between soul and soul, and of our life with them and of their lives with each other. We cannot help the coming of redemption if life does not redeem life."

Rabbi Mendel was silent. Whenever he was silent as he was now, he was accustomed to lower his eyes, and this lowering of the eyes had the effect of robbing him who spoke of his voice. The conversation soon broke off. They said farewell to each other.

Hirsch, the "servitor" who had shown the Yehudi no respect in Rabbi Mendel's house, nor accompanied him home, went to the inn after evening prayers. His master had gone to bed early, as he always did, in order to be able to get up at midnight. Hirsch had been told on the way that the guests had departed. Nevertheless, he thought he would be able to pick up some gossip about their goings-on. When he arrived, the string of vehicles of those who wanted to accompany the Yehudi was no longer there. The driver of the foremost wagon had been of the opinion that the guests had driven ahead. In point of fact, the Yehudi and his disciples were still here. Now the two, the Yehudi and the "servitor," were walking up and down the street in converse. The Yehudi, according to a favorite custom of his, held the girdle of his companion. Later on, when Hirsch would tell the story, he would say at the end: "He got nothing out of me; I got everything out of him that I wanted to know." After the conversation Hirsch had begged the Yehudi to bless him in order that he might be able to pray with true fervor. "What more do you want?" the Yehudi answered. "All greatness and honor are in store for you." Thereupon the guests departed.

CANDLES IN THE WIND

Rabbi Benjamin writes:

"When, that summer, news concerning the journey of the Holy Yehudi came from Rymanov, the Rabbi summoned me to his presence. Upon my entering he said to me without salutation: 'I forbid you to enter my house hereafter.' I said: 'All I ask you to do is to tell me why.' He said: 'You have divulged the messages, which you wrote down according to the words of my mouth.' I said: 'I have not divulged them. And though you are the leader of this generation and I less than nothing, may God, Lord of Spirits, judge between you and me!' And I went out. What I now set down in this book concerning events in the house of the Rabbi I know only from the lips of others. That applies to the following.

"Rabbi David related to me that late in the afternoon on the eve of Yom Kippur, which this year fell on a Sabbath, the Rabbi had lit two candles and set them in candlesticks. Then he had opened a window and had placed on its sill the holders with the burning candles. There they had stood and stood and the flames of the candles had not been extinguished. That year, as every year, Rabbi David passed the Days of Dread in Lublin. When, as annually at the close of the festival, he entered the Rabbi's house in order to take leave of him, the Rabbi came forward to meet him and said: 'A good

[257]

week to you, dear Rabbi David! Yesterday I girded myself
to uproot two mountains, but I did not succeed.' Rabbi
David said farewell and journeyed on to Pshysha, as he did
every year to pass the feast of Succot there. The holy Yehudi
met him on the threshold of his own house. 'Rabbi David,
my dear comrade,' he cried, 'hear what I have dreamed!
A storm wind was blowing through the world and two candles
stood in the great wind and burned. And the one candle
was you and the other was I.' "

KOSNITZ AND NAPOLEON

On the eve of Purim, 1812, when the *Maggid* of Kosnitz
in reciting the Book of Esther reached the words *napoi tippol*,
"fall, thou wilt fall," which Haman's wife and his friends
addressed to him, he interrupted himself and exclaimed:
"Napoleon *tippol*," (Napoleon, thou wilt fall). He paused
for a while; then he resumed the recitation of the *Megillah*.

It was at this time that Napoleon divided the *grande armée*
for the invasion of Russia, which was announced a week later.
First there was named the Polish corps, which was under
the command of Prince Josef Poniatowski, the nephew of
the last king of Poland. "Poniatowski," Napoleon observed
later on at St. Helena, "was the real king. He combined all
the necessary claims and gifts; yet he remained silent."
This meant that the prince remained loyal to the end to the
man whom he had decided to follow, without asking for
himself what he might have asked.

At the end of March he received the news of the imperial
command in Warsaw. He had just undergone a serious illness and his convalescence was slow. When the news came
he immediately set up a will "for the possibility of a sudden
death." Before he began mobilizing his troops he took a

short trip. It is related that he took this trip to Kosnitz and that his only companion was his Jewish bodyguard. It was not the first time that he had visited the *Maggid*. He never confided to anyone the subject of their consultation. But there is a rumor, based apparently on utterances of the bodyguard, that the *Maggid* not only foretold to the prince the events of that campaign, but also told him that he would soon fall in battle, and that he addressed him as marshal — a title which was given to Poniatowski, only one day before he fell, for his distinguished conduct during the battle of Leipzig. What is certain is this, that Poniatowski, hitherto a man who delighted in life, passed the period between this interview and his own death in a mood of somber resignation. As in the anecdote concerning the visit of Czartoryski to the *Maggid* we hear of a brown dog, so in this anecdote concerning the prince we hear of a dark gray mare of whom the *Maggid* predicted that she would drop a snow white foal. It is further related that it was this white horse which, eighteen months later, bore the mortally wounded marshal into the Elster river.

Several weeks after Poniatowski had received the imperial command in Warsaw, that is, on the evening of May 16th, Napoleon reached Dresden. Not only the people but the soldiers boasted that he would march across Russia to India. On all the roads pyres were lit to light his march. He stopped in Dresden, before joining his army, to meet the monarchs of Austria and Prussia. "After a battle or two," he said on that occasion, "I shall be in Moscow and Alexander will be on his knees before me."

On the very morning of that day, which was the day of the eve of the festival of Revelation, Rabbi Abraham Yehoshua Heshel had come to Kosnitz to visit the *Maggid*, who was a friend of his youth. A tradition tells us that this man was the one to whom, in addition to those other three, the Rabbi Elimelech on his deathbed had passed on one of his powers, namely, the power of that mouth from which issued reconciliation and judgment. It was said of him that he had a goldsmith's scale in his mouth. This includes his characteristic of speaking nothing unnecessary, although he esteemed as necessary such strange and mysterious fabulation. With the *Maggid*, to be sure, he could communicate without many words.

When he entered the room in which the *Maggid* was reposing they looked at each other in silence. Nevertheless, Rabbi Heshel asked how he felt.

"At present," the *Maggid* answered, "I am a man of war. I guard here in my bed the five pebbles which the young David took from the brook for his sling when he went forth against Goliath, the Philistine."

During the night following that day, which had been passed in study and prayer, the two friends remained together. Two hours after midnight the *Maggid* said to Rabbi Heshel: "Pray with me." It is related that the *Maggid* stood in front of his praying stand for the space of thirteen hours. Early he prayed the morning prayer; he read from the Scripture; he recited the liturgical additions of the Festival, and again stood in prayer from two o'clock that night until three o'clock the following afternoon. When he was asked to lie down and rest, he answered in his favorite verse: "They who wait for God receive strength in return."

On the next day, which was the second day of Shavuot, Alexander received Napoleon's ambassador. Upon a map he pointed to the extreme limit of his Asiatic realm, where straits sunder the continents, and said with gentle pride: "If the Emperor Napoleon is determined upon war and fortune does not favor the cause of justice, he will have to go to this point in order to find peace." The Frenchman characterized the attitude of the Czar as "dignified without any braggadocio," wholly different from that which he had shown during similar negotiations earlier in the war.

[260]

Four months thereafter, in the night before Yom Kippur, a grandson of the *Maggid*, the young Chaim Yechiel, stood on the street in front of his grandfather's house. He was a pupil of the Seer, but in his heart he was devoted to the Yehudi. He used to tell how one glance had sufficed him to recognize what manner of man the Yehudi was. The thought of the irreconcilable conflict between Lublin and Pshysha troubled his heart with particular intensity on this night. After returning from the synagogue he sat for hours in his white shroud, which he had worn according to the regulation, in his room and sadly reflected on these circumstances which were so inaccessible to the goodness of his will. Finally he could bear no longer to be indoors and, still clad in his shroud, went out into the September night and walked up and down for a long time. When he returned home and stood in front of the *Maggid's* house, he saw in the latter's bedroom, on the floor above, a broad bright red reflection rise from the floor to the ceiling. It was too straight and too rigid to be taken for fire. It could have been the reflection of a flame. He ran upstairs and opened the door. The room was in total darkness, and his grandfather was obviously asleep. Yechiel went out and softly closed the door behind him. In the morning he told the *Maggid* all about it.

"You had a glimpse of the vision in my dream," the latter said.

Uncomprehending the youth stared at him.

"I dreamed of the Prince of Fire," the aged *Maggid* added. Beyond this he said nothing.

That was the night on which the city of Moscow, which Napoleon had just entered at the head of his army, was swept by that mighty equinoctial storm which blew a conflagration from street to street and from quarter to quarter.

About three months later Rabbi Naftali, just as he had done in 1809, journeyed to Rymanov, Lublin, and Kosnitz, in the same order as on that other journey. When he heard the news of the battle of the Beresina River, the feeling that blood enough had flown took entire hold of the soul of this man who had become a changed man since that table conversation of the year before. But since he was aware of his own powerlessness in the matter, he sat out on the road to Rymanov. Rabbi Menahem Mendel had been his teacher before the Seer; even now he could not do other than begin with him. Also, he was of the opinion that Rabbi Mendel must by now have recognized his error and so would be the more easily moved to lend his influence toward bringing to an end the destruction raging in the world. But when he stood before the Rabbi of Rymanov he was frightened. That countenance which had once reflected the very peace of heaven was cruelly contorted. Looking upon it, he dared hardly to utter his request. In point of fact the Rabbi soon interrupted him.

"He will get on top again and make them suffer for this!"

"But Rabbi," Naftali objected, "can his cause be identified with our own? Is it not written: 'Not by arms and not by might, but by My spirit?' Dare we wage or support any combat save that of the spirit against force?"

Again he was shocked, for he observed that the Rabbi had not heard him, but was, as it were, listening for a sound in the distance.

Next Naftali repaired to Lublin. Here he was quite differently received. The Rabbi welcomed him with so great a readiness of spirit as though he had expected him. Soon after their meeting he took him upstairs to his room. And now, as though it had all been a few weeks ago, he took up the conversation where it had been left off thirteen years before.

"I told you, did I not, Rabbi Naftali," he reminded him, "that 'North' as used by Ezekiel in his prophecy concerning Gog is to be understood in its literal meaning. Thither he had first to go, before being brought to the hills of Israel where the bow was to be wrenched from his left hand and the arrows from his right be hurled upon the earth."

"It would seem to me, Rabbi," Naftali answered tentatively, "as though he had lost both bow and arrows already."

"There you err," said the Rabbi, "he will arise again in his might."

"Is it, then, not yet approaching the end?" Naftali asked. His heart contracted. Once again he was surprised when he became aware of it. For his heart had been a hard heart, and ever and again he was surprised when it was stirred. But already the Rabbi broke the silence which had lasted several instants.

"Let us not speak of the end," he cried, "ere the end comes!"

Then Naftali did a thing which he would not have believed himself capable of doing only a little while ago. Turning to the Rabbi he spoke the word which no one had hitherto spoken. "Have not our sages warned us?" said he. "Have they not warned us: 'Seek not to press for the end!'"

From under his lifted brows the eyes of the Rabbi reproved him. But Naftali was inviolable now.

He was journeying to Kosnitz. "How often have I set out on the road to Kosnitz," he reflected on the way, "but never do I reach it. I really get to Rymanov and even as far as Lublin, but never do I reach Kosnitz!"

But when he stood in front of the *Maggid*, the latter saluted him as follows: "How is it with you, Rabbi Naftali? Your forehead gleams like purest silver."

Naftali understood that he was being accepted, and once again he was astonished. And another thing was revealed to him, that here there was no need of words, as there had been in the other two places. And yet he knew that it was well and right that he was here.

On Friday evening, before the *Maggid* intoned the Sabbath psalm: "It is a good thing to give thanks unto the Lord," he said: "The whole world is still discussing how the French were forced back across the Beresina River. But we do not speak thereof. We say" — and now with great emphasis he intoned the verses of the psalm — "we say: 'When the wicked spring up as the grass, and all the workers of iniquity flourish, it is that they might be destroyed forever. But Thou, O Lord, art exalted in world-time. For, lo, Thine enemies, O Lord, for, lo, Thine enemies shall perish; all the workers of iniquity shall be scattered.' "

Later on at table he said: "We have nothing to do with Frenchmen and we have nothing to do with Russians; we ask only who is the wicked, who works iniquity, who is God's enemy. We arise against that power which awakens and nourishes wickedness and iniquity and hostility to God in the souls of men. For wickedness and iniquity are in the souls of all men, in ours as well as in theirs. The combat against God's enemies is the combat against that power which causes wickedness and iniquity to wax great in the human soul. When we see them burgeon and bloom, then we know what they would be at. As they fade, all the powers of evil which they have concentrated are scattered. But Thou, O Lord, art exalted in world-time. There is no covenant between God and Belial."

The Sabbath thereafter was the one on which is read that section of Scripture which treats of Jethro's visit to Moses. When the *Maggid* came to the words of the Scripture: "*Nabol tibbol*, thou shalt wither and all this people that is with thee," he repeated the words thrice, and only then read on. But he concluded as follows his discourse at the third Sabbath meal: "It is written: 'Thou shalt wither and all this people that is with thee.' This saying is said to us. We, the hasidim of the land, we shall wither if, in our attempt to press for the end of things, we neglect the struggle against the enemies of God, each in his own soul and in his own life, and all of us together in our souls and in our lives, until the victory is won."

"I have truly reached Kosnitz at last," Naftali reflected. When he went to say farewell, a messenger from Lublin stood in the room. Naftali was about to withdraw, but the *Maggid* bade him stay. In front of him lay an open letter which he was reading. He read very slowly. It was obvious that he reread certain sentences twice or three times. His face wore an expression of melancholy; but there was no anger in it. Finally he folded the letter again and closed it.

"Give this message to my friend, the Rabbi of Lublin," he said to the messenger, "that it is not fitting for such a creature as man to return an answer to such a question as his. There is an Other who must answer it."

CONCERNING THE TELLING OF PARABLES

After the homecoming of the Yehudi from Rymanov, the community of Pshysha drew more closely together. It was, as though, according to its feeling, it had extended itself too daringly into the world and must now reintegrate itself. And this inner life was intensified for quite a period thereafter. Never had the sense of communion between the master and his disciples, never had that of the disciples among themselves been so strong and so intimate as during this year in which the Kosnitzer *Maggid* fought to the finish his fight against Napoleon. It was clear that it had been more deeply recognized than ever before that nothing can be concretely realized in the world if the individual does not find his realization in the community.

One thing there was that Pshysha had taken over from Lublin: the telling of stories in the night after the Sabbath, after the "farewell repast of the Queen"— with this difference, that in Pshysha it was not only the Rabbi who told tales, but everyone. Thus they sat together on a certain winter night, soon after Naftali's visit to Kosnitz, and spoke to each other in parables. David of Lelov, too, was at that time the guest of his old friend and comrade. The series was begun by the youngest this time. The parables were genuine similitudes, that is to say, each had a meaning which concerned the community, either all the members or individuals among them, but it was shaped in such a fashion that whatever concerned any at the very core of his being also concerned all.

Mendel of Tomashov prefaced his parable with the observation that he had heard it from an itinerant preacher. He spoke in his terse manner, pausing after each few words. "Two merchants had brought their wares to a city in a single wagon, each having his in a separate wooden box. The boxes were of about the same size. In the one box, carefully wrapped in cloths and bedded on straw, there was a small casket filled with precious objects; the other box was packed with iron utensils. When they had arrived in the city the dealer in jewels ordered a porter to bring his box to his house. When he was about to pay the porter, the latter complained. He demanded a higher payment for having carried so heavy and wearisome a burden. 'The boxes have been exchanged,' answered the merchant. 'If the box was as heavy as all that, it was not mine.' That is, as it is written: 'Not me hast Thou called, Jacob, that Thou hast troubled Thyself for my sake, Israel.' If you grow weary, says God, you have not had Me in mind. My wares are no burden that wearies."

Delighted and anxious at once, all eyes turned to the Yehudi. A tranquil seriousness, serene rather than stern, lay upon his countenance; his glance had become that of one who knows, but no, he was not weary. And there was none who was weary among them all.

One disciple after another told his tale. The last to tell

one was Bunam. Slowly he raised his eyes, which were threatened with blindness, and looked about him.

"Once upon a time," he said, "there was a great lord who had a race horse in his stables, which he treasured above all his other possessions and which he caused to be well guarded. The door of the stable was latched and locked and a guard stood continuously in front of it. On a certain night a restlessness overcame this lord. He went to the stable. There sat the watchman quite evidently reflecting intensely upon some matter.

" 'What are you pondering about?' the lord asked.

" 'I am wondering and wondering about this,' answered the man. 'When a nail is driven into the wall what becomes of the mortar?' "

" 'That's a fine thing to think about,' said the lord.

"He went back into the house and went to bed. But he could not sleep. After a while he could endure it no longer and went back to the stable. Again the watchman sat in front of the door and meditated.

" 'What are you thinking about now?' asked the lord.

" 'I am wondering,' said he, 'what becomes of the dough that should have been in the holes of the doughnuts?'

" 'That's a fine thing to think about,' the lord agreed with him.

"Again he went back and again he could not rest and for the third time he went to the stable. The watchman was sitting in his place and thinking ever so hard.

" 'And what are you thinking so busily about now?' the lord asked.

" 'I am just wondering,' the other answered. 'There is the door, well locked and latched, and here I sit in front of it and watch, and the horse is stolen. How did that come about?' "

The story was received with joyous acclamation. For it did in very truth embody in image the teaching of Pshysha:

delusive is every thought which deflects man from the service of the Everliving One.

The last one to tell a story was David of Lelov. As always, when he narrated, his hearers felt that there was no other possible expression of what he desired to express than through the tale he told.

"Even as Mendel," he began, "so I can only repeat what was told me. Once upon a time I was going, as I did year after year, along the long road from Lelov to Lisensk to Rabbi Elimelech. Over my shoulder I was carrying two meal scoops which I was taking to him as a Pesach present to be used for the baking of the unleavened bread from the wheat well guarded and selected out of the last harvest. Not far from the end of my journey I passed through a forest which was familiar to me from my having so often pursued the self-same path. And what do you think? All of a sudden I was lost. I ran hither and yon and found no way and no outlook. Hour followed hour and I was still wandering about. And what do you think I did in the end? I actually wept.

"While I was weeping a man came along and asked me: 'Why do you weep, my dear son?'

" 'Oh,' I lamented and did not cease from weeping, 'year after year I go on this same road to visit my teacher and know every inch of it and I am as well acquainted with this forest as with the street in which I live, and suddenly I get lost and know not where to turn. There must be more here than meets the eye and very evidently there is something within me which is not as it should be.'

" 'Be comforted,' said the man, 'and come with me; together we shall find a way out.'

"Hardly had we gone a few paces when I observed that we approached the edge of the forest.

" 'Do you understand now,' the man asked, 'what that means: together?'

" 'I know it now,' I replied.

[268]

" 'I will tell you something else to remember on your way,' he added. 'If you want to join two pieces of wood to each other in such a fashion that they become one, you must first smooth them both down. But if the protuberances in the one piece fit exactly into the hollows of the other and vice versa, then no smoothing down is necessary. Such is true togetherness!' "

"Yes, such is indeed togetherness!" they all cried.

But Yissachar Baer added: "That man was the prophet Elijah!"

They talked and fell silent and talked again. Then they all begged the Yehudi that he too should tell a tale.

"I will gladly do so," he said with a smile, "but it is no parable that I tell you today.

"A hasid after his death came before the Heavenly Judgment Seat. He had strong advocates and a favorable decision seemed assured, when a great Angel appeared on the scene and accused him of a sin of omission.

" 'Why did you omit to do what you were bidden to do?' he was asked.

"The hasid found no answer but this: 'My wife was the cause of it.'

"The Angel laughed at the top of his voice: 'That is, to be sure, a very fine justification!'

"Sentence was pronounced. A punishment was meted out to the man for his sin, but the Angel was forced to undergo the test of being incarnated on earth and of becoming the husband of a woman."

The Yehudi himself laughed at his story. The laughter was clear and mild.

Several weeks before Pesach there was a great tumult in the house of the Seer. Confidential messengers were sent forth to all the great *Zaddikim* of the period, who had studied with him under the *Maggid* of Mesritsh or under Rabbi Schmelke of Nikolsburg or under Rabbi Elimelech. A messenger was sent to only one of his own disciples, and that was the Yehudi. The message sent forth was a single message. All of its recipients were invited to fix their entire souls upon the coming of redemption all during the celebration of the *Seder*, during each part of the ceremony and each utterance, and to do so in a very special way, according to very special attitudes and aims concerning which the Seer provided precise directions. In this message the beginning of the celebration and the time which was to be devoted to each part of it were determined by hours and minutes. With an emphasis which rose to a cry of adjuration, an appeal was made and a command was issued to the common will that, in spite of separation in space, all this should be done by universal consent, so that nowhere there should protrude a personal expression or gesture. Usually the conduct of this night was largely left to the impulses of the master of the house; this time a perfect circle unified in attitude, action, and speech was to bind together place to far place. The thing which our narrator, Rabbi Benjamin, had perceived twice seven years ago, on the day of the battle of Megiddo, namely, that the souls of the assembled hasidim, melting into one, stretched out mighty hands into the darkness of the decision, this thing was now to take place in the houses of the great hasidim. But this time the concentrated soul of the community could not be fixed upon a simultaneously occurring event. The only way of offering to all a common goal of vision, upon which every soul could concentrate, was to offer them that which from the beginning was the aim of their common and passionate desire: the coming of redemption, come as it may. At bottom, in fact, nothing other was demanded than that which everyone as a rule attempted on this night, namely, by the might of one's yearning to throw a bridge between that deed which God performed in the liberation from Egypt to that awaited deed of His, which as yet has no name. Only in this sense was it possible for the Rabbi to address himself to all, including the Yehudi. Many of the recipients of the message were not wholly unaware of the renunciation, though but for a single night, inherent in this kind of demand; all perceived that such a message could have been sent forth by none other than the acknowledged leader of the generation.

None of the messengers who returned brought a refusal. The *Maggid* of Kosnitz, to be sure, had received the communication in silence, but he had offered no objection. The Yehudi had said nothing but: "Thank God that I may obey." One man only had reacted in an almost incomprehensible way. That was the Rabbi of "Kalev," which is the North Hungarian small town of Negy-Kallo. While the message was being communicated to him he had, according to his custom and seeming scarcely to listen, hummed to himself a little song. He gave the document which described the special attitudes desired only a cursory glance.

"Oh well, we do it just about that way," he had then said. With that the messenger had to content himself.

Rabbi Yitzchak Eisik of Kalev was a singer of love songs. The songs treated of love and of the yearnings of parted lovers. He heard them from Hungarian shepherds, whose company he liked because in his childhood he had himself been a herder of geese. Then delicately he re-wrought the songs. It was not his intention to add an alien element to them but to reconstitute their great original meaning which had been transformed among the shepherd people and which was this, that the origin of all love is God's love for His

Shechinah; all love points to this love and may receive its consecration therein. The shepherds sang of their far-away sweethearts. Now it was a great dense forest which separated the lovers, and now it was a high steep mountain that arose between them; but always the song ended with the removal of the obstacle and the uniting of those who belonged together. Not much needed to be added to this imagery. Was not our exile in very truth a dark forest in which one wandered and wandered and saw no end; was it not an immeasurably high mountain which one climbed with wounded feet only to see arise above one more jagged crag?

> "Were I but snatched from exile's pain,
> So that we two might meet again!"

Thus sang the Rabbi of Kalev. But it was not his singing alone. Every gesture of his expressed the deeply felt desire that those who are parted be united again. Among all the periods of the year the night of Pesach was the most precious to him; for it was evident that this, above all others, was the time of liberating grace. The daughter of Rabbi Hirsch of Zydatshov, the disciple of the Seer, who had married a son of the Rabbi of Kalev, once told her father that on the last Pesach night her father-in-law had waited until eleven o'clock to begin the *Seder* ceremony. At that hour he had opened a window. "Thereupon," she narrated, "a carriage came driving up, drawn by two horses silvery white. In it sat three aged men and four aged women of princely aspect and clad in princely garments, and the Rabbi went out to them and I saw how they embraced him and kissed him. Then I heard the crack of a whip and the carriage clattered off. The Rabbi closed the window and sat down at the *Seder* table. I did not dare ask him who they were."

"They were the arch-fathers and the arch-mothers," Rabbi Hirsch had explained to his daughter. "The *Zaddik* of Kalev had not been willing to sit down before the breaking of the dawn of redemption and besieged with his prayers the highest worlds. And so the Fathers and the Mothers had to come and make him understand that the time was not yet."

The Seer himself was accustomed to saying that in all the world there was no light such as the light which radiated from the *Seder* of the Rabbi of Kalev.

The Rabbi of Lublin celebrated the *Seder* more consecratedly and with all the attitudes and motivations which he had himself prescribed. During the repast he explained, as was customary, the eating of the paschal lamb and ended his instructive discourse with the traditional saying: "This is the command concerning the eating of the paschal sacrifice. May the All-Merciful find us worthy of partaking of it even in our days in the city of our sanctuary and may thus be fulfilled the Scripture that is written: 'For not in haste will ye set forth, nor in the manner of flight will ye go. For before you goes the Lord and your rearguard is the God of Israel!' As in the days of our exodus from the land of Egypt will He cause us to see wonders. The word of our God will stand fast in world time. His right hand is lifted up to perform dreadful things."

Scarcely had he uttered the last word than there issued from his throat a wild and dreadful cry. Before anyone knew what was happening all throats were beset by the same loud cry. "It has failed!" he cried. "The *Seder* is disturbed! The *Seder* is pain-riven! It was so from the beginning!" Gasping he fell back in his seat. No one knew what he meant. After a while he whispered: "Pshysha!" And once again: "All is lost!" Long he remained without stirring in his seat.

It was after midnight. According to the regulation he brought forth the half of a cake of matzah set aside at the beginning of the celebration for the dessert, the *Afikoman*, and said in a trembling voice before he ate thereof and distributed it: "Herewith I am prepared and arrayed to fulfill the command of the eating of the *Afikoman* to the unification

[273]

of the Holy One, Blessed be He, and his *Shechinah*, through Him, the Hidden One and the Secret One, in the name of all Israel." Then, ever and again forced to pause, he pronounced grace; he leaned toward his left side, as it is ordered, for the purpose of marking those who had been liberated from the Egyptian yoke, grasped the beaker with still trembling hands, pronounced the blessing over it, drank of it and, singing the songs of praise against his custom with but half a voice, he completed the ceremony. It was evident to those about him that all he spoke and did was spoken and done, contrary to his annual custom and especially to his attitude at the beginning of this night, without fervor or fixed inner direction. When he arose and went slowly forth, one saw that his steps were faltering and difficult. But he would have no one support him.

Immediately after the two festival days the Seer sent out the messengers to the same places to inquire how the *Seder* had gone.

The first news came from Pshysha. It crossed with the messenger sent thither. And this is what took place on the night of *Seder* there:

When the mother of the Yehudi prepared to take her seat, as she did every year, at his side, Schoendel flew into a rage. "That is my place!" she cried. "I will no longer be pushed out of my place!"

"What are you talking about, daughter?" said the old woman. "Will you not let me sit beside my son?"

"I demand my due," Schoendel shrieked.

"If you feel in your heart that it is your due," answered the mother, "I shall yield the place to you in peace."

"It's too late now!" Schoendel shrieked again. "I won't sit down at all unless you leave the table."

They all stared at her, incapable of speech. She rushed forward, tore the cushions and covers from the seats around the table and threw them into an adjoining room. Then she

[274]

ran in after them and shot the latch. For the first time the Yehudi was seen to weep. The hasidim were about to remove their long coats in order to refurnish the seats with them, when Mendel of Tomashov hastened to the latched door of the adjoining room.

"*Rebbitzin*," he cried, "come and look at your child!"

Instantly the latch was opened and Schoendel rushed forth. She looked at the boy Nehemya who, pale as death, trembling all over, was regarding his weeping father. Beside him his brother Asher, who was twelve years older than the little boy of six, sought in vain to soothe him. Nehemya uttered little cries of fright. They made one think of the young of birds whose nest is menaced by a hawk. Schoendel ran up to the child. But so soon as she took him by the hand, he tore it away; he threw at her a glance of fear and anger. When she tried to approach him again he struggled wildly with his hands and feet. For an instant Schoendel stood stock still. Then she ran back into the other room and tugged at the pillows and covers and began to array the seats anew. The hasidim helped her. Everyone sat down. There was still another delay because Schoendel now begged her mother-in-law to take the place of honor; the old woman was inclined to insist upon her renunciation; finally she was persuaded to take her place. Now the ceremony proceeded. The Yehudi sought to fulfill all the directions of the message from Lublin. But the lost time could not be retrieved.

The messengers who returned to Lublin brought one strange piece of news after another. Everywhere disturbances had taken place. In one single house, namely, the famous "Court" of the *Zaddik* of Tshernobil, everything had gone well — up to the moment when the *Afikoman* was to be eaten. No one could find it! But the strangest report of all came last on account of the long distance. It came from Kalev.

Superficially as he seemed to have listened and read, the Rabbi of Kalev had precisely followed the directions of the

Seer. But he had spoken every word which was to be spoken in Hungarian, as was his custom. He used to say: "Not in vain is the totality of that which is spoken on this night called *Haggadah*, that is to say an account. An account must be communicated in such a manner that all who hear it understand it. I render this account to all, including the poor man who is my guest this evening and has crossed my threshold in order to eat and drink with me, as well as to the servants who join me and mine in this celebration. All are to understand the account, even as they all went forth from Egypt with us."

In Lublin this custom of the Rabbi of Kalev had either not been known or not thought upon. Only when the news reached the house of the Seer there was an old hasid who remembered and whispered to his fellow: "Do you know that Rabbi Shmelke of Nikolsburg, the teacher of him of Kalev, would listen to all the places where on the *Seder* disciples of his recited the *Haggadah*? In the year after his disciple Yitzchak Eisik had been made Rabbi of Kalev, Rabbi Shmelke said: 'How does it happen that I do not hear the Rabbi of Kalev recite the *Haggadah*? Is it possible that he recites it in Hungarian?' "

The Seer had received the report from Pshysha with a singularly strained expression of countenance. "He looked," the bearer of the report said later on, "like a lion who was about to leap upon his prey."

"Do you know," it was objected to him, "how a lion looks?"

"I know it now," said the other, and that had to suffice them.

The Rabbi accepted all the later reports with great equanimity.

It was on the day after that Pesach night that Napoleon Bonaparte set forth from Paris upon that decisive campaign which put an end to his dominion.

Concerning the feast of the New Moon of the month of Sivan of that year (toward the end of May) as it was celebrated in Lublin, the relation comes down to us from Rabbi Chaim Yechiel of Mogielnica, that grandson of the *Maggid* of Kosnitz who had seen the red flare in the bedroom of his grandfather during the night before the conflagration of Moscow. He told it to his hasidim.

"I stood on that occasion," he told them, "next to the spotless table of the Rabbi, about which sat thirty in their white coats and among them was the Holy Yehudi. I did not take my eyes from him for a moment. His face bore no resemblance to any that I knew. But it had also changed from the aspect which it had had on previous occasions. It seemed extinguished; yet, when one looked more closely, it radiated light. Suddenly knowledge came over me; *there* will *he* be at the head of all. So I stood and kept looking at him. I did not touch the food which was given me. How could I have eaten?

"The Rabbi called to me. 'Chaim,' said he, 'why eatest thou not?'

"I answered: 'Because I'm not hungry.'

"I was not lying; it was the truth; that which I looked upon satisfied me.

"He, however, asked again: 'Why art thou not hungry?'

"I was silent.

"The Rabbi continued: 'Chaim'l, if thou couldst eat — knowedst thou what "eating" means, eating for the sake of God — then things of that kind would not spoil your appetite. I would like to ask the Yehudi after his opinion, but . . .'

"He ceased and did not complete his speech, but a slight smile appeared on his lips. After the meal he summoned me to his room.

" 'Tell me,' he began, 'why do you come here? Simply to pass the time? If you were not the grandson of the *Maggid* and if I did not have an affection for you I would bid you come here no more. I would have my people love you, too; but if you go on this way they will speak to me against you.'

"But I knew in my heart that the Rabbi himself, in spite of everything, loved the Holy Yehudi and gave ear to his calumniators against his own will. For this reason I went straightway to the Holy Yehudi in his inn.

"He said to me: 'Well, my dear man, you were well scolded by the Rabbi. Tell me what he said.'

"I did not want to tell him; an honorable man must not be a tale-bearer. Thereupon he repeated to me everything that the Rabbi had said. 'Be of good courage,' he continued, 'you will learn how to eat; you will not neglect that; but if we want to look at each other it were better that we did so today. And one other thing I would say to you. You are not to think that those who persecute me do so out of an evil heart. The heart of man is not evil; only its "imagination," is so; that is to say what it produces and devises arbitrarily, separating itself from the goodness of creation, that is the thing called evil. Even so it is with those; the fundamental motive of their persecution of me is to serve Heaven. What is their predominant intention? Since it has been long known that Rabbi Israel will decline the succession, they desire to secure it for Rabbi Joseph. And why is that their intention? Because they believe that the succession of son to father in the function of *Zaddik* is the desire of Heaven. Assuredly, they are in error. They will effect nothing for Rabbi Joseph, and as for me, it is not I who stand in his way; I stand in no man's way.'

"I looked up at him and I understood him. My eyes grew dim from looking at that tranquil, radiant countenance. I could say no more. When I bade him farewell, he took my hand and held it until we had issued forth from the door of the inn. He pointed to the sky.

" 'Does it not look as though there were no more moon?' said he. 'It always looks this way when a renewal of things is about to take place.' "

THE LAST TIME

This is the close of the memoirs of Rabbi Benjamin.

"I am writing this three days before the New Year. My hand trembles and so does my heart. I know not how I will be able to write down even the little that I want to write.

"During this summer Rabbi Meir told me that the Rabbi of Lublin had said from time to time that he must 'send a messenger.' I did not understand his meaning. He is accustomed to sending messengers; I myself served him as one on an occasion, of which I shudder to think, and he never spoke of the matter until the message and the mission were ready. But I did not ask Rabbi Meir. I no longer put questions to those people.

"But yesterday the Holy Yehudi (the only one whom I shall confess to have been my teacher before the Courts of Heaven) was here. Nowadays he always visits before the New Year, since he spends the feast itself with his congregation. The Rabbi of Lublin summoned him and they were together long in the Rabbi's study. Soon after he came out I went to visit him at his inn. I found him pale and lost in thought. The situation became clear to me at once.

" 'Rabbi,' I asked him, 'what did the Rabbi of Lublin say to you?'

" 'Don't, Benjamin,' he replied, 'it is not permitted to ask.' "

" 'Rabbi," I persisted, 'did he tell you that he wanted you to be his messenger?'

"He was silent.

" 'Rabbi,' I asked again, 'did he tell you that after all the failures he knew no longer what was to be done?'

"Still the Holy Yehudi was silent.

" ' 'Rabbi,' I cried, 'did he propose to you that you should die and bring him a message from Heaven?'

"He was startled. 'Benjamin,' said he, 'what need have I to speak, seeing that you know!'

" 'Rabbi,' I asked him, 'what answer did you make?'

" 'Benjamin,' he replied, 'I have known for all of four years, that I am not destined to grow old. But I had hoped for two more years, that is, until my fiftieth year, for thus something could be completed. That must remain uncompleted now.'

" 'Have mercy upon us, Rabbi!' I cried.

" 'What do you think I should do?' he asked.

" 'Do not obey him!'

"He tapped my hand lightly. 'Do you really not know, Benjamin,' he said, 'what it means to be a hasid? Will a hasid refuse to give his life?'

" 'But Rabbi,' I insisted, 'how can it be that you bring him a message? Are you not opposed to all his goings-on?'

" 'How foolishly you speak, Benjamin,' he replied and smiled; yes, truly, he smiled. 'If one is permitted to bring a message from the world of truth, it is bound to be a message of truth!'

"This is the last entry which I am making in this book. Enough of scribbling and too much! Help me, my God! Help him, him, Jaacob Yitzchak, son of the woman Dajka, Thy servant! Help this world of Thine! Tear it out of the hands of Gog and Magog!''

PEREZ

On the day before New Year, Perez, the younger brother of Yekutiel, disciple of the Yehudi, was attacked by an apparently light feverish chill. He made his final dispositions and went to bed. The Yehudi went to see him and sat down beside him and stroked his forehead.

"Perez," said he, "your time has not yet come."

Perez said: "Rabbi, I know it well, but I beg to be permitted to speak on a certain matter."

"Speak," said the Yehudi.

"I have come to see," said Perez, "that you must soon take leave of the earth, and I would not stay here without you."

Next day he died.

THE YEHUDI OBEYS

In the days between the Day of Atonement and the feast of Tabernacles the Yehudi had a series of conferences with his familiars. Yet any hasid, who had a question to put or a desire to express, was given a hearing, even as always, and none had the impression that the master's hours were numbered.

On the eve of the festival, on the threshold of the *Succah*, the leafy tabernacle, he invited the arch-fathers to be his guests according to the prescribed formula. Then he entered the tabernacle and pronounced the prayer. When he came to the words: "And mayest Thou give me the grace to be sheltered under the shadow of Thy wings at the time of my farewell to the world," he was seen to bow down three times. Then he sat down to the meal with his comrades and with the seven poor men who symbolize the seven invited arch-fathers.

When, next morning, he called upon God in prayer as Him who "is faithful to quicken the dead," Bunam, who stood beside him, could see, in spite of his badly impaired eyesight, that the vein behind the Yehudi's ear, which often trembled softly while he prayed, was throbbing violently.

In the afternoon Bunam came to see him in the *Succah*. They sat together for a long time in silence. Now and then one looked at the other. Now and then one took the other's hand. They knew in common all that was to be known. More than that. He who was remaining behind accompanied his friend even unto that narrow highland path which no two can tread together. From this point, separated and yet together, they took a common view of their world. Finally it was the Yehudi who broke the silence.

"Apothecary," said he, "I have a difficult case for you. It is you, yourself." Bunam lowered his head.

"You will resist assuming an office," the Yehudi continued, "for which you are destined. But I say to you what you once said to me: You will be compelled. We need not discuss it further now."

Later the Yehudi summoned Mendel of Tomashov.

"Mendel," said he, "be a friend to Rabbi Bunam, when I am no longer here. Ask not," he added when he saw that Mendel was about to speak, "I could not answer you. But listen. Rabbi Bunam needs you and you need him. Learn of him what you can learn from no other. Nightly does our Rabbi say of him that he is a sage. But all his wisdom is his love of the world. And you, Mendel — the world will make you suffer, even as it has made me suffer, only in an even more somber way. There is nothing that can be said in this matter, nor anything that can be done. Only try not to be angry at the world. The world and all of us who are in it exist by grace."

On the second day of the festival the Yehudi gathered his disciples about him and spoke to them concerning the Seer of Lublin. "Heaven has bestowed great power upon the Rabbi," he said, "and he has tirelessly devoted this power to the redemption of the world. Even those who oppose him must revere him. We are all his disciples. Pshysha strives after another aim than Lublin, but without Lublin it would be unthinkable. Insofar as I am anything at all, I have become it through him. He who speaks against him, speaks against me."

That evening in the *Succah* his children were gathered about him: Yerachmiel with his wife, the two daughters by Foegele with their husbands, Asher and his wife and the little Nehemya. Schoendel sat at the side of her mother-in-law. Since that unhappy *Seder* she had become strangely silent. The Yehudi spoke to his children concerning their affairs; he gave them advice and support. In a very special way he turned to Yerachmiel.

"It is a good trade that you drive," said he to him, "and you are master of it. But in the end you will not be able to withdraw yourself from learning and from our hasidim. So I bid you to remain loyal to my friend, Rabbi Bunam. Do you remember you were here once when you were ten years old, and you were indignant because Bunam had told such idle, worldly anecdotes concerning Danzig. When he had left I said to you that what he had told me reached from the bottom of the great abyss even to the Throne of the Divine Majesty. Do not forget!"

Last of all, the Yehudi turned to his wife. "And you, Schoendel Freude," he said, "I said it to you all alone before the beginning of the Day of Atonement, and I **say** it to you once again in front of your children and of Foegele's children —forgive me!"

Schoendel started up, but the tears burst from her eyes and silenced her again. She choked. "I have been a bad wife to you, Itzikel," she stammered.

"You have been a good wife," said he. "You were zealous

on the side of Foegele. And it was right and handsome of you to be zealous on her account."

On the next morning a great ecstasy of prayer took hold upon the Yehudi. From early youth on he had had this experience and had sometimes been brought by it to the edge of the grave. All those about him knew concerning this thing, and so someone always remained near him in order to give him refreshment when he fell into a state of exhaustion.

On this morning, even as on the mornings of the first days of penitential prayer, he repeated again and again the whispered words in which God the Redeemer is besought to redeem. Even when Bunam came to see him later, he could only whisper.

"Bunam," said he, "you once asked me, what is the meaning of those three hours of which the beseeching prayer speaks:

> Resoundingly
> Come the hours, the three!
> O haste, set free!

And I answered you, that those are the three hours of speechless horror after the tumult of the wars of Gog and Magog and before the coming of the Messiah, and that they will be much more difficult to endure than all the tumult and thunder, and that only he who endures them will see the Messiah. But all the conflicts of Gog and Magog arise out of those evil forces which have not been overcome in the conflict against the Gogs and Magogs who dwell in human hearts. And those three hours mirror what each one of us must endure after all the conflicts in the solitariness of his soul."

By evening his breathing and his glance were tranquil. Very slowly he repeated a number of times the saying of Obadiah: "And saviors shall come up on Mount Zion to judge the Mount of Esau; and the kingdom shall be the

Lord's." Schoendel, who was with him at the time, went out for a little, because she heard the little boy crying. On the way back she heard something fall in the *Succah*. She ran in and saw her husband lying on the ground. He kept repeating: "There is none besides Him!" And with that he raised his arms and then stretched them forth on both sides with a gesture of one who spreads out something that had been over him to his two sides.

This new state of ecstasy lasted thirty-six hours. Toward the dawn of the third day of beseeching penitence, Yerachmiel, who was watching beside him, heard him whispering the words of the prayer: "She is like the palm tree. She who is slain for Thy sake. And considered as a sheep on the butcher's block. Scattered among those who wound her. Clinging and cleaving to Thee. Laden with Thy yoke. The only one to declare Thy oneness. Dragged into exile. Stricken on the cheek. Given over unto stripes. Suffering Thy pain." No further sound was to be heard, but his lips continued to move, though ever more slowly. Then they stopped. Suddenly Jaacob Yitzchak raised his hands gently, as though he wanted to hand something to someone near him, and his lips moved once again. Yerachmiel put his ear close to his father's lips. He heard: "The only one to declare Thy oneness." And at the same time those two raised hands were folded.

A CONVERSATION

It is related that, on that morning, Rabbi Kalman of Cracow and Rabbi Shemuel of Korov, likewise a disciple of the Seer but attached to the Yehudi, happened to meet on the road as they were traveling in opposite directions.

Kalman said: "I am worried about the life of the Yehudi. There is a secret Unification which may be accomplished on this day. But none can accomplish it and live, save in the land of Israel. And it seems to me as though the Yehudi were daring to accomplish it."

"Well," said Shemuel, "it may be that this is the day of the approach of which he had knowledge quite a long time ago. And assuredly he has sought to accomplish a matter which cannot be accomplished, save in the land of Israel, without the incurrence of death. But when will one accomplish it in the land of Israel?"

They did not continue this conversation but proceeded on their respective journeys.

LAMENT IN LUBLIN

Rabbi Chaim Yechiel of Mogielnica, the grandson of the *Maggid* of Kosnitz, related as follows:

"I happened to be in Lublin when the news of the passing of the Holy Yehudi reached me. Weeping overcame me. I wept and wept without ceasing, and since I did not desire that the Rabbi be told thereof and question me, I ran into the forest and wept my fill. Nevertheless it was brought to the Rabbi's attention and he summoned me. When I came to him he embraced me and said: 'My Chaim'l, for the love of me do not weep any more! After all that has come to pass I miss the Yehudi more than you do. When I was told that he was no more among us, I rolled myself in the ashes. I have had no hasid like him and I will not ever have.' "

THE LAUGHTER OF DAVID OF LELOV

The winter after that David of Lelov fell ill. A physician whom he knew called on him. When he had examined him, he uttered nothing but a friendly phrase. Then he turned to David's friends who had been standing aside and spoke softly to them. Rabbi David called him back.

[286]

"Do you think I don't know what you are telling them? You are telling them that it is not well with David. What kind of talk is that? I am going home. How could I be better off?"

The hasidim, who surrounded his bed later on, saw that he was laughing.

"Why do you laugh, Rabbi?" they asked.

"I laugh," he answered, "because the people who were so busily concerned with us two, with me and my comrade, the Yehudi, are now getting rid of me, too."

Soon thereafter he laughed again. When he was asked for the reason he said: "I laugh because the tractate *David, the son of Solomon* will now be read no more until Messiah comes. Except the Yehudi no one ever opened it, not even the Rabbi."

And once again he laughed. "You want to know," said he, "why I laugh? I laugh toward God, because I have accepted His world exactly as He made it."

Therewith he turned to the wall and breathed his last.

Sometime before this he had given an order that after his death his silver *Kiddush* cup should be given to the Rabbi of Lublin. His son Moshe, he who was married to the daughter of the Yehudi, executed the command. Next Friday evening, exactly a week after the death of David, the Seer bade the beaker to be placed on the Sabbath table in order that he might pronounce the blessing over it. But when he lifted it up his hand trembled so that he had to put it down again. This thing happened a second time. Not until the third attempt was he able to hold the beaker and to drink from it.

"Woe," he cried thereupon, "woe unto us because of those who are lost to us and cannot be forgotten!"

Then he turned to Simon Deutsch, who sat next to him. "Rabbi Simon," he said, "you are a liar."

Simon Deutsch arose and went out and was never again seen in Lublin.

EPILOGUE

BETWEEN LUBLIN AND KOSNITZ

The news of the defeats of Napoleon dampened, as they could not but do, the Messianic movement among the hasidim. It goes without saying that what weighed so heavily upon their hearts was not the fact that he was defeated, but that the life of earth slipped back into its accustomed grooves. Nothing pointed to extraordinary consequences of the things that had come to pass. The man had been viewed as a phenomenon of superhuman or of unhuman stature; as the Gog of the land Magog, he had stamped his way over the supine and beaten nations. A thing so monstrous ought to have been the prelude to some decision of all decisions. And now there was nothing notable except that men breathed more easily. Everywhere men were happy that they had come home, as it were, from the horrors of history into the common course of things in which death occurred on the same wholly human plane as birth. The hasidim saw this thing and felt it and were stunned. Now was it possible that, in spite of all these things, nothing presaged the coming of the Messiah? Had all those daring things, of which whispers were heard, failed utterly? The stodgy life of every day spread over the world. What had become of God?

Only in Pshysha and in Lelov and in other places where men's hearts were of the same temper did they know that all things were as they had to be. Rabbi Bunam who, though he was now almost blind, had assumed the headship after a resistance of several months, gave forth the following watchword: "One does not go to the Messiah; one comes to him."

[291]

Therewith the matter was settled. All knew that the heritage of the Yehudi was being rightly administered.

In contrast to this the mood of Rymanov was dark. All knew that Rabbi Menahem Mendel had expected of Napoleon's conquest of the whole world the turning point of fate. One of the hasidim of Rymanov had once heard it said that in all battles the emperor had seen a little red man go in front of him. Since then it seemed certain that that could have been none other than the red-haired Rabbi Mendel. Now the opponents of the hasidic way, who even prior to this had called Rymanov "Napoleon's second headquarters," jeered and asked whether the Rabbi was still going forth to war. His power to achieve victory was evidently over. Rabbi Mendel did not reply to the jeers which were reported to him. But to his intimates he said at times: "Pray for me, that I may survive this coming year. In that case you may be sure that you will hear the ram's horn of the Messiah."

Most curious was the situation in Lublin. The Seer had accepted the news of the various defeats with apparently imperturbable equanimity. He was not visibly surprised until the abdication of Bonaparte was reported to him. For two weeks he went about in a scarcely repressed rage — "like a lion in his cage," observed that disciple who had once after Pesach brought the message from Kalev. He treated everyone who crossed his path so irritatedly as though that one and that one alone was guilty of the whole thing. Then came the news that Napoleon had been banished to the Island of Elba. It gave the Seer a new lease on life.

"The Sidonian has an island under his feet," he said to Meir. "Now the way is open again."

Soon thereafter, in the week following Shavuot, he went on a journey to Kosnitz.

Of what passed on that occasion between these two aged men, the huge unbowed one and the small and delicate one,

[292]

only a very little has come down to us through the relation of Rabbi Chaim Yechiel, the *Maggid's* grandson.

Soon after the salutations had been passed and they were sitting on a bench in front of the house, the Seer said that it was his intention precisely now to risk the decisive attempt.

"That chapter is ended," answered the *Maggid*.

"The essential thing is still to come," said the Seer.

"If something is still added, it will be only in the form of a note to elucidate the meaning."

"The true meaning, which concerns both us and the world, has not yet become apparent."

"What you're thinking of, Rabbi Yitzchak, is not the meaning of this chapter."

"Must not things so monstrous point to the coming of redemption?"

"Everything points to the coming of redemption, but otherwise than we are inclined to think."

"Can you deny that what happened before our eyes introduced the birth pangs of the Messiah?"

Before the *Maggid* could answer, a young man joined them who had overheard their last words. The Rabbi of Lublin recognized him at once, although that face had aged strangely since he last beheld it. It was Mendel of Tomashov, who had been here since Shavuot. He began to speak at once, more boldly and violently than even he had ever done.

"What do we know of the birth pangs of the Messiah?" he cried. "How do we know when he will come? Perhaps it will be when no one calls him and no one expects him any more, on a gray day among other days, when Jews run hither and yon confusedly knitted into the web of their cares to make a living, and no one is thinking of aught but of the next hour, and then, then . . .!" his voice broke.

"Mendel," said the *Maggid* calmly, "it is not well thus to disturb a conversation the deep roots of which you cannot possibly know."

[293]

"Forgive me, Rabbi," said Mendel and left them.

"You ask me," said the *Maggid* turning to the Seer, "whether I can refute your assertions. I can refute nothing and you may not assert anything. There is here nothing to assert and nothing to refute."

"Do you remember, Rabbi Israel, how twenty years ago you said to me that Leviathan would devour all the fishes of the sea?"

"And you asked me, whether it was Gog."

"And you answered me that his name would not be written until the world was lying in the birth pangs."

"And you asked me in your turn whether what was now happening did not constitute those pangs."

"And you answered me that it depended on whether a place had been prepared for the child."

"It is so," said the *Maggid* tranquilly. "And is it prepared? Is it prepared where it ought to be prepared? In the street? In the house? In the heart?"

"What do you mean by that?" asked the Seer.

"Do you remember, Rabbi Yitzchak," the *Maggid* replied, "how at our leavetaking that time I gave you the sheet with the prayer of Rabbi Elimelech upon it? And do you remember how five years later I came on an evening to Lublin and talked with you all through the night of that disciple of yours who is now dead? And do you remember what once more, again years later, I said to your wife Beile, when she came to me to ask that I pray for a child for her? It has always been the same thing!"

It was with difficulty that the Seer held his great head erect. He spoke no word.

For a while the *Maggid* seemed to be waiting for something. Then he stretched out his hand and with his index finger touched the breast of him who was sitting beside him but turned toward him. "He is here," he said calmly. "Do you remember how twenty years ago, as Rabbi Naftali told me much later, that disciple of yours who is now dead asked you at your own table what was the nature of this Gog; he could exist out in the world only because he exists already within the human breast? In there he is." His index finger was still touching the breast of the Seer.

The Seer's head sank almost to his knees. He had to hold it up with both his hands.

Suddenly a twitching went through his whole body. He looked up. The *Maggid* was now holding his finger over his own heart. "And in here he is," said he.

A long silence ensued.

"I am guilty," the Seer said at last. "I have said it time and again: woe to the generation whose leader I am! Pray for me, Rabbi Israel."

"I will pray for us," answered the *Maggid*. "But do not believe that I did not know how lofty was your aim in your conflict with that disciple who opposed your undertakings. Nevertheless did you feed the heavenly fire with mortal substance."

Upon that day they spoke no more.

Next morning, however, when the Rabbi of Lublin appeared with all his usual superior calm, it was the *Maggid* who began to speak.

"I cannot abet you in your undertaking, Rabbi Yitzchak," he said.

"I desire nothing but this," the Seer replied, "that on the feast of the Rejoicing in the Law there should reign in Kosnitz a joy as perfect as in Lublin."

"It is well," said the *Maggid* thoughtfully. "So far as in me lies the joy shall be perfect."

When the Seer returned to Lublin he found, instead of an answer to the letter which he had sent by special messenger to Rymanov upon the reception of the news of Napoleon's banishment, that Rabbi Menahem Mendel had come in person. The latter, who was usually a man of the most restrained demeanor, approached him with unbridled violence.

"He must be liberated," he said.

THE *MAGGID* WITHDRAWS

As was the annual custom in Kosnitz on the eve of the Day of Atonement, so this time, too, the entire Jewry of the town, men and women and even little children, assembled in front of the *Maggid's* house. He appeared on the threshold. When they saw him they all burst into tears. They wept aloud so that their sins might be held to be expiated and that the sentence in the heavenly court might seal them for a good life. And he, too, wept. "I am a greater sinner than are you," said he and laid himself down in the dust. Then they all went together clad in their white garments, the men in their shrouds, into the house of prayer, and any who had neglected on that day to ask forgiveness of another whom he had hurt during the past year by so much as a thoughtless word, any such ran now on the way to the synagogue over to that other. But from time to time all of them, even to the little children, looked over at the *Maggid*. For when he had stood on the threshold it had been evident that he needed every ounce of strength to hold himself erect, whereas now he walked among them with firm tread like one who was young and of abundant health.

When now the scroll of the Torah had been lifted out of the Ark and pardon had been asked of the Word for every sin against Its honor, and the saying of the Psalmist, "Light is sown for the righteous and joy for him who is straight of heart," had been repeated again and again, the *Maggid* was

[296]

seen to raise high his head, and once again he cried in a loud
voice: "Joy!" And when thereupon there was read a para-
graph from one of the books of secret wisdom and the words
were uttered in which the *Shechinah* in exile is first compared
to a woman in the days of her uncleanness, whom her husband
may not approach, and next with a leper, who must remain
beyond the habitations of men, the *Maggid* kneeled both
times upon his knees and bowed himself down to the very
earth. Never before had he done the like.

When next he stood in front of his praying stand and
recited the formula, "All the vows," *Kol Nidre*, and had
already pronounced the words: "Forgive the errors of this
people on account of the greatness of Thy mercy and even
as Thou hast borne this people from Egypt unto here," he
stopped and did not say the words that now follow: "And
the Lord said: 'I have forgiven according to thy speaking,' "
but instead repeated everything from the beginning on and
again stopped and did not continue with the liturgy. And
suddenly he spoke out of his own heart to God.

"Lord of the world," said he, "the greatness of Thy might
is known to none but Thee alone, and my weakness also is
known to none but Thee. And yet this is the first time that
I have not spent this day, as I have spent each day during the past month, in front of my praying stand. And Thou
knowest that I have done what I have done not on my account, but for the sake of Thy people Israel. And so I ask
Thee, what is it that has made it easy for me, the feeblest
of mortals, to take upon myself the yoke of Thy sons, the
sons of Israel, and what makes it possible that it is difficult
for Thee, O Almighty One, to pronounce the words: 'I have
forgiven according to thy speaking'?"

Then he adduced the merits of the *Zaddikim* of his generation -- Rabbi Menahem Mendel's sense of justice and the
devotional power of the Rabbi of Lublin.

"If there be a lack of those in the world who would make

[297]

atonement," he added, "behold me who, despite the weakness of my body, am willing to make atonement for the entire community of Israel. And now I beseech Thee . . ." For the third time he repeated: "And so forgive . . ." up to the words: "And the Lord spake." Again he stopped and was silent and waited. Then he turned to the people and cried in a loud voice: "And the Lord spake: 'I have forgiven according to thy speaking.' "

On the fifth day thereafter, the day preceding Succot, for the end of which, that is, for the festival of Simchat Torah, the Seer had demanded the perfection of joy, the *Maggid* summoned his people immediately after the hour of awakening and said to them: "And now I may fall asleep."

And having said that, he fell asleep forever.

THE DAY OF REJOICING

In his two previous undertakings the Rabbi had bidden all his assistants — the first time these were the assembled hasidim of Lublin, the second time all the comrades all over the land — to exercise the most precise inner and outer conformity in the hour of ceremonial action. This time he required of the few, to whom he addressed himself, nothing other than "the perfection of joy."

"Do you expect joy to be effective, Rabbi?" Meir asked.

"Nothing is equally effective," was the reply, "in the matter of the marriage of the higher worlds, on which everything depends. Melancholy divides, joy unites." He declared that he had chosen the day of the Rejoicing in the Law, because now, after the days of judgment, all Israel, being free of the weight of sin, could truly rejoice once again.

The path to that day seemed, to be sure, to lead through a period of melancholy. During the time of preparation the

Rabbi said to Meir and to others that he was horrified at the thought of those of whom Moses speaks: "For horror overcame me at the anger and the fury."

"They stare at me with their terrible eyes," said the Seer.

It is to be noted that usually he did not associate himself with Moses, but rather with the adversary of Moses, with Korah, the violent rebel, whom the earth had opened to devour. "My grandfather Korah," he was wont to say, wherewith he desired to express the fact that the soul of Korah had come to life again in him. Not more than two weeks after his visit to Kosnitz, on the Sabbath on which the *Sidra* dealt with Korah, had he in his table talk, as he did annually, justify Korah and explained that the man's intention had been a good one except for the fact that he had arrogantly emphasized his freedom from sin as against Moses and Aaron who had incurred sin.

On the eighth day of Succot, after the noon meal, the Rabbi assembled a number of his familiars in his study. Mead was drunk and the empty bottles placed on a window sill.

"If we celebrate a happy Simchat Torah," said the Rabbi, "we will also have a good ninth of Ab."

They all understood him. If this autumnal feast went right, then would the summer day of Ab, the day of the great mourning over the destruction of the sanctuary and of the holy city, be transformed into a day of joy under the reign of the Messiah. Never before had the Seer placed the hope for consummation at a period so close.

Evening came. In the synagogue all the Torah scrolls were taken out of the Ark, as was done every year, and the chiefs of the congregation led by the Rabbi, each one a scroll in his hands, went dancing and rejoicing seven times around the platform. They sang:

"Angels gathered themselves together,
Each standing opposite the other,
And each one spoke unto the other:

[299]

'Who is it and what is he, who stretches out his
    hand to the front of the Throne?
He has covered him with His cloud!
Who has climbed to the summit?
Who has climbed to the summit?
Who has climbed to the summit?
And brought us a strong shelter down?
Moses it was who climbed to the summit,
Moses it was who climbed to the summit,
Moses it was who climbed to the summit
And brought us a strong shelter down.' "

The death of the *Maggid* was not yet known to the Rabbi.
The news had reached Lublin but had been kept from him.

After the processions and songs and prayers, the hasidim
united in a great and festive meal of rejoicing. For a while
the Rabbi remained among them. Then he bade his familiars
either to come into his study with him or to remain at the
door of it and to watch carefully over him. Curiously enough,
it was as though they did not take in his words. They nodded
but did not stir from their seats. He repeated his command
again and yet again. They nodded in assent and one of them
cried out: "Yes, yes, Rabbi." But they all went on drinking
and screeching. He looked at them in amazement; they did
not observe it. He went over into the dwelling house and
told Beile to watch over him. She accompanied him to his
room.

An hour later Beile heard a knocking at the door of the
house, soft but pertinacious. From the threshold there came
to her the sound of a child weeping. She recognized the voice
and ran out. No one was there. When she came back she
did not find the Rabbi in his room. She looked for him all
over the house. In vain. Now she went to rouse the hasidim.
They hastened into the Rabbi's room. No one was there, but
nothing had been disturbed. On the window sill which was
as high up as a man's shoulder — thus the story comes to us —

still stood the rows of empty mead bottles. The threefold window was closed. Only the small lookout pane in the middle was open, the one which the Rabbi was accustomed to use when he peered into distances unreachable by other eyes, as on that day when he had seen Beile in Lemberg in her many-colored frock.

After a long search a certain hasid, who was circling the house at a distance of more than fifty ells, heard a feeble moaning from the earth.

"Who is here?"

He heard a weak voice: "Jaacob Yitzchak, son of the woman Matel." The hasid screamed with terror and ran senselessly up and down. Soon others came and surrounded the prostrate Rabbi. His intimates cast lots to determine who was to carry his feet, who his rump, who his head. The lot of permission to carry the head was drawn by Shemuel of Korov, who had been a close follower of the Yehudi. On the way back to the house he observed that the lips of the Rabbi were moving. He inclined his ear and heard the words of the psalm of midnight lamentations: "Deep calleth unto deep." It was the exact moment at which the Rabbi was accustomed on every night to recite that psalm.

They sent for Doctor Bernard, a celebrated physician, who, having been converted by David of Lelov, had become a passionate hasid. He had desired to relinquish his practice and remain at the court of the Seer; the latter had dissuaded him, saying that it was his duty to do what he had been doing, but now in the right way.

Bernard asked the Rabbi whether he felt any pain.

"There is a pain in my left hip," he answered with difficulty. "The whole 'other side of things' has thrown itself upon me. All my bones would have been broken, had not the *Maggid* spread his coat under me. Why did no one tell me that the *Maggid* is dead? I did not learn it until I saw him. Had I known it before, I would not have ventured so far."

[301]

After a while he added: "The Yehudi would have watched over me. He would not have let me fall."

And again after a space and also with great difficulty but very clearly, he said: "Once upon a time when I and the *Maggid* and the others were assembled in the house of the Rabbi Elimelech, he came from the synagogue and walked up and down and peered into the countenance of each one of us. Finally he said to me: 'Be sure that we should go on praying: *Cast us not down in the time of our age!*' "

The Rabbi was weary and said no more. They asked the physician how it stood with him. The latter shook his head; he could not say.

But the Rabbi lived four and forty weeks longer, to the ninth of Ab.

THE END OF THE CHRONICLE

As the news of the disaster spread, all the great ones, who had been the disciples of the Seer, fared to Lublin from all directions. They remained there; day after day they went together into the house of their teacher and sat at his bedside. Only Naftali of Ropshitz was missing. He had been notified at once, but had not come.

Autumn and winter passed and the illness seemed to be alleviated. But around Purim, the Rabbi having just been told that Napoleon had returned to France, a turn for the worse set in. A special messenger was sent to Ropshitz. Soon, thereafter, on the New Moon of the month of Nisan, two weeks before Pesach, Naftali came to Lublin. From then on he stayed uninterruptedly, even by night, near the Rabbi during twelve days. No one saw him sleep. These were the twelve days of the twelve sacrificial offerings of the twelve princes of the tribes, each corresponding to one month of the year.* At the dawn of the thirteenth day Naftali left the house of the Rabbi and went to an inn. From then on he visited the Rabbi no more.

When on the day of the festival of the New Moon Naftali had approached the Rabbi's bed, the latter had regarded him in so friendly a fashion as though they had parted but yesterday. But when on the thirteenth of Nisan, one day before the eve of Pesach, Naftali did not come, the Rabbi said to Meir: "Naftali knows a great deal, but he does not know enough yet."

After Pesach Naftali set out for home. Soon thereafter, however, he proceeded to Rymanov.

In Rymanov Rabbi Menahem Mendel had continued the processions, with his ten hasidim bearing scrolls of the Torah around the Ark, from the beginning of the feast of the Rejoicing in the Torah until the feast of the Reconsecration of the Temple (Hanukkah), that is to say, every night for nine weeks. When the townspeople came to the synagogue to perform their morning devotions, they met those ten going home. A strange period set in in Rymanov. The Rabbi asked everyone who came from out of the city, what he had heard about Napoleon. He was finally informed that the Emperor had left the Island of Elba. On the next evening he again assembled those ten and again, every night, until the preparations for Pesach, a mysterious ceremonial took place.

Rabbi Mendel of Rymanov was a very pertinacious man, even stubborn. He did not incorporate many things into the innermost core of his will; those which he did so incorporate were sheltered as nowhere else. Thus long ago, in his youth, he had appointed the *Seder* evening as the time of the great hope of his heart. At no other time than on this night, on which once the faring forth of the hosts took place and

*See Numbers 7.12–83.

on which this event was annually renewed, would the great new faring forth be prepared.* Much later his soul had laid hold upon an entirely different matter, namely, the fantastic undertaking of a usurper, which was bound to accumulate gigantic masses of might and victory, in order to provide the prelude for the great faring forth. Two things — the full moon of the night of spring and the recurrent dream-image of this man with the tousled hair and the sulphur-colored skin (the skin had long ago lost that color, but it was the young Napoleon who appeared to Mendel in his dreams) — these two were blended in the directed aspiration of this steady heart. He did not abandon his aspiration even when that of the Rabbi of Lublin had gone down in disaster. On the contrary, now that it was no longer disturbed by his two great fellows, did he develop it to its utmost capacity. The *Maggid* had been his open opponent and when he died he seemed to have conquered. In his last daring undertaking the Seer had not been able to prevail against the dead. Now it was Menahem Mendel's turn. The two "king's sons" whose windows he, the "peasant," watched, as he had once said, that they might not break each other's panes — those two had yielded the field to him. Now he needed no longer to submit as in those days when the message from Lublin came to him. His people clove to him; that was enough. Already the Emperor had started on his second and definitive conquest of the world. The night of *Seder* was near.

Unlike the Seer, Rabbi Menahem Mendel sent out no messengers and sought no one's help. If there was such a being in the world as the people Israel, then in this night of *Seder* the wishes of all those flaming souls everywhere must arise and coalesce on high. More was not needed. Nothing was to be commanded or to be prescribed. If either were to be necessary, then the one thing needful simply did not exist.

*The reference is to the Exodus from Egypt and to the final Exodus con-
nected with the Messianic Redemption.

[304]

"This is the beaker of salvation for all Israel," said Rabbi Mendel when he raised up the first cup of the *Seder*. Nothing else has been handed down to us concerning what took place on that night.

Pesach passed by. After the festival Rabbi Mendel's strength seemed to decline. When Naftali came he found him in such a state of decline that he was shocked. Mendel grew weaker and weaker until the twenty-third day of the counting between Pesach and Shavuot. That morning in the ritual bath he indulged in special purifications and sanctifications. Then he sat down on the chair from which he was accustomed to receive his hasidim and to straighten out their affairs.

"Alas, I feel the weight of a whole world upon me," he sighed with closed eyes. Then, without opening them, he commanded that after his death there should be a window giving on the city in his sarcophagus.

Naftali wept aloud. "Rabbi," he cried, "teach me to know when Messiah will come!"

Rabbi Mendel opened his eyes. "Green worms with trunks of iron will come upon you," he cried out to Naftali, "before Messiah comes."

Thereafter he spoke no more; it seemed to them all as though he were dying. But the lamentations of his hasidim held his soul in its tenement and he kept on breathing until the next morning.

Soon after Shavuot the Seer sent to Pshysha and summoned Bunam, who had not been in Lublin since the death of the Yehudi, to come to see him. Bunam accompanied the messenger back. When the Rabbi saw him enter, with the spectacles to help cataracts over his eyes, but otherwise unchanged, he sent everyone else out of the room.

"Bunam," he said, "we say in the hymn: 'Approach, leader of the bride!' Who are those leaders of the bride?"

"Fear and love," said Bunam.

[305]

"What is the nature of this fear?"

"When a man feels as though in his trembling hand he held both heart and brain and both tremble close to each other."

"And what is the nature of love?"

"When the hand trembles no more but holds out both to Him, blessed be He."

"So it is," said the Rabbi. "It is written: 'Is he to make a whore of our sister?' And the Poles say: 'A whore is no sister.' Why did the brothers of Dinah assert that the strange chief's son, who wanted to take her as his wife, wanted to make a whore of her? When a woman is uniquely and perfectly inclined toward her husband with brain and heart, this thing is the making of oneness; but if she is not thus, then she is a whore. And in the sayings of Solomon it is written: 'Say to wisdom: Thou art my sister.' But a whore is not a sister. If wisdom is a whore, it cannot be a sister. Hail to that wisdom, which is not a whore!"

After a period of silence he said: "This too is written in the Proverbs: 'As countenance is to countenance in clear water, so is the heart of man to man.' Why does it say 'in water' and not 'in a mirror'?"

"In the water," Bunam replied "a man sees his image only when he approaches very near to it. So, too, the heart must come very close to another heart, before it sees its image therein."

"It is even so," said the Seer. "Come nearer to me, my son Bunam."

Bunam went to the side of the bed.

"Bunam," said the Seer, "why did disaster overtake me?"

"Rabbi," Bunam said, "with your permission I will relate a tale. Rabbi Eleazar of Amsterdam was faring over the sea to the Holy Land, when a storm brought the ship near to being wrecked. Before dawn Rabbi Eleazar bade his followers go on deck and blow the ram's horn at the first gleam of dawn. They did so and the storm subsided. But do not think that it was the intention of Rabbi Eleazar to save the ship. In fact, he was certain that it would sink. He merely desired that he and his followers before they died should fulfill the holy command of blowing the *shofar*. Had he intended to perform a miracle, they would not have been saved."

After another interval of silence the Seer said: "Give me your hand, my son Bunam."

Bunam took the emaciated hand which lay on the coverlet into his own.

"Bunam," said the Seer, "I realize now that judgment has been passed on me in heaven. But does not a man pass judgment on himself here on earth every night?" And again after a while: "Do you know, Bunam, that from the first to the last hour I loved your friend incessantly?"

"I know it," said Bunam.

"But not enough, according to you?"

"Yes, Rabbi, not enough."

"I am making up for it now," said the Seer. "Do you think that there is a special meaning in the fact that I am making up for it now?"

"I believe," Bunam replied, while his strong hand which held the Rabbi's feeble one quivered, "that there is a great meaning in that fact."

"But why was it," asked the Seer, "that they first sent me that enemy who called himself Jaacob Yitzchak, the son of Matel, and did not send him at once?"

Bunam reflected. Then he spoke hesitantly: "It is written: 'The mystery of the Lord is for them who fear Him.' With those who fear Him, God communicates by means of mystery."

"Bunam, Bunam," cried the Seer, "is it possible that I have feared Him, blessed be He, more than I have loved Him?"

Bunam lowered his head. After a few moments he raised it again. Through his lenses a radiance streamed out of his purblind eyes into those of the Seer. He spoke softly: "It is written: 'The world is built by virtue of grace.' What is here called grace, *hesed*, is the mutual love between the Lord and His vassals, his hasidim. In every moment of life up to his very last moment, the world can be rebuilt for a hasid by *hesed*."

He fell silent. After a while the Rabbi whispered so softly that Bunam could but just hear him: "Bunam, that friend of yours, who was named even as I am, said to me once that grace had played a game with me."

For yet another hour Bunam sat at the bedside of the Rabbi and held his hand. "And now, my son Bunam," said the Rabbi, "go home. You are to remain here no longer."

On the Sabbath after Bunam's return home, the weekly portion "Korah" was read. In his table talk he spoke of Korah. "In every generation," said he, "the soul of Moses returns and the soul of Korah returns. When the day comes that the soul of Korah will willingly subject itself to the soul of Moses, then will Korah be redeemed."

Soon thereafter Naftali, who had gone home to Ropshitz after the death of Rabbi Menahem Mendel, returned to Lublin. But he did not visit the Seer, urgently as the others pressed him to do so. There was a rumor among the disciples that he expected an invitation from the Rabbi which was never sent. Others, on the contrary, declared that, during his previous visit, the Rabbi had demanded that he undertake for him a new attempt in the realm of active Cabala, but that Naftali had refused to participate in anything of that kind. At all events it was apparent that during that first period, when Naftali had spent twelve days and nights at the Seer's bedside, an abyss had opened between them.

Three weeks after the reading of the *Sidrah* "Korah," on the Sabbath of the *Sidrah* called "Pinhas," the Rabbi gave the order that Meir, in accordance with his Levitical descent, should be called up as the second one for the reading of the Torah, and that he was not to read only the portion appropriately to be read by a Levite, but that he was to read what follows up to the relation of the appointment of Joshua as the successor of Moses. For at that moment, in which he was to read the words of Moses to God: "So let the Lord command, the God of all spirits in all flesh, that there be a man above the congregation, who fares forth before them, who returns before them, who leads them forth, who leads them back, that the congregation of the Lord be not like sheep, who have no shepherd" — at that moment he was to be appointed to the succession. And even so it came to pass.

Four and twenty days thereafter was the ninth of Ab.

On the eve thereof, when the mourning begins, new strength seemed to inspire the Rabbi. In a voice, which recalled his better days, he said to his faithful who sat by him: "It is said in the Talmud, that Rabbi Yehuda, the patriarch, had desired to abrogate the ninth of Ab when it fell on a Sabbath. But the sages were not in accord with him. The Rabbi did not desire to abrogate the day of fasting for that one time only. Because on that occasion it fell on a Sabbath, on the day of grace, he wanted to draw down redemption on man and thereby abrogate the day of mourning entirely. But his comrades refused their help. What does that mean, that comrades refuse to help you? How does it happen that they do not see what you are doing, nor hear when you address them? Do they do it out of a lack of knowledge and good will?" And suddenly he cried in a strong voice: " 'For My plans are not your plans, neither are your ways My ways, is the saying of the Lord.' " He spoke no more for the rest of the night.

Early in the morning the Rabbi demanded of Beile that she promise to become the wife of no other man; he would effect things in Heaven in such a manner that she, though she had borne no child, be permitted to dwell in the tent of the arch-mothers. She refused to promise.

[After the death of the Seer none of the rabbis dared to marry her. In the end she married a citizen of that neighboring little city called Tshechov or Vieniava, in which the Seer had dwelt before he came to Lublin. The hasidim showed so violent a bitterness against her that she soon gave up going out of the house. But when Simon Deutsch turned up one day in Lublin — it was the first time since he had left it after the death of David of Lelov — she sought him out in his inn. She had a basket in her hands.

"What do they want of me?" she cried weeping. And from the basket on the table she emptied the linens of her dead child. "Why do they throw it up to me that Schoendel Freude did not remarry? She is the mother of two sons!"]

After his conversation with Beile the Rabbi was silent until noon. Then a red glow came into his face and his eyes opened wide as in immense astonishment. He cried: *"Sh'ma Yisrael!"* and died.

At the same moment Naftali, who a little while before had left his inn and started slowly on the way, stepped on the threshold of the house in the Broad Street. When he was asked later on how it had come to pass that he knew so precisely the time of the Rabbi's death, he said: "When I watched by the Rabbi's side for those twelve days, which correspond to the tribes and to the months, he said to me on the fifth day, which corresponds to the month of Ab: 'I can see the ninth of Ab only until noon, not beyond.' I observed that the Rabbi meant that Messiah would come at noon on the ninth of Ab. I did not contradict him. Yet my attitude must have shown him that I did not share his opinion,

for he mentioned the matter no more. What I did understand at once was that in this manner the time of his death
was being made known to him."

What grips me now and has always gripped me concerning
the events assembled in this chronicle, since first long years
ago I heard of them and read of them, are the dates — the
dates of the actions and the deaths of sundry men. The few
generations, which separate me from that time, have told
and retold these events. Thence came into being the flesh
and blood of this chronicle. What I have added may be called
its garment. But the dates are the mighty skeleton beneath.

The adversaries of the hasidic way in Lublin had as their
chief the Rav, that is, the official city rabbi, the extremely
learned Rabbi Asriel Hurwitz, whom they called "The Iron
Head." The conflict between him and the Seer had dragged
on for many years and reached its climax since a chance
meeting between the Seer and Rabbi Asriel.

The latter had asked: "How does it come that such
crowds seek you out? I am far more learned in the Law
than you and yet the crowds don't gather about me."

The Seer answered: "I am no less surprised that many
come to me to hear God's word, seeing that I know myself
to be a man of small worth, and that they do not seek it of
you whose learning can move mountains. But the matter
may be thus, that they come to me because I am surprised
that they come, and that they do not come to you because
you are surprised that they do not come."

Finally it came to the point that The Iron Head asked of
the Yehudi, in the last year of the latter's life, why the Seer
did so and so in such a matter and not otherwise, and to this
too an emphatic answer was given. Now after the death of
his opponent he gave an order to the Burial Society that
no place of honor be reserved for the grave of the Seer. When

Naftali was told of this, he said: "Seeing that I once disguised myself in order to drink of the Rabbi's beaker, it is
but fair that I now do the same thing in his honor." He
put on a ragged garment; he knotted together a gravedigger's
spade and an axe and hung them over his shoulder. Thus
looking like a hired laborer, he set out on his way. "Thus
a man looks who goes to bury a rabbi," he said to himself
and laughed. First he sought out the gravediggers. He gave
them so much money that they blinked at him distrustfully;
he told them that all he asked of them was this, that when
he gave them the sign they were to begin digging at once
and not stop digging till the grave was ready. They gave
him their solemn promise. Then he went to the president of
the Burial Society. It was a strange mid-summer day. The
whole previous night and all day long it had poured continuous torrents, such as usually occur during this season
only after a short thunderstorm. The earth had turned into
slime. When Naftali came to the president the rainstorm
was still at its height and the heavens deeply overcast. It
was toward twilight and one could barely see one's path.

"I come to you," said Naftali in the broad idiom of an
illiterate worker, "in order that you point out to me a place
for the grave of this rabbi of the hasidim. Those people
are bold and insolent! They say it must be in a place of
honor! What does that mean, a place of honor? They
ought to be glad to get a grave at all!"

The president went with him to look for the gravediggers.
The latter had meanwhile, as Naftali had foreseen, lost no
time in spending the money on drink and were not easily to
be revived. By the time they reached the gate of the cemetery
it was dark. With their dim lanterns in their hands they
made their way with difficulty through a veritable swamp.
Naftali and the president preceded. He arranged it so that
they were soon lost in the confused tract of ground. Naftali
kept talking emphatically to the president.

[312]

"It really doesn't matter a bit," he chattered, "it doesn't make any kind of difference; wherever it is it'll be all right."

Leading them through the bushes hither and yon, he finally succeeded in leading them, accidentally as it were, to a place which he had carefully picked out and which the president, according to the path which they seemed to have pursued, was bound to take for a very undesirable one.

"For all I care let it be here," cried Naftali. "What's the difference!"

The exhausted and confused old president, whose beard and earlocks and eyebrows and even eyelashes dripped with water, did not contradict him. In the meantime Naftali had given the signal agreed upon and himself set to work. It was not only because the men had given their promise. They were drenched to the skin and worked with unaccustomed zeal in order to get back as soon as possible to their warming brandy. Meantime the president had taken thought. He peered around by the light of his lantern and observed that they were quite otherwhere than he had assumed, namely, near the grave of the great sixteenth-century rabbi, Shalom Shachna. Naftali had chosen this spot, because in bad times the Seer had bidden his people pray at the grave of this man who had not, like so many others, fared to the land of Israel to die there, but had wanted to lie here in Lublin so that even after his death he might watch over the welfare of his congregation. Dismayed, the president scolded Naftali and the gravediggers. But the work was done.

"What do I care?" said Naftali. "Didn't I keep saying you could do exactly as you liked? Now, of course, there's nothing to be done. Though I am an ignorant man, I know this much, that one may not change the location of a grave nor leave a freshly dug grave unfilled. But you can go to the Rav; if he gives his permission it's all the same to me. The president ran to him of The Iron Head, but, though he was most unwilling, he could not depart from prescription and tradition and had to leave the matter as it was.

After the burial it came over Naftali: how is it possible that he exists no more and that the world still stands? From that time on he could rid himself of this thought no more.

Many hasidim turned to the eldest son of the Seer, Israel, and besought him to take his father's place. Calmly and decisively he declined. A group gathered about the second son, who had always remained near his father and enjoyed his father's frequent confidence. But they were not able to procure the leadership for him. The care of the "Doctrine of Lublin" remained in the hands of Meir, whom the Rabbi, shortly before his death, had clothed with his mantle. But Meir did not dwell in Lublin, but in Apt, the city of the Yehudi's youth. Thus, though the teaching of Lublin was preserved, the school died with its master. When Rabbi Chaim Yechiel of Mogielnica, the grandson of the *Maggid*, heard the name of Lublin named, he was wont to say: "The true Lublin never saw the light of day. One can kill a child in its mother's womb."

It is related that, after the death of Simon Deutsch, the latter's spirit took up its dwelling in a boy. He was brought before Rabbi Chaim Yechiel of Mogielnica.

"I cannot help you," he upbraided the spirit, "until you have received forgiveness from the sons of the Holy Yehudi.

The *dibbuk*, that is to say the spell-dweller, as the spirit dwelling in the possessed one is called, refused to address himself to those.

"In that case, O impious one," cried the Rabbi, "you shall fare into the depth of the great abyss."

At that the *dibbuk* had to yield. A messenger took the boy to Rabbi Asher, the son of the Yehudi. Not until he had forgiven him, could Rabbi Chaim Yechiel effect his redemption.

THE END

[314]

GLOSSARY

AMORAIM — *See* Tannaim.

BA'ALE BATIM — Householder, plural of *ba'al bayith*.

BA'AL-SHEM-TOV — Israel *B(a'al)-Sh(em)-T(ov)* (*Besht*), c. 1700–1760, was the founder of Hasidism.

DAYS OF DREAD OR DAYS OF PENITENCE — The Ten days beginning with *Rosh Hashanah* (New Year) and ending with *Yom Kippur* (Day of Atonement).

GABBAI — Trustee, manager; in hasidic circles the director of the Rabbi's office.

GOG AND MAGOG — According to Ezekiel, chapters 38 and 39, the wars of Gog of the land of Magog will precede the messianic salvation.

GOYIM — Nations, peoples of the world, Gentiles.

HAGGADAH — The order of the service read at the *seder*, on the first and second evenings of Passover.

HIGHER SOUL — An additional soul, נשמה יתרה, the mystics believe, visits a Jew from sundown on Friday to the end of the Sabbath.

MAGGID — Literally "preacher." The *Maggid* of Mesritsh was the immediate successor of Israel *Ba'al-Shem-Tov*, and therefore the second in line of hasidic leaders. In some respects he was the real organizer of Hasidism. In the next generation, Rabbi Israel of Kosnitz was also called "the *Maggid*."

MELAMED — Teacher of children.

PETITION — A statement in writing which was handed to a hasidic rabbi, or to his *gabbai*, outlining the request for prayer or advice which the visitor sought.

[315]

REDEMPTION MONEY — The gifts which hasidim left with the rabbi's household in return for advice and spiritual comfort which they received.

SANCTIFICATION OF THE MOON — A ceremony observed on one night of full moon every month. It consists of Bible quotations and some prayers recited in the open.

SHECHINAH — The Presence of God; sometimes used as a synonym for God. A rather old rabbinic statement speaks, poetically, of the *Shechinah* having accompanied Israel into exile.

TALLIT — A prayer shawl.

TANNAIM AND AMORAIM — The Tannaim were the scholars of the Mishnah (edited about 200 C. E.). Their successors were the Amoraim (from 200 to 500 C. E.) whose discussions were called *Gemara*. The Mishna and the *Gemara* constitute the Talmud.

TEFILLIN — Phylacteries.

TESHUVAH — Repentance.

THIRTY-SIX ZADDIKIM — The number of righteous men existing in every generation, for whose sake God extends His mercy to the world. The Thirty-six generally assume the guise of poor workmen, so that their holiness remains unknown even to their intimates.

ZADDIK — Literally, "righteous;" the name applied to the Rabbi, or leader, of a group of hasidim.

ZOHAR — The Book of Brightness, the foremost work of Jewish mysticism. The *Zohar* was compiled in the thirteenth century in Spain. It is in the form of a commentary on the Pentateuch.

MERIDIAN BOOKS

published by The World Publishing Company
2231 West 110 Street, Clevelana 2, Ohio